A Short Hi
Todmorden

With some account of the Geology and
Natural History of the Neighbourhood

Joshua Holden

Alpha Editions

This edition published in 2020

ISBN : 9789354175633 (Hardback)
ISBN : 9789354176241 (Paperback)

Design and Setting By
Alpha Editions
www.alphaedis.com
email - alphaedis@gmail.com

As per information held with us this book is in Public Domain. This book is a reproduction of an important historical work. Alpha Editions uses the best technology to reproduce historical work in the same manner it was first published to preserve its original nature. Any marks or number seen are left intentionally to preserve its true form.

PREFACE.

This book has been written at the suggestion of Professor Findlay in order to interest Todmorden boys and girls and their parents in the history of their own neighbourhood. It often happens that school subjects are outside the range of home interests. Local history, however, may be interesting to young and old alike, and this book is intended for all those, whether in school or out, who call themselves Todmordians and wish to know how the Todmorden of to-day has grown out of the conditions of the past.

For pupils in day and evening schools this book has a fourfold aim. First, to direct attention to the most important periods in our local history, and to arouse an interest that may continue long after school days are over. Second, to furnish local illustrations of the great movements described in ordinary English histories. Third, to unite children and parents in a common intellectual interest, the absence of which is so often to be regretted in the home. Fourth, the earlier chapters are intended to serve as an introduction to out-door science. The identification of local rocks, fossils, plants and birds will help to foster among boys and girls a habit of careful observation, create fresh and enduring sources of enjoyment and give some insight into the meaning of scientific method.

I am indebted to the Rev. John Naylor for the account of local plants and animals given in Appendix II.

I have to express my obligation to Professor Tout for a detailed and very helpful criticism of many chapters and for valuable advice as to the book as a whole; to Mr. Whitehead, Clerk to the Todmorden Education Committee, who permitted me to make the fullest use of his unique collection of papers and documents relating to Todmorden; to Mr. Sutcliffe, Borough Librarian, Mr. Jackman, Assistant Overseer, and Mr. Hollinrake, Clerk to the Guardians, for help in dealing with various local records; and to Ald. William Ormerod, J.P., and Mr. J. B. Brown, of Hebden Bridge, for the loan of books and papers. My thanks are due to Mr. John Lister, M.A., of Shibden Hall, for helpful criticism, and to Mr. Hugh P. Kendall, of Sowerby Bridge, for photographs of the Roman road over Blackstone Edge and of Heptonstall Old Church and for Civil War documents.

With regard to the illustrations in the book, I am

PREFACE

indebted to Mr. Herbert Crabtree, of The Mount, for the reproduction of Mr. Holland's picture, in the Frontispiece, and to Mr. John Barker, of Friths, for the sketch of Cross Stone Church given in Fig. 21; to Mr. Knox, Lecturer in Mining, Manchester University, who kindly drew for me the map to illustrate the Carboniferous Period (Fig. 1); to Mr. Jackman, for the photograph of flints (Fig. 8); to Dr. Russell, for the photograph of urns (Fig. 9); and to Messrs. King, of Halifax, for the block of the gibbet (Fig. 16). Figs. 13, 19, 20 and 21, as well as the Frontispiece, were taken from photographs kindly supplied by Mr. Clapham, of Todmorden. The Ordnance Maps (Figs. 2 and 24) have been reproduced by kind permission of the Ordnance Survey Department.

The publication of this book has been greatly facilitated by the kindly help of Professor Findlay and of Ald. Robert Jackson, and I desire gratefully to acknowledge the assistance they have rendered.

JOSHUA HOLDEN.

Whitcliffe Mount School,
    Cleckheaton,
        June 1912.

CONTENTS.

		PAGE
Preface		vii
List of Illustrations		xiii

Chapter
- I. Introduction — 1
- II. The Story of the Hills — 5
- III. The Vale of Todmorden — 12
- IV. Local Drift Deposits — 18
- V. Neolithic Man — 21
- VI. An Ancient Graveyard — 25
- VII. Todmorden During the Roman Occupation — 29
- VIII. Angles and Danes. A Chapter about Place Names and Dialect — 35
- IX. Domesday Book — 46
- X. Todmorden in the 14th Century — 55
- XI. Mediæval Churches and Law-Courts — 66
- XII. An Old Poll Tax Return — 78
- XIII. Todmorden during the Reformation Period — 84
- XIV. Cavaliers and Roundheads, or, Days of Strife — 95
- XV. Three Centuries of Trade and Industry — 108
- XVI. Social Life and Superstitions after the Reformation — 115
- XVII. The Beginning of Nonconformity — 126
- XVIII. Todmorden Schools and Churches during the 18th Century — 135
- XIX. The Management of Local Affairs in the 18th Century — 143
- XX. The Industrial Revolution and the Story of Mr. John Fielden, M.P. — 154

CONTENTS

XXI.	Todmorden on the Eve of the Railway System	169
XXII.	Local Politics in the 19th Century	180
XXIII.	Educational Progress in Todmorden in the 19th Century	196
XXIV.	Todmorden in Recent Days. How Todmorden became a Borough	207
XXV.	To the Reader	216

Appendix

I.	Todmorden of To-day	219
II.	Flowers and Animals in Todmorden. By Rev. John Naylor	223
III.	Parliamentary Representation of Todmorden during the 19th Century	228
IV.	Genealogies of the Families of Radcliffe and Fielden	231
V.	Local Maps and Records	234
Index		236

LIST OF ILLUSTRATIONS.

"Todmorden from Stannally Stones." *Taken from a picture painted by John Holland about 1870* - Frontispiece.

			PAGE
Fig. 1.	Diagram of Ancient British Gulf, Carboniferous Period	- - - - - -	6
Fig. 2.	Geological Map of Todmorden and District	-	8
Fig. 3.	Diagram of Carboniferous Rocks, as first laid down beneath the sea - - - -		12
Fig. 4.	Diagram of Carboniferous Rocks, bent upwards into an arch - - - - -		13
Fig. 5.	Diagram of Carboniferous Rocks, showing valley formation due to weathering - - -		14
Fig. 6.	Diagram of Rocks in the Vale of Todmorden	-	15
Fig. 7.	Section across Country from Todmorden to Halifax - - - - - -		16
Fig. 8.	Local Flints - - - - - -		22
Fig. 9.	Urns found in the Earth Circle above Butt Stones		26
Fig. 10.	Roman Road over Blackstone Edge - -		30
Fig. 11.	Diagram of Section across the pavement of the Roman Road - - - - -		31
Fig. 12.	The Forest of Elmet and the Settlements of the Angles at the beginning of the Seventh Century A.D. - - - - - -		36
Fig. 13.	Mount Cross - - - - -		39
Fig. 14.	Facsimile of the portion of Domesday Book that refers to the local Townships in the Manor of Wakefield - - - - - -		49

LIST OF ILLUSTRATIONS

Fig. 15.	Map to Illustrate Domesday Period	50
Fig. 16.	The Gibbet, Halifax	76
Fig. 17.	Heptonstall Old Church, Lady Chapel	84
Fig. 18.	Map to illustrate Civil Wars	101
Fig. 19.	Carr House Fold	122
Fig. 20.	Chapel House	129
Fig. 21.	Cross Stone Chapel	137
Fig. 22.	First Carriages used on the Lancashire and Yorkshire Railway	179
Fig. 23.	Map of Local Townships	218
Fig. 24.	Map of Todmorden and District	at end

History of Todmorden.

CHAPTER I.

INTRODUCTION.

IN the following pages the story will be told of Todmorden and the surrounding district, and some account will be given of the way in which the hills themselves have come into existence. Todmorden lies in the heart of the Pennine Range, far removed from the most noteworthy scenes of English history. Enough, however, is known of the past history of this district to make a continuous narrative possible of the events that have occurred during the last two thousand years. Hills and valleys, villages and farms will reveal some of the secrets of the past.

The best idea of this neighbourhood may be gained from some point of vantage on the moors, such as Stoodley Pike or Whirlaw. These places are situated at the edge of a moorland plateau more than 1,300 feet above sea level. Five hundred feet below are flat terraces of upland out of which there have been hollowed three narrow and deep valleys that lead through the hills to Burnley, Halifax and

Rochdale. The town of Todmorden stands where these valleys meet, on a level tract nearly one thousand feet below the level of the moors. From Summit to Hebden Bridge the valley is often exceedingly narrow, but it forms one of the most important links between Lancashire and Yorkshire; road, railway, river and canal run side by side between steep hills the whole distance. Burnley valley presents a broader expanse of landscape, before the valley narrows to a ravine at Lydgate. Its northern slope, topped with rocks at Whirlaw, Bride Stones and Orchan Rocks, overlooks green fields and clustering trees, whilst beyond Centre Vale, Scaitcliffe Wood clothes the opposite hill slope.

The town fills the central space and extends for more than two miles along each of the valleys. From the uplands may be observed the large number of mill chimneys and the dull grey of the housetops. The great railway viaduct and embankment join two of the valleys and block the entrance to the third, whilst above the mills and houses a few church spires are visible. Though Todmorden has little in itself that is picturesque, it is most picturesquely situated among the folds of the hills. On a moonlight night from one of the hill slopes, instead of streets and houses, a valley of stars may be discerned, where gleaming points of light mark out the railway and the streets that mount the uplands, or indicate the more distant windings of the valleys.

The landscape that surrounds the town is full of beauty. There are green uplands with hamlets and scattered farmsteads. From the main valleys branch off narrow ravines or cloughs, their sides clothed with trees that overhang running streams and waterfalls. On the hilltops, moorlands extend for many miles; range after range of hills becoming fainter and fainter in the far distance.

This district can be divided into three parts along the three levels of valley, upland and hill-top. To-day Todmorden lies almost wholly in the valley or along the lowest level. Farmers on the uplands are well aware of this fact. In winter they often enjoy days of cloudless sunshine when the town's folk are enveloped in a thick, cold mist. The mist divides the land; beneath it Todmorden and its inhabitants are hidden; above, only a few farms and hamlets are visible. This can have only been the case for about a hundred years. During the preceding centuries Todmordians lived above the mist line. Todmorden Hall, Scaitcliffe Hall and the church of St. Mary's were in the hollow, but on the uplands, Sourhall and Cross Stone, Mankinholes and Bottomley, Blackshaw Head and Shore, Heptonstall and Old Town were centres of population and industry. Earlier still, in days that go back to prehistoric times, the inhabitants lived at the highest level on the hill tops and moors.

The main outline of this narrative may now be clearly understood. First, the story of the hills themselves will be told and an explanation given of the way in which the rocks that make up the hills were laid down millions of years ago. Next, some account will be given of the different races of men who lived on the moorlands in days before the dawn of history. Then the progress will be traced of those small civilised communities that settled on the uplands, and during twelve centuries gradually laid the foundation of the language, social customs and industries that exist in Todmorden to-day. Finally, the great changes brought about by canals, factories and railways will be described, when men left the villages on the uplands and established themselves in the valley below.

CHAPTER II.

THE STORY OF THE HILLS.

The Todmorden district lies in that part of the Pennine Chain which separates the Lancashire and Yorkshire plains. It is marked by an abundance of sandstone. Lines of crag are visible on the tops of the hills, at Bride Stones and Blackstone Edge. Big rocks occur on every moorland and there are many quarries. Todmorden and Hebden Bridge are built almost entirely of stone, and place names such as Stansfield (Stonesfield), Stones, Hardcastle Crags and Cragg Valley are numerous throughout the district.

In addition to sandstone there are thick beds of hardened clay or shale. Todmorden is built on clay, and beds of shale are exposed along the hill-sides and in the cloughs. Seams of coal occur at Dulesgate and Cliviger.

Millions of years ago this country was not in existence, but where England now is, there was a sea with several islands in it. Fig. 1 shows how very different the geography of the British region was in those days. The present geographical outline is put in lightly for comparison. The shaded lines represent the coast. The shore line skirting the Grampians belonged to a great continent that included the whole of North Europe and the greater part of the North Atlantic area. On the other hand, an ocean occupied the southern half of Europe, the sea that covered most of the British region being

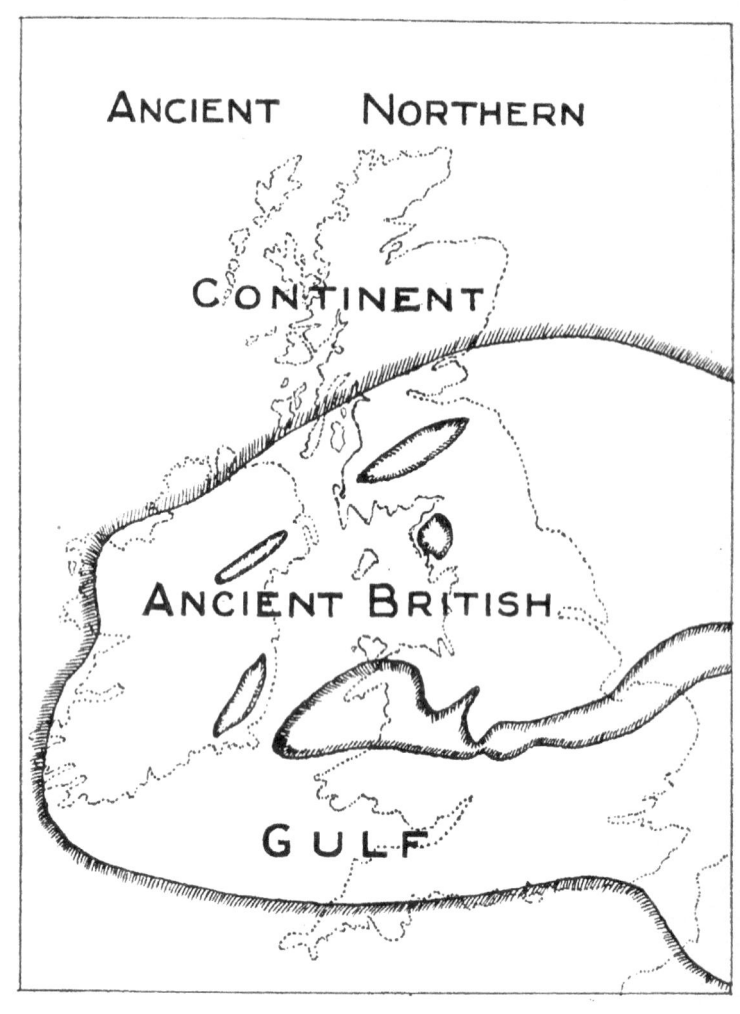

Fig. 1. DIAGRAM OF ANCIENT BRITISH GULF, CARBONIFEROUS PERIOD.

one of its gulfs. It was in this ancient sea that the rocks composing the Todmorden hills were first laid down. Geologists call the whole of the rocks thus deposited the Carboniferous Series. It took millions of years for their formation, and during this long period the following changes probably took place.

1. At first the ancient sea, shown in the map, was deep enough to allow marine animals to live in its clear waters. Shells of the dead animals accumulated on the sea floor until thick beds of chalk-like ooze were formed, known as Carboniferous Limestone. These rocks may be seen at Clitheroe and in Derbyshire, but they are not visible in Todmorden. They lie buried beneath the ground.

2. An upward movement of the land made the sea become shallower, part of the British Gulf being replaced by land and the limestone beds being thus brought nearer to the new shore line. The consequence was that the sand and mud brought down by the continental rivers covered the beds of limestone. In clearer water bands of limestone might still be formed, but most of the rocks then deposited were sandstones and shales. These rocks are called Yoredale rocks (also Pendleside beds), and in the Todmorden district they consist of two thick beds of shale with a bed of sandstone between them. The town itself stands on Yoredale shale. Yoredale sandstone may be seen in the quarries at Longfield, Hollins and Butt Stones, in Ravensnest Hill and behind Waterside Mill. Stone from most of these quarries has been obtained for building purposes. Yoredale rocks flank both sides of the Calder valley to Hebden Bridge, branching up Hardcastle Valley

8   HISTORY OF TODMORDEN

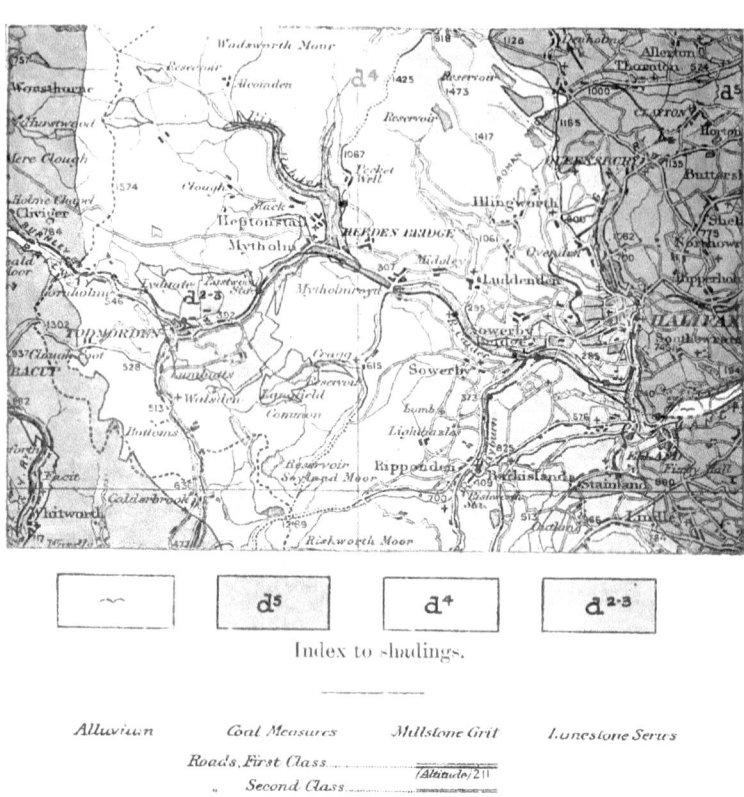

Index to shadings.

Alluvium   Coal Measures   Millstone Grit   Limestone Series

Roads, First Class ....
   „   Second Class .... (Altitude) 211
   „   Third Class ....
Railways .... Station
County Boundaries ....
Church .... +

Reduced from the One-Inch Maps of the Geological Survey, 1906.
Published 1907.   J. J. H. Teall, M.A., D.Sc., F.R.S., Director.

Fig. 2. GEOLOGICAL MAP OF TODMORDEN AND DISTRICT.

Reproduced from the Ordnance Survey Map, with the sanction of the Controller of H.M. Stationery Office.

and Horsebridge Clough. Yoredale rocks (referred to in Fig. 2 as Limestone Series, d 2–3), however, do not reach to the hill tops on the Yorkshire side of the district, and on the Lancashire side they are entirely absent.

3. After the Yoredale rocks were deposited, a further upheaval of the land brought the continental shore line still nearer the British region and made the water that covered it still shallower. Great mountain ranges rose towards the north and north-east; and big rivers, flowing south, brought down coarse sand and pushed forward their deltas into the shallow sea. Enormous deposits of coarse sandstone and shale were then deposited. So coarse were the sandstones that the name *grit* has been given to them. Excellent grindstones and paving stones are made from them, and the series of rocks deposited is known as Millstone Grit. These rocks are found in abundance in the Todmorden district. (Fig. 2.) The bed of grit first deposited and lying above the Yoredale rocks, is called Kinderscout grit, because a fine example of it occurs at Kinderscout in Derbyshire. It crops out at Bride Stones, Whirlaw and on the Gaddens Moor. Kinderscout grit underlies Heptonstall and forms the side of Nut Clough. The Crag at Hardcastle and the rocks above Widdop reservoir also consist of the same very coarse grit.

Other beds of sandstone, called Middle grits, are found above the Kinderscout grit. Good examples occur in the quarries below Stoodley Pike, at Warland, Light Hazels and Long Lees in Walsden, in Ramsden Clough, Dulesgate and Green's Clough. The rocks at Watty and Eagle Crag consist of Middle grits. Further to the east, Middle grits may be traced from Wood End, near Hebden Bridge, to Luddendenfoot.

Above the Middle grits, at the top of the Millstone Grit series, is another bed of coarse sandstone, known as Rough Rock. It may be seen at Cloughfoot and in Green's Clough on the western side of the neighbourhood, but on the east is not met with until Halifax is reached. (Fig. 7.)

4. After the Millstone grits had been formed, the land began again to sink, so that the whole of England and most of Ireland were changed into immense swamps scarcely lifted above sea level. Similar mud flats covered a large part of Europe. The climate was warm and moist, and enormous forests grew on the swampy ground. The trees were very tall and resembled gigantic ferns, clubmosses and horsetails; others were more like fir trees. Then a series of changes took place in the level of land and sea. The land slowly sank until forests were submerged beneath the water and buried under deposits of sand and mud. Next the land again began to rise; the sea once more became a swamp and forests again flourished luxuriantly, until they in turn were buried beneath the sea. The trees and vegetation that were thus entrapped between beds of shale and sand were changed at last into seams of coal. The rocks that were deposited during this last stage of the Carboniferous period are called Coal Measures. Beds belonging to the lower Coal Measures are found in the Lancashire portion of the Todmorden district, in Dulesgate, Cliviger and Walsden. At Dulesgate there are seams of coal 2 feet and 4 feet

in thickness. The principal trees that lived in the Carboniferous period were Lepidodendron, Sigillaria and Calamites. The Sigillaria had long branching roots called Stigmaria. The fossil remains of these trees may be found in the local Coal Measures. Underlying seams of coal, there are often beds of clay from which good bricks can be made, and at Cloughfoot, not far from the colliery, a brick works has been built.

CHAPTER III.

The Vale of Todmorden.

After the Coal Measures had been laid down under the shallow seas of the ancient British Gulf, great earth movements gradually but completely altered the arrangement of land and water described in the last chapter. The North Atlantic continent sank beneath the sea to form the bottom of the Atlantic Ocean, whilst on either side rocks were slowly piled up into great mountain ranges. These changes also must have taken many millions of years. During the process rocks were smashed and split asunder; beds, at first level, were tilted in all directions and so powerful were the forces at work, that great thicknesses of rock were often wrenched from their places and pushed into new positions. In some such fashion the Pennine Chain gradually rose into a wide arch of rock.

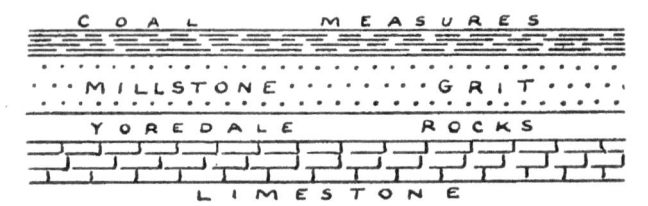

Fig. 3. Diagram of Carboniferous Rocks, as First Laid Down Beneath the Sea.

The changes that took place may be roughly represented in a series of diagrams. Let Fig. 3

represent the Carboniferous rocks in the Todmorden district when first laid down beneath the sea. By the action of earth forces these beds were pushed out of the horizontal position into a wide arch, as shown in Fig. 4.

During this upward movement the surface of the land was continually being acted upon by wind and rain, snow and frost. The greater the height to which the beds of rock were lifted, the more powerful the action of these agencies became. Rivers and streams ran swiftly down the hill sides, and

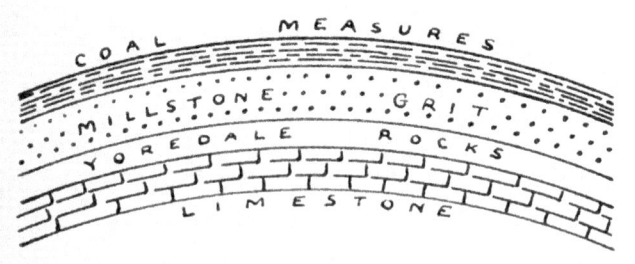

Fig. 4. DIAGRAM OF CARBONIFEROUS ROCKS, BENT UPWARDS INTO AN ARCH.

valleys were gradually hollowed out of the land. But the Coal Measures were uppermost and therefore the rocks composing them were first washed away. Then the Millstone Grit and Yoredale rocks were laid bare and last of all the Carboniferous Limestone. In Todmorden, however, the process was never completed. A thickness of several thousand feet of rock has been removed, reaching to the Kinderscout grit on the Yorkshire moors, and exposing the Yoredale rocks along the Todmorden valley, but the Carboniferous Limestone is still beneath the surface. (Fig. 5.) The Todmorden hills are situated along the central axis of the Pennine Chain. They form, as it were, one of the keystones in a great arch of rock many miles broad. On the Yorkshire side the rocks in every quarry or cutting may be observed sloping gently eastward; on the Lancashire side the rocks dip westward. (Fig. 5.)

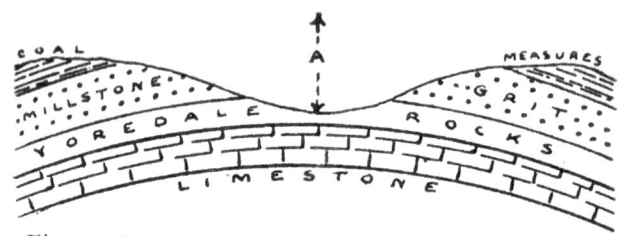

Fig. 5. DIAGRAM OF CARBONIFEROUS ROCKS, SHOWING VALLEY FORMATION DUE TO WEATHERING. (A represents the thickness of rock washed away.)

The above diagram needs one important correction before it can represent even roughly the position of the rocks in Todmorden. The rocks on each side of the valley at Centre Vale belong to quite different beds. At Bride Stones, on the *summit* of the Yorkshire slope is the lowest bed of Millstone Grit; whereas, at the *bottom* of the opposite slope rocks are exposed belonging to the Middle grits. In other words, along the line of the Burnley and Walsden valleys, when the Pennine Chain was being formed, the enormous forces at work split the rocks and threw down the beds on the Lancashire side hundreds of feet below the corresponding beds on the Yorkshire side of the district. Such a displacement

VALE OF TODMORDEN

is called a Fault. Fig. 6 gives a rough idea of the general position of the rocks that make up the Todmorden hills. In addition to this great fault running in a direction from north to south, a large number of smaller faults have complicated the geology of the neighbourhood.

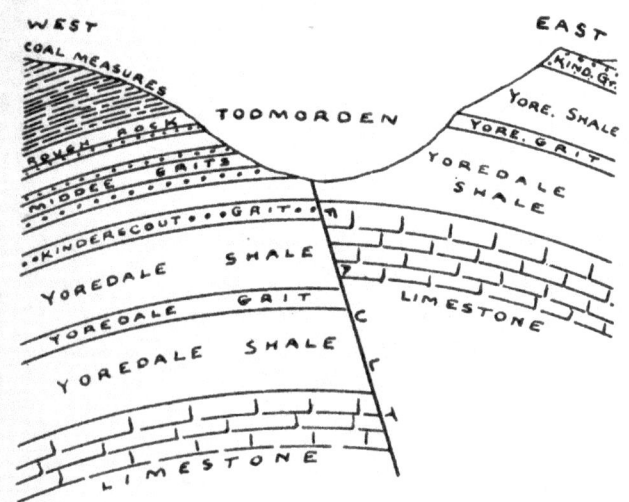

Fig. 6. DIAGRAM OF ROCKS IN THE VALE OF TODMORDEN.

On the west side of Todmorden it will be observed there are neither Yoredale rocks nor Kinderscout grit, but only Middle grits, which are soon followed by Rough Rock and the lower Coal Measures. Eastwards the Coal Measures do not appear until Halifax and Elland are reached. The diagram in Fig. 7 shows the succession of rocks from Todmorden to Halifax.

The story of the hills has been briefly outlined,

beginning with the quiet deposition of limestone ooze in a gulf of an ancient European ocean and ending with the upheaval of enormous thicknesses of rock into the Pennine Chain. Since that remote period this district has probably never been completely submerged beneath the sea. On the contrary in the earlier stages of its history the Pennine Chain was much higher than it is to-day. The present hills are merely the remnants of a mightier mountain range.

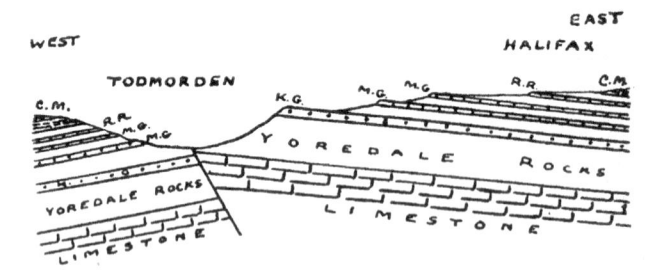

Fig. 7. SECTION ACROSS COUNTRY FROM TODMORDEN TO HALIFAX.

NOTE.—The following exercises may be suggested for "Out of School" excursions on the hills or in the cloughs.

1. Collect specimens of the sandstones found in the different quarries, etc., in the neighbourhood (Yoredale grit, Kinderscout grit, Middle grits, Rough Rock, Coal Measures). Compare the different specimens, noticing which are coarsest (with quartz pebbles in them); which are smoothest.

Label each specimen, giving the *exact position* and date when found. If possible, make a note of the kind of beds above and below the one from which the specimen was taken.

Is the coarseness of the sandstone any indication of the bed from which it comes?

2. In the Millstone Grit quarries (in Walsden valley, Dulesgate, Green's Clough, below Stoodley Pike, etc.) look for thin bands of coal. In the beds near them, search for fossils. What sort are they?

3. Make a collection of fossils from the Coal Measures. Besides the fossil remains of trees, specimens may be found of different shells (Goniatites, Lingula, Aviculopecten, etc.), and of various fishes.

On each specimen put a label saying exactly where it was found. The *names* of the fossils may be found out later by comparing them with specimens in the Free Library or in the museums at Halifax and Rochdale.

4. Carefully notice the character of the trees, plants and flowers that grow on the different shales and sandstones in the cloughs and on the uplands and the moors. Verify, as far as you can, the list of local plants given in Appendix II.

In obtaining specimens of flowers, etc., take the greatest care *not to uproot* the plants.

CHAPTER IV.

Local Drift Deposits.

The story of the Todmorden hills will not be complete unless some account is given of several interesting deposits found in many parts of the neighbourhood. These deposits lie on the surface of the ground above the Yoredale beds, Millstone Grit or Coal Measures as the case may be. For the most part they consist of clay or sand and contain a large number of pebbles and boulders. The pebbles and boulders are not arranged in layers, but are scattered in a haphazard fashion through the clay. Also, although most of the pebbles consist of sandstone, a large number are composed of granite and volcanic rocks, being entirely unlike any boulders in the Carboniferous beds in Todmorden, but exactly resembling granitic and volcanic rocks found in some parts of Cumberland.

These deposits are found in the following places. (1) Walsden valley.—In the quarries at Warland, Long Lees and Light Hazels, and in the Summit brickyard there is a bed of clay with granite boulders above the third Millstone Grit. (2) Todmorden—Near the Gas and Electrical works a similar bed of clay occurs. Beneath the clay on which the town is built, there is a layer of blue clay which is neither Yoredale shale nor river deposit. (3) Calder valley.—Between Hebden Bridge and Mytholmroyd there

LOCAL DRIFT DEPOSITS

occurs a great thickness of sand, with granitic and volcanic boulders. (4) Burnley valley.—At Lineholme, nearly 20 feet below the ground, many limestone boulders have been found. In Sheddin and Cant Cloughs (and along the north-west slope of Boulsworth Hill) big deposits of limestone have been left, that resemble the rocks in the Craven district of Yorkshire.

These deposits are never found on the higher level of the moors, but are confined to their lower slopes and to the valleys.

Similar beds consisting of clay filled with strange boulders are spread over most of England and Ireland. Lancashire is covered with them: the beach at Blackpool is strewn with pebbles from the Cumbrian mountains. It is only reasonable to expect, therefore, that the same explanation may be given of the formation of them all.

Very long ago most of the United Kingdom, together with a large part of North-west Europe, was covered with ice. This took place during a period of intense cold, known to geologists as the Ice Age. Big glaciers moved down the mountain sides and spread over the plains. Some glaciers in Cumberland travelled south or south-east across Lancashire; one from North Yorkshire skirted the eastern side of the Pennine Chain. On the way, the bottom of each glacier scraped the ground underneath to fine mud or sand, whilst boulders and pebbles from the mountain sides fell on the top of the glacier and were carried south. The glaciers, however, were not able to climb over the Pennine Chain. They covered the lower slopes of the hills and pierced through the gaps at Summit, Cliviger and Widdop, filling the Todmorden valleys with ice and mud and boulders from the northern mountains.

Then a change came; the climate became milder, the ice fields gradually disappeared and a thick mantle of mud and boulders or of *glacial drift* was left in the valleys and on the lower hills. There were many boulders from the granitic and volcanic rocks of Cumberland, and from the limestone rocks of North Yorkshire that had travelled in this way a long distance from their starting point. In this neighbourhood rain has long since washed away most of these deposits. A few, however, have escaped the process of weathering and still remain as local memorials of the distant Ice Age.

The Glacial Drift at Millwood is probably part of a larger deposit that once blocked up the narrow outlet of the valley at Lobmill and changed the Todmorden basin as far as Lineholme and Walsden into a beautiful lake. On the bottom of the lake the blue glacial clay left by local glaciers was first deposited. Then sand and mud from the hill sides covered the clay and raised by many feet the level of the Todmorden valley. A series of lakes, in all probability, extended along the valley as far as Hebden Bridge.

EXERCISE.—Obtain specimens of granitic and other pebbles, that are not sandstone, from the Glacial Drift overlying the quarries in Walsden valley; also specimens of limestone in the valleys near Hurstwood. Notice whether any *flint* nodules are to be found in the local drift deposits.

CHAPTER V.

Neolithic Man.

Man first appeared on the earth during the Ice Age. In England his bones and roughly chipped stone tools, as well as the bones of animals he had killed, have been found under the limestone floor of many caves. The Victoria Cave near Settle, and Kent's Cavern, near Torquay, are two well known examples. No traces, however, of this earlier race have been met with in Todmorden, but the remains of a later and cleverer race are still scattered over the moorlands.

These remains consist of a large number of bits of broken flint together with occasional specimens of beautifully carved flint arrow heads and of other tools and implements. Mr. Robert Law, F.G.S., collected thousands of flint chippings, including many good examples of worked flints, whilst more recently Mr. Luke Fielden and Mr. Jackman of Todmorden have obtained many fine specimens. This early race made knives, scrapers, borers and arrow heads of different shapes, composed of flint or some hard stone such as quartz. (Fig. 8.)

Thousands of flint chippings still lie on the Todmorden moors, but anyone who looks for them should bear in mind the following facts. First: worked flints occur on the top of the moors or on the slopes of rounded hills skirting the moors. They are always found near beds of peat, especially on bare ground from which the peat has been washed away. Second: flint chippings never occur above a peat bed, but in the soil underneath the peat.

In this district peat beds cover the moors to a thickness of several feet. Peat consists of decayed vegetation, and the formation of so great a thickness of it must have taken many thousands of years. Moreover, in the soil underneath, where flints are

Fig. 8. LOCAL FLINTS.

found, stumps of oak trees occur that show there were forests on the hills before the peat was formed. Hence there can be no doubt that the race of men who carved the flint implements found on the Todmorden moors lived many thousand years ago when forests that have long since vanished covered the hills.

These early workers in stone are known to-day as the men of the Neolithic or New Stone Age, because their tools are more perfectly made than those of the race that lived during the Glacial Period. They are said to have belonged to the Iberian race; one that resembled the Basques who live to-day in the north of Spain. Neolithic men lived on the hills; their knives and arrow heads are most abundant in places commanding an extensive view. It is impossible to tell when first they reached this district, but the scene they looked upon was very different from the present landscape. Hills and valleys were covered with woods; rain was excessive and in flood time the swamps in the valley must have been changed into a gleaming lake. In the woods roamed wild boars and wild oxen, wolves and wild cats, foxes and badgers. Under such circumstances, clothed in the skins of wild beasts and seeking shelter in caves or under rocks, the men of the Neolithic Age maintained a wretched struggle for existence.

They were small of stature (the very tall were not more than 5 feet 6 inches high) and had long shaped heads and dark hair and eyes. They were herdsmen as well as hunters, and had begun the domestication of animals. Gaunt, fierce dogs were their companions; herds of swine gathered near their rude dwellings and horses either gave them food or served them in the chase. Flint scythes reaped only the scantiest harvests of spelt* and wild barley in clearings on the uplands. Food consisted mainly of the flesh of animals or of fish and wild fruits. In summer men searched for lumps or

---

* Spelt is a kind of wheat that grows on poor soil.

nodules of flint or for pieces of quartz. The nodules found in this neighbourhood are small compared with those in beds of chalk, so that the tools found on the Todmorden hills are smaller than those discovered in East Yorkshire. Sometimes the number of broken nodules, flint tools and chippings is so large as to suggest that the place where they occur was the site of a Neolithic workshop. A fine flint nodule was found on Inchfield Moor by Mr. Luke Fielden and near it was a flake that had been chipped from it by a Neolithic workman thousands of years ago. Occasionally bits of charcoal and burnt flint point to the existence of an ancient hearth.

Neolithic men were very artistic and some of the smallest flints were probably used as graving tools for delicate work. Others were used for drilling eyes in bone needles. Neolithic men were also very superstitious and wore tiny flint amulets to keep them safe from evil spirits.

NOTE.—Where did the Neolithic men in Todmorden find the flint nodules for making tools?

CHAPTER VI.

An Ancient Graveyard.

In a field above Butt Stones in Stansfield there is a portion of ground enclosed by a circular bank of earth thirty yards across. Except for the regularity of the raised circle there is nothing to distinguish this part from the remainder of the field. Some years ago, however, Mr. Wilkinson of Burnley, Mr. Law of Halifax, and Alderman Crossley of Todmorden examined this circle, and found near its centre, not many inches below the ground, three vases of baked clay buried in charcoal and burnt bones. The rim of each urn was ornamented with a simple geometrical pattern. There were also two small clay cups and several flint implements, including a few scrapers and a leaf-shaped arrow-head. The urns were filled with charcoal, charred soil and bits of calcined bones. A small earthenware cup, found in the largest urn, also contained amber and jet beads, a bone pin, a *bronze* knife blade (or possibly brooch), three inches long, and a small *bronze* pin.

A more thorough examination of the ground was undertaken by Dr. Russell of Todmorden, and a carefully drawn plan (now in the Free Library) shows the position of every object of interest discovered. Three more large urns, one covered with an inverted earthenware vessel, and two small earthenware cups were obtained in an excellent state of preservation. (Fig. 9.) The remains were also detected of nearly a score of urns that had crumbled away. Most of the urns were situated near the centre of the ring. At some distance below the surface there was a hard floor of baked clay with abundant remains of charcoal. Stones were also grouped round the circumference at the four points of the compass, those to the south resembling a stone seat. Among the bones found in the urns there was part of a human jaw with a large number of teeth, as well as parts of a hand and wrist. A primitive

Fig. 9. URNS FOUND IN THE EARTH CIRCLE ABOVE BUTT STONES.

whetstone, with grooves still plainly marked in the sandstone, gives a touch of reality to the workmen who once sharpened their tools and made clay vases on these uplands.

The earth circle just described is the remains of an ancient graveyard. It was in use at a time when men burned the bodies of the dead and placed their ashes in rudely ornamented urns of baked clay.

AN ANCIENT GRAVEYARD

It is the bronze implement and bronze pin, however, found in one of the urns that are of special importance, for they serve to point out by whom and at what time the urns were probably placed in the ground.

Bronze is an alloy of copper and tin, and its use indicates a great advance in civilisation beyond that of the New Stone Age. In this country the Bronze Age lasted for more than a thousand years. This length of time, however, may be divided into three periods, according to the mode of burial that was practised. First, the bodies of the dead were buried in big round funeral mounds or barrows; this period continued till about 900 B.C. Second, earth circles were used instead of barrows; and lastly, a circle of stones (usually seven in number) marked the place of burial. Moreover, funeral urns were not used until somewhat late in the Bronze Age. It is plain, therefore, that the graveyard on the Stansfield upland belongs to the second period of the Bronze Age, and its funeral urns show that it is considerably later in date than the ninth century before Christ.

At that time a race of Celts, known as the Goidels, invaded this country, a race that was noted for its use of bronze weapons. Gradually the Goidelic Celts overthrew the Neolithic men in this island and took possession of the interior. Long afterwards it took the Anglo-Saxons nearly two centuries to reach as far inland as the Pennine Chain; the Goidelic Celts, therefore, can hardly have encamped on these uplands before the seventh or sixth century before Christ.

The Goidels were a tall, blue-eyed race with round-shaped heads and long reddish hair. They established themselves as the ruling class over the conquered Neolithic race. With better weapons they hunted and fished, tamed animals or fortified their rude settlements against attack. In religion they were powerfully influenced by their Neolithic subjects. The medicine men of the earlier race were replaced among the Goidels by the Druid priesthood. Religious worship was conducted in the open air beneath the branches of oak trees, or near huge rocks or within the precincts of an earth circle. When a chieftain died, his relatives were killed and their ashes were mingled with his in the urns buried within the sacred enclosure. Many such barbarous rites may have been celebrated on the Cross Stone upland amid the silence or savage exultation of the assembled tribe. It is possible that the group of weathered rocks at Bride Stones served as a Celtic temple, but there is no evidence that marriage rites were ever performed there.

CHAPTER VII.

TODMORDEN DURING THE ROMAN OCCUPATION.

Several centuries after the coming of the Goidels, another branch of Celts, known as Brythons, invaded this island. They were a fierce, warlike race, and conquered the country as far north as the Clyde. Their weapons were of iron; they wore their hair long, painted their bodies blue and were clothed in skins. From the language they spoke, modern Welsh has been derived. Different tribes took possession of different parts of Britain, one of the most powerful being the Brigantes who occupied the Pennine Chain. Hence at the beginning of the Christian era this district was in the hands of the Brigantes. They have long since vanished, but a few relics of the language they once spoke may be discerned in some of the local place names and in the local dialect.

The Roman conquest of Britain occurred during the first century after the birth of Christ, when a succession of Roman generals gradually subdued the various Celtic tribes. It was Agricola who overcame the Brigantes and established a military supremacy over the whole country. The Roman dominion lasted for more than three centuries. During this period towns were built and a great system of roads was established. In the neighbourhood of towns the Romans greatly influenced their British subjects, but on moorlands or in remote forests the Celts were able to elude the Roman legions and hold fast to their own tribal customs.

It is not likely that the Romans ever settled in the Todmorden district or exerted an appreciable influence on its inhabitants. No important fort existed such as had been built on the edge of the Cheshire plain at Mancunium (Manchester) or on the Ribble at Ribchester, or on the Wharfe at Tadcaster. All that the Romans desired was a swift passage over the hills, and on Blackstone Edge there still remains an excellent example of a Roman

Fig. 10. ROMAN ROAD OVER BLACKSTONE EDGE.

roadway. The relics of the Roman occupation that still exist in the Todmorden neighbourhood may be grouped under the three heads of roads, entrenchments and coins.

I.—*Roman Roads.*

Within a few minutes' walk of the White House, Blackstone Edge, an ancient paved roadway leads straight over the crest of the hill in a direction roughly parallel to the present road to Ripponden. The road may be traced on both sides of the hill top, especially up the steep Lancashire slope, where it is visible at intervals for a distance of several hundred yards. Its appearance is shown in Fig. 10. The construction of the stone pavement may be gathered from the diagram in Fig. 11. The pavement is about 18 feet broad and is made up of three principal parts. Along the centre are large stone blocks (*A*, Fig.11), 3 feet 8 inches across and hollowed out so as to form a continuous trough along the middle of the road. A slightly raised ridge along the centre of the trough divides it into two separate grooves

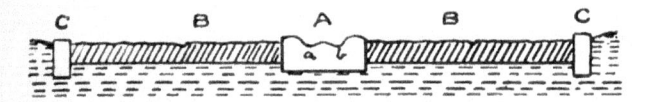

Fig. 11. DIAGRAM OF SECTION ACROSS THE PAVEMENT OF THE ROMAN ROAD.

(*a* and *b*). There is a level pavement (*B*), about 6 feet wide, on each side of the trough, flanked at the outer edge (*C*) by stones set up on end. Along many portions of the pavement distinct ruts or wheel tracks may be traced, in some places to a depth of three or four inches. Their position makes it probable that they were produced by wheeled vehicles, with wheels 4 feet 6 inches apart. The central trough stones are found only at the steepest part of the road, and the grooves running along either side were produced by skidded wheels that scraped along the sides of the trough where it was most needful to apply a brake.

The road over Blackstone Edge formed part of the Roman road between Mancunium and Olicana (Ilkley), thus connecting stations situated on opposite sides of the Pennine Chain. It was a branch of Watling Street. North of Todmorden and skirting the moors from Burnley to Midgley a highway known as the Long Causeway is believed to be on the site of an old Roman road between Burnley and Halifax. Some years ago portions of the road were still preserved near Ringstones Camp beyond Worsthorne and also in Warley. Coins have been discovered near Holme, and at High Greenwood and in Stansfield, belonging to the reigns of Trajan (98—117 A.D.) and Hadrian (117—138 A.D.).

II.—*Entrenchments.*

At Ringstones, on Worsthorne Moor, is a small Roman camp, now completely embedded in earth and long grass. Its walls, not quite square in outline, may still be traced and there are indications of a ditch outside. The angles of the fort face the chief points of the compass, and openings in the north-western and south-eastern walls, nearly opposite to each other, still mark the position of ancient entrances. A small handmill for grinding corn was found in the camp, as well as a large stone oven.

III.—*Coins.*

In addition to those already mentioned, coins have been discovered at Mereclough, Stoodley Pike and Kitson Wood. Most of them belonged to the reigns of Hadrian, Antoninus Pius (138—161 A.D.) and Gallienus (260—268 A.D.).

In the third century the power of the Roman

emperors was so small that for many years they were little more than puppets of the soldiery, who raised them to power and deposed them in quick succession. The consequence was that in many provinces the garrisons set up rival emperors of their own. The legions of Gaul and Britain, for example, during the years A.D. 259—273 elected Posthumus, Victorinus and Tetricus as sovereigns, and it is interesting to note that relics of these usurpers have been found in Todmorden in the shape of coins bearing the names of Victorinus and Tetricus (269—273 A.D.).

Such are the local memorials of the Roman occupation, but roads, camps and coins are silent as to their individual histories. The reader must imagine, as best he can, the story attached to each. We have already observed that the Blackstone Edge road was merely a passage across inhospitable moorlands for soldiers and traders. Within the woods lurked bands of Brigantes, devoted to their chiefs, fearless of danger and inured to hardship. The news of the advancing legions roused them to the fiercest resistance. We can imagine their murderous onslaught as they issued swiftly from the woods and fell on the flank of a Roman cohort or surprised a detachment of soldiers building or repairing the road. The coins left on these hills may have been the fruit of victory over the Roman legions, or they may mark the abandonment of treasure during some sudden retreat in the later days of the Roman occupation. Doubtless the Roman soldiers kept a sharp look out in their march over Blackstone Edge and breathed more freely when they reached the Romanised villages on the plain.

This district, therefore, in Roman times may be thought of as a sort of Celtic island, surrounded but never submerged by the influences of Roman civilisation. The dwellers on these hills preserved almost without a break traditions handed down from their Neolithic and Celtic ancestors, and only with the coming of our Germanic forefathers did the civilisation of the Celts finally give place to one entirely different both in language and in social organisation.

CHAPTER VIII.

ANGLES AND DANES. A CHAPTER ABOUT PLACE
NAMES AND DIALECT.

The English invasion of Britain took place during the fifth and sixth centuries. Saxons and Jutes from north-west Germany took possession of the south and south-east coasts, whilst bands of Angles sailed up the rivers along the east coast from south of the Wash to the Firth of Forth.

The Angles who sailed up the Humber drove the Celts in East Yorkshire into the great forest of Elmet that covered most of the West Riding and stretched on its western borders along the Pennine Chain from the Peak to Settle. The Anglian kingdom thus founded was known as Deira. Farther north, other Angles conquered the eastern coast-line from the Tees to the Firth of Forth and established the kingdom of Bernicia. During the sixth century, however, the Britons held all the land westward, so that a way of retreat lay open from Yorkshire into Lancashire and North Wales.

Early in the seventh century a powerful king, Ethelfrith, united Bernicia and Deira into one great kingdom of Northumbria. He then crossed South Lancashire and took Chester by storm (A.D. 613). The consequence was that the Celts on the Pennine Chain were cut off from their allies in North Wales. Meanwhile other bands of Angles had sailed up the Trent and settled in the valleys of the Dove and

36   HISTORY OF TODMORDEN

Derwent, so that the Celts in Elmet were again hemmed in on every side. (Fig. 12.) Previously the Romans had kept them in subjection by a ring of fortified towns on the plains, but there had been

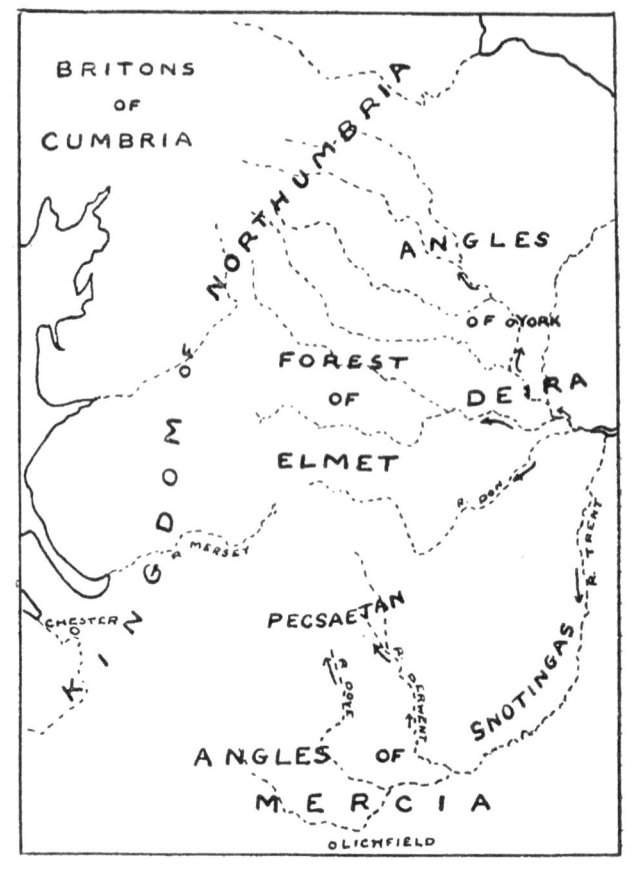

Fig. 12. THE FOREST OF ELMET AND THE SETTLEMENTS OF THE ANGLES AT THE BEGINNING OF THE SEVENTH CENTURY, A.D.

little direct intercourse between Romans and Celts. Now, however, the advancing Angles were lovers of an open air life and came of set purpose to find new homes in the forest. Nor could they permit so extensive a forest as that of Elmet to remain unsubdued. Edwin, the next King of Northumbria (A.D. 617—633), conquered the Celts in Elmet and built fortresses near Leeds and Huddersfield.

Before the end of the seventh century Anglian warriors must have reached the Todmorden district. Under brave leaders they advanced along the uplands that skirt the banks of the Calder. In caps and tunics, with spears, two-edged daggers and wooden shields, these early English soldiers fell on their foes and drove many of them on to the moors round Todmorden. The names of *Wal*shaw and *Wals*den (Anglo-Saxon, wealas, foreigner) may point to the time when on the western moorlands the Celts were sufficiently numerous to make those districts seem to the early English settlers full of strange Celtic people.

When the victory was won the Angles laid aside their weapons and on the hills were heard sounds that are familiar to English colonists in Canada to-day. Forest trees were felled, camp fires were lit, rude huts were built and the land was cleared for ploughing.

Meanwhile another all important event had taken place. Augustine and his monks had introduced Christianity into Kent, and converted King Ethelbert. His daughter Ethelburga was married to Edwin, and after the conquest of Elmet, he also became a Christian, through the preaching of

Paulinus, his wife's chaplain. Many legends have gathered round the person of Paulinus. Ancient crosses at Godley Lane in Burnley and in the parish church of Dewsbury are still known as Paulinus preaching crosses. At Dewsbury Edwin had a royal palace and the church is said to owe its foundation to the preaching of Paulinus. After Edwin's downfall in battle, a period of confusion prevailed. Then under his successors, Oswald and Oswy, the gospel was preached in Northumbria by Scotch missionaries from Iona and the land was won from heathendom. Soon afterwards Christianity was introduced into nearly all the Anglo-Saxon kingdoms, and Theodore of Tarsus, the first Archbishop of Canterbury, mapped out the country into dioceses with a bishop over each (A.D. 670). Yorkshire and Lancashire were included in the great diocese of York, and it is probable that the Todmorden district formed part of the extensive parish of Dewsbury. On the moor above the village of Shore, not far from Stiperden, there stands a monument known as Mount Cross. (Fig. 13.) In appearance it somewhat resembles the Paulinus cross at Burnley, and may be a very early preaching cross, possibly dating back to Saxon times.

It has already been pointed out that the Britons in the Todmorden neighbourhood were left undisturbed until the coming of the Angles. After the introduction of Christianity wars of extermination ceased and Angles and Britons lived side by side as conquerors and conquered. In some respects Celtic usages were like those of the Angles. The Britons lived in tribes on land that belonged to the tribe instead of to any one person. They gained a livelihood by hunting, rearing livestock or ploughing the common lands. Similarly the free-born Angles who came as conquerors to the uplands settled in small communities, holding their lands in common. Strips of land were distributed annually among the freemen, but they united to help each other in ploughing and harvesting. The Britons would find little

Fig. 13. MOUNT CROSS.

difficulty in adopting such methods. The Angles, however, differed in their methods of government. In each village or township the freemen transacted the town's business at the village moot or meeting-place. Bigger districts, known as Hundreds, were under the control of larger gatherings, consisting of representatives from each of the townships within the Hundred. These gatherings were held at the Hundred Moot.

During the ninth century, the peaceful development of the Anglo-Saxon communities all over England was disturbed by the fierce raids of Norse and Danish rovers. They sailed up the rivers, as the Angles had done three centuries before, and once again Yorkshire and part of Lancashire were conquered. The course of the Danes along the Calder is marked by the names of Ravensthorpe and Sowerby, and reasons will be given later (pp. 42 & 51) for the belief that they reached the Todmorden district. The Northmen established a military supremacy over Yorkshire and divided it afresh into districts known as *Wapentakes* instead of Hundreds. The name still survives, inasmuch as Todmorden to-day is included in the Wapentake of Morley.

The invasion of the Northmen had important consequences. It compelled the Anglo-Saxons to maintain soldiers in readiness for fighting at a moment's notice. The poorer freemen who cultivated the town lands no longer formed a sufficiently strong militia, but had to leave warfare to those who were able to devote all their energies to it. Hence there arose two distinct classes: one, engaged in military service that was esteemed honourable; the other, restricted to agriculture and considered menial. Further, the necessity of leadership in war made both classes more dependent on the great thegns who were the chief followers of the king. A different style of dress marked the difference in social rank. A freeman who followed his thegn to battle had long fair hair and flowing beard; he wore a belted tunic and pointed shoes. A servile tenant was known by his cropped hair, plain smock and bare feet. It should be noted, however, that in districts where the Northmen settled in large numbers, the freemen were more independent than the English peasants.

The power of the Northmen reached its height towards the close of the ninth century. Then bit by bit Alfred and his successors extended their dominion over the Midlands and the northern counties. The region between the Ribble and Mersey was conquered from the Northmen in A.D. 923 and added to the central kingdom of Mercia. The consequence was that for the first time the Lancashire part of the Todmorden neighbourhood was separated from the part in Yorkshire. The former was henceforth in Mercia; the latter in Northumbria. It followed also that people living on different sides of the Calder were brought under the jurisdiction of two different bishops. On the west, they were in the huge Mercian diocese of Lichfield; on the east, in the Northumbrian diocese of York.

Neglecting for the present the coming of the Normans, the story of invasion may be regarded as complete. Neolithic men, Goidels, Britons, Angles and Northmen, encamped in succession on the Todmorden uplands. Nor could any one of them sweep away its predecessors. An intermingling of races— Neolithic, Celtic, Teutonic—has been the result, and from this intermingling the present generation of men and women has come into existence.

As with race, so it has been with language. The dialect spoken in the Todmorden district is the direct outcome of the languages spoken by the various races who have lived on the uplands during the last two thousand years. A careful examination of local place names and dialect will reveal the presence of many words that are simply survivals from the forgotten speech of earlier races.

The subject is a difficult one, but the following derivations have been taken, for the most part, from the English Dialect Dictionary edited by Professor Joseph Wright.

Place names derived from Anglo-Saxon (A.S.) or Old Norse (O.N.):—

(*a*) Hills.
    1. *Hough* Stones. O.N. haugr, a 'how' or mound.
    2. Whir*law*. A.S. hlœw and hlāw, a mound or hill.

(*b*) Valleys.
    1. Todmor*den....Dean*, etc. A.S., denu, valley.
    2. *Clough*foot. A.S. clōh, ravine.

(*c*) Woods.
    1. *Hurst*wood. A.S. hyrst, a wood or copse.
    2. *Shaw* Wood. A.S. scaga, a copse.

(*d*) Forest clearings.
    Friths. A.S. fyrhth, a wood.

(*e*) Meadow Lands, etc.
    1. *Holme*, My*tholm*. A.S. holm, land rising from water.
    2. *Ing*bottom, Hall *Ings*. O.N. eng, meadow.
    3. Cross *Lee*, Town*ley*. A.S. lēah, untilled land.

(*f*) Settlements.
    1. Sowerby. Danish, by, town or village.
    2. *Thorpes*. A.S. thorp, throp, a farm or village.

The names "Todmorden" and "Calder" have been variously explained. Perhaps the most probable meaning of Todmorden is "the marshy valley of the fox"; tod meaning fox; mor, a heath or fen; and den, a valley. The name was first applied only to the north-western portion of this district, as distinct from Stansfield, Langfield and Walsden. Canon Taylor in his "Words and Places" suggests that Calder means "cold" (Norse, kalldr, cold).

Equally interesting survivals of ancient languages may be traced in local dialect expressions. Dr. Ellis, an authority on English dialects, mapped out this country into districts corresponding to the different varieties of dialect spoken in each. Todmorden is on the border line between three separate divisions in the North Midland division of English speech, viz.:—

1. Southern North Midland division: south-east Lancashire, including Rochdale.
2. Western North Midland division: Lancashire, south of the Ribble (excluding No. 1), and including Burnley.
3. Eastern North Midland division: the southern half of the West Riding of Yorkshire, including Halifax.

The following expressions are mentioned as being of common occurrence in one or more of these three districts:—

(a) oo or hoo, meaning she.
(b) au'm, meaning I am.
(c) Plural verbs ending in -en, such as thinken.

These expressions are obviously characteristic of the Todmorden dialect.

The following illustrations, taken from the local dialect, may also be added:—

(1) *Celtic.*
    " Heaw theaw duz *cam* thi clogs at th' eel." How you do *wear down* your clogs *on one side* at the heel. Welsh, Irish, Gaelic, *cam*, crooked.

(2) *Anglo-Saxon.*
  (a) "*Ax* 'im." *Ask* him.
      A.S. ācsian, to ask.
  (b) "*Oo* did *flite* 'im." *She* did *scold* him.
      A.S. heo, she.
      A.S. flitan, to chide.
  (c) "'As ta *steyven'd* the meat?" Have you *spoken in good time for* your meat?
      A.S. stefn, voice.
  (d) " What art a *threäpin* about?" What are you *quarrelling* about?
      A.S. thrēapian, to reprove.

(3) *Norse.*
  (a) " Go into th' *laithe.*" Go into the barn.
      O.N. hlatha, barn.

Mention may also be made of the following words:
  brat. A.S. bratt; O. Irish bratt, apron.
  barm. A.S. beorma, yeast.
  neive. O.N. hnefi, fist.
  attercop. A.S. attorcoppe, spider.
  arran web. O. French, araigne, spider.

These examples show how valuable a light may be thrown on the movements of vanished races by a study of place names and dialects. It is also note-

PLACE NAMES AND DIALECT

worthy how accurately old words are reproduced after the lapse of a thousand years. Our forefathers had little to do with books or newspapers, but depended almost entirely on the *spoken* language for a knowledge of spelling and pronunciation. The township records of Stansfield and Erringden during the 18th century (see Ch. xx.) show how men were often guided by the *sounds* of words rather than by any knowledge of spelling obtained from books. No one can mistake the pronunciation of the following words as written by the churchwardens, constables, and surveyors of that day :—kays (keys), saxton (sexton), chimley (chimney), quishins (cushions), roäp (rope). Phonetic spelling is manifest in such words as plastring, whitning, carrige and Crismas. Sometimes amusing attempts are made by the constables to spell unusual words: fisak (physic), lisanes (licence), and nessasrys (necessaries).

These examples serve also to show how from one generation to another, old ways of speaking are handed on with little or no change. To-day with compulsory attendance at school and an ever-widening intercourse between different districts, local dialects are rapidly changing and run a danger of being blotted out. Their value, however, should be fully recognised, and every care taken to preserve with accuracy the various dialect expressions used by old Todmordians living on the hills. An excellent collection of local dialect words was compiled by Mr. Joseph Crowther, of Walsden. His manuscript is now in the Reference Department of the Todmorden Free Library.

CHAPTER IX.

DOMESDAY BOOK.

Before the coming of the Normans most of the land in this country had passed into the possession of the king and his thegns. Moreover the distinction between men of honourable rank and such as cultivated the soil was clearly defined. A thegn's retainers received estates in return for military service; the peasants who were occupied in farming these estates, were not slaves, but they could not choose their own masters and were compelled to remain on the land given to them. There were in addition a number of slaves.

The Norman conquest gradually affected all classes of society. Saxon thegns and their retainers were wholly or partially deprived of their estates to make room for Norman knights and barons. The peasants were attached still more closely to the land, but slavery disappeared. Towards the end of William I's reign almost the whole of England had been divided among his followers. In the year 1086, at the command of the Conqueror, a great survey was made of most of the country. Royal commissioners visited nearly every shire. The men of each hundred or wapentake were summoned to meet them and give information about the estates in their neighbourhood. The king's officers wished to know, for example, who had been the owners and what had been the value of each estate in Edward the Confessor's reign; who then held the land (A.D. 1086) and what it was worth; how much of the land was waste and how much under cultivation. An inventory was also made of the number and character of the tenants on the different estates. So searching was this enquiry that " not a hide or a yard of land, nor . . . an ox nor a cow, nor a swine was left " that was not included in the king's writ. All these details were recorded in the Book of Winchester or Domesday Book. In its pages may be found the oldest description that exists of the Todmorden district. Before giving this description, however, it will be well to give a brief explanation of some of the terms employed in Domesday Book.

Norman estates were known as *manors*. This name was applied both to large districts such as the Manor of Wakefield or the Hundred of Salford, and to smaller estates that comprised only a single township. The latter were also called *berewicks*.

The part of a manor specially reserved for the Lord of the Manor and managed by an agent was termed *demesne* land.

Different classes of tenants were distinguished by different names. Free tenants, such as were numerous in districts where the Northmen had settled, were known as *sokemen*. Servile tenants were divided into villeins and bordars. *Villeins* owned about 30 acres of land and had one or two oxen for the plough team of eight oxen needed by the village community. Villeins were required to cultivate the demesne land of the Lord of the Manor, as well as their own farm. They ground their corn at the Lord's mill, made his park palings and drove the deer through the forest during the hunt. *Bordars* or cottagers had not more than 5 to 10 acres of land, and in addition to their work as labourers, they had to supply eggs and poultry. The services thus rendered by villeins and bordars were known as week-work and boon-work; at a later period rents were paid in money instead of work.

Two different terms were employed for the measurement of land. In counties like Yorkshire, conquered by Northmen, the usual standard was the *carucate*, or the amount of land (Lat. carucata) ploughed by a team of eight oxen in one season. Its usual subdivision was the eighth part, called a *bovate* or *oxgang*. The area of a carucate was about 120 acres. In Anglo-Saxon districts, where Northmen had not settled, the usual measure was the *hide*. Its value was different in different counties, but broadly speaking, it represented the amount of land needed by a single township. In South Lancashire, at the time of the survey, a hide was equal to six carucates.

Domesday Book was written in abbreviated Latin. Fig. 14 is a facsimile of the chief passage referring to the Todmorden district. The description of this district is found in two different parts of the book, as Todmorden was on the borderland, partly in one of the Yorkshire wapentakes and partly in what is now Lancashire. The most important extract refers to the Yorkshire portion (Fig. 14), and in modern English reads as follows:—" Yorkshire. King's land. In Wakefield with nine berewicks, Sandal Magna, Sowerby, Warley, Halifax, Midgley, Wadsworth, Crottonstall (?), Langfield and Stansfield, there are 60 carucates and $3\frac{1}{3}$ bovates on which danegeld has to be paid. Thirty ploughs may till this land. This manor was in the demesne of King Edward; now it is in the king's hands. Four villeins are there and 3 priests and 2 churches and 7 sokemen and 16 bordars. Together they have 7 ploughs. Woods pasturable, 9 miles in length and 6 miles in breadth. In the time of King Edward it was worth sixty pounds; now, fifteen pounds."

Sandal Magna is near Wakefield, and is described

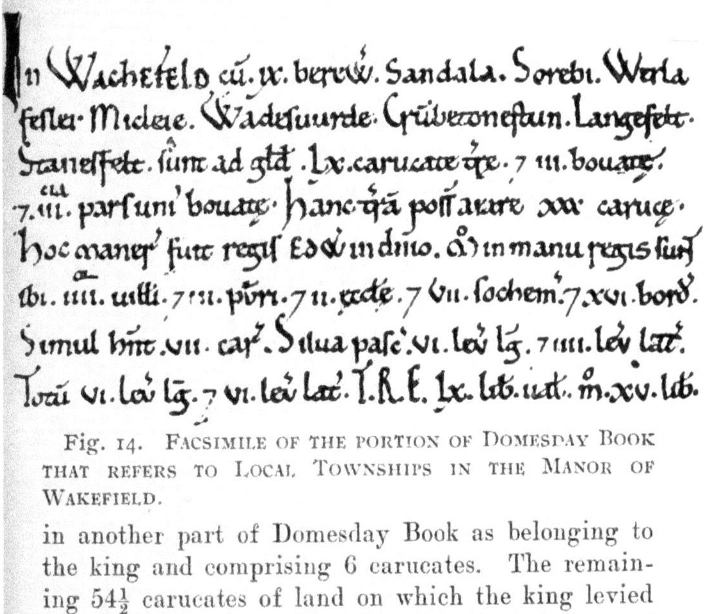
In Wachefeld cū. ix. berew. Sandala. Sorebi. Werla
fesley. Micleie. Wadesuurde. Crubeconestun. Langefelt.
Stanesfelt. sunt ad gld. lx. carucatae træ. 7 iii. bouatæ.
7. iii. pars uni' bouatæ. hanc trā poss arare xxx carucæ.
hoc maneri' fuit regis Edw in dnio. modo in manu regis sunt.
ibi. iiii. uitti. 7 iii. pbri. 7 ii. æcctæ. 7 vii. sochem. 7 xvi. bord.
Simul hnt. vii. car. Silua past. vi. leu lg. 7 iiii. leu lat.
Totū vi. leu lg. 7 vi. leu lat. T.R.E. lx. lib. uat. m. xv. lib.

Fig. 14. Facsimile of the portion of Domesday Book that refers to Local Townships in the Manor of Wakefield.

in another part of Domesday Book as belonging to the king and comprising 6 carucates. The remaining $54\frac{1}{2}$ carucates of land on which the king levied taxes were all situated within the ancient parish of Halifax. Five settlements skirted the uplands north of the Calder, viz., Stansfield, Wadsworth, Midgley, Warley and Halifax; on the south side were the three settlements of Langfield, Crottonstall (?) and

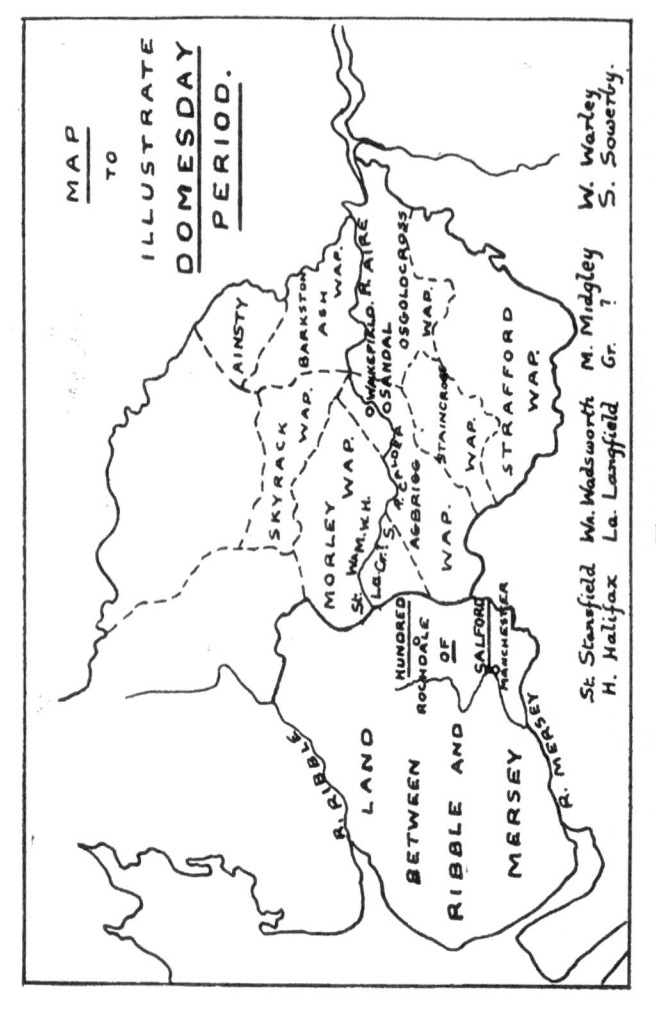

Fig. 15.

Sowerby. (Fig. 15.) Bordering these greener terraces and covering the moorlands were extensive woods that served as swine pastures.

Only seven ploughs were in use, so that only a small proportion of the land was under cultivation at that time. The value of the manor was only one quarter what it had been in Edward the Confessor's reign, viz., £15 instead of £60.* Moreover it seems to have been the opinion of the commissioners that the taxation paid was excessive (on 60 carucates) and that payment on 30 carucates (represented by 30 ploughs†) would be fairer. The lessened value of the manor and the smaller proportion of it under cultivation were the result of the terrible punishment that William I. inflicted on Yorkshire after the third northern revolt (A.D. 1069); a revolt in which men from the Todmorden uplands would be likely to take part.

The two churches were situated at Wakefield and Sandal Magna, and probably the three priests were also stationed there. A church at Halifax is not mentioned before the twelfth century, although a chapel may have been built even in Anglo-Saxon times.

The presence of seven sokemen points to the conquest of the Calder valley by the Northmen; a conclusion already reached from a consideration of local place names and dialect (pp. 42 and 44).

The number of tenants specified is 30, representing

* These amounts should be multiplied by 20 to obtain the value they would represent now.
† This is the probable meaning of " 30 ploughs may till this land."

a total population of about 150. This number is small, but with seven ploughs, only seven carucates, or rather more than a square mile of land could be cultivated. Moreover an acre of land in those days produced only six bushels of barley or about one-fifth of the present yield.

It is possible that in Stansfield or Langfield there were several farmsteads occupied by a free tenant, a villein and one or two bordars; all being under the supervision of the king's agent. Patches of brighter green indicated where the homesteads lay, separated from one another by woodland or marsh, and solitary amidst the surrounding moorlands. Food was probably abundant, although coarse in quality; oat or rye bread, fresh meat in summer, salted meat in winter, and plenty of ale. Each homestead was protected by stout palisades of felled timber from the wolves and boars that roamed over the hills. As for the world outside, wandering harpers were the likeliest persons to bring news of public affairs to this remote part of the country.

In the eleventh century the "county" of Lancaster did not exist, and in Domesday Book its southern half is described as "the land between the Ribble and Mersey." (Fig. 15). This district was divided into several Hundreds, among which was the Hundred of Salford.

The following passages occur in the account given in Domesday Book of the Salford Hundred:—

"Roger of Poitou held the land between Ribble and Mersey.

"To the Hundred (or Manor) of Salford belonged

21 manors held by as many thegns, in which there were 11½ hides and 10½ carucates of land. The woods there were 14 miles long and 8 miles broad. One of these thegns, Gamel, held two hides of land in Recedham, and was free of all customs but these six; viz., theft, heinfare, forestel, breach of the peace, not keeping the term set him by the reeve, and continuing a fight after an oath given to the contrary. The fine for these was 40 shillings.

"Of this manor (of Salford) there are now in the demesne 2 ploughs, and 8 serfs and 2 villeins with one plough. Of the land of this manor these knights hold by the gift of Roger of Poitou, Nigel 3 hides and half a carucate of land . . . . and Gamel, 2 carucates of land. In these there are 3 thegns, 30 villeins, 9 bordars, 1 priest and 10 serfs."

In the above narrative the following points may be noted:—

1. The Hundred of Salford had been granted to one of the king's vassals, Roger of Poitou, who lost it before 1086, but recovered it after the Conqueror's death.

2. A portion of the manor, cultivated by three ploughs, was reserved as demesne land. The rest of the land was granted to various knights and thegns, including a thegn called Gamel. In Edward the Confessor's reign Gamel had been the most important landowner in the Hundred, holding twelve carucates of land in Recedham or *Rochdale* (Fig. 15). He was highly privileged, escaping the usual burdens, such as rent. He was, however, responsible under severe penalties for repressing the following offences:

theft, assault on the king's highway (forestel), breaking into a man's house (heinfare), quarrelling or fighting, and disobedience to the lord's bailiff or reeve. For each of these offences the heavy fine was imposed of 40s. (equal to-day to £40).

3. Roger of Poitou took from Gamel most of his estate, leaving him only one-sixth of his former possessions.

4. The Normans objected to slavery, and after the Conquest slavery was abolished in this country. In the Hundred of Salford, however, this change had not taken place at the close of the Conqueror's reign.

5. The portion of the Todmorden district included in the Salford Hundred was probably part of the wood 14 miles long and 8 miles broad, mentioned in the description.

The total impression left by a consideration of the Domesday survey is that eight centuries ago this neighbourhood was mainly woodland, with several settlements on the Yorkshire uplands. On the foundations laid by the Normans this district gradually developed a more vigorous life during the later Middle Ages.

CHAPTER X.

TODMORDEN IN THE FOURTEENTH CENTURY.

During the reign of William the Conqueror the Manor of Wakefield belonged to the king, but the Hundred of Salford was granted to Roger of Poitou. These estates soon passed into other hands. In 1107 Henry I. bestowed the Manor of Wakefield on William, second Earl Warren, as a reward for the capture of Robert Courthose, the king's brother, in Normandy. The Earl's father, who came from the neighbourhood of Rouen, held a large number of estates in twelve counties, including Sussex and Yorkshire. His descendants, usually known as the Earls of Surrey, retained possession of the Manor of Wakefield for nearly 250 years. After several changes, portions of the Hundred of Salford were granted to the family of Lacies, lords of the castles of Clitheroe and Pontefract, and later Earls of Lincoln. In this way the western half of the Todmorden district passed under their jurisdiction during the 13th century.

Norman earls did not spend many days in a year on these inhospitable hills, for both food and accommodation were too scanty for their immense households. The Earls of Surrey, however, jealously guarded their right to follow the chase in their manor of Sowerby. No sport was more keenly indulged in by kings and barons than that of hunting, and for this purpose forests and chaces were set apart. All game was held to be the property of the king, whose permission barons had first to obtain before they might hunt even on their own estates. Strictly speaking, forests were reserved for kings; an earl's stretch of woodland was termed a chace. When Edward I. demanded of the fifth Earl Warren by what right he treated the various parts of his estates in Stansfield, Langfield, Wadsworth, etc., as a forest, the Earl replied that he claimed no forest rights in those lands, but he and his ancestors from time immemorial had had free chace therein, and Henry III. had confirmed those rights.

In the 13th century Erringden was enclosed as a park for breeding deer, and continued to be used for this purpose until Henry VI.'s reign. The park is mentioned several times in 14th century documents. In 1335, for example, William of Langfield granted to John of Methley and Henry of Langfield all the lands held of Earl Warren in "Withens, Tornelymosse and Mankanholes" outside the "park of Heyrikdene" (Erringden); whilst in 1370 "John by the Water, Thomas del Oldfield, Thomas by the Brokebank and Richard de Whitelee" had to see to the repair of its palisades.

Foresters or keepers were employed to look after the game and to preserve trees, shrubs and coverts. The Earl's keepers lived in the forest; among other places, probably at Old Chamber, near Hebden Bridge, and the Lodge in Erringden. It was their duty to prevent stray cattle from wandering into the forest, and to protect both game and timber from robbers. Offenders were brought before the Manor Courts. Hence the position of forester was an

IN THE FOURTEENTH CENTURY 57

important one; nor was it unattended with danger, for foresters were often assaulted and even killed.

A few examples will serve to illustrate the punishment inflicted for various offences by the Manor Court:—

Court at Wakefield, June 29, 1275. Thomas, son of John, son of Hugh de Mankanholes, was fined 6d. for the escape of pigs into the forest.

Court at Halifax, November 6, 1296. William de Stodelay, for the escape of two beasts in le Berndackeres, was fined 4d. John de Routonstall for 7 beasts in the same place, was fined 6d.

In 1296, Richard the fuller of Sowerby, was fined 2d. for collecting nuts in Sowerby wood; and John of Midgley 2s. for carrying away the Earl's timber.

About this time the Earl's chief forester killed a hart and sent it (without the Earl's permission) to the Vicar of Rochdale, in the hope that the latter would prevent poachers from the Rochdale parish coming into the Earl's chace. This secret action having been discovered the forester was tried at Wakefield, but the Court acquitted him.

Not many years later a Vicar of Rochdale was himself fined 20s. for hunting and killing deer in Sowerbyshire.

In 1305, the Earl of Lincoln received £1 18s. for the impoundment of free cattle that had escaped into the forest.

The above instances show how carefully intruders were kept out of the forest. Nor can we wonder at it, for hunting was not merely a pastime, but a necessary means of procuring food for the Earl's table. Local place names still point to those early hunting days; as, for example, Wolf Stone in Cliviger, Hawkstones in Stansfield, and Swines-head Clough in Langfield. Deer were also plentiful in the woods covering Walsden, within the domain of the Earls of Lincoln.

Both the Earls of Surrey and of Lincoln were often busy in the king's service. The fifth Earl Warren, who was Regent of Scotland during Edward I.'s reign, was defeated by Wallace (1297) and driven over the Border. The following year Henry de Lacy, Earl of Lincoln, led the van of the English army at Falkirk, and with a thousand men from Lancashire (including a contingent from the Rochdale parish) swept the army of Wallace from the field. It may well be that after following their respective lords, men from both sides of the Todmorden neighbourhood returned from the Scotch wars and poured into wondering ears tales of Border forays, of the daring of Wallace and the terrible vengeance of the king.

Meanwhile on each Earl's estate the ordinary business of life was being diligently pursued. Bailiffs were superintending the work of the tenants, holding manor courts, and collecting rents and various dues that had to be paid each year to the Earl's receiver. In the Middle Ages earls were often exceedingly wealthy. From his Lancashire and Cheshire estates the Earl of Lincoln received £1,146 (roughly, £23,000 to-day) during the year ended September 30, 1305; similarly Earl Warren's northern manors yielded an annual income of £666 (or £13,000). But a correspondingly great expense was incurred in the maintenance of many castles and manor houses and the payment of an enormous number of servants.

In the Todmorden district the income of the Lord of the Manor was derived chiefly from rents, agricultural produce, manorial mills and mining. The following examples will serve to illustrate the conditions under which men lived five or six centuries ago.

I.—*Rent and the tenure of land.*

A.D. 1274. Thomas of Langfield held directly of Earl Warren in the "town of Mancanholes" 13 oxgangs of land (about 200 acres), paying yearly 3s. 4d. (or £3 10s. to-day).

In Edward II.'s reign (1307—1327) the following tenants held estates of Henry de Lacy in the district of Cliviger:—

Gilbert de la Leghe (Towneley), 140 acres for 46s. 11d. (=£50).
William de Middlemore (Holme), 60 acres for 21s.
Stephen of the Grange, 18 acres for 6s. 6½d.
Adam of Ormerode, 8 acres for 1s. 1½d. and a pound of pepper.
Adam the Wright, 16 acres for 3s. 8d. and one pair of spurs, price 1½d.

Cliviger was sufficiently cultivated to permit 34 freeholders to rent farm lands.

It will be observed that the above rents were paid almost entirely in money: the older method survived in the following instance:—

A.D. 1372. Otto de Rivill gave to Richard of Stansfield for his homage and service, one oxgang (or 15 acres) of land in Wadsworth.

II.—*Agricultural produce.*

On the uplands large farms for cattle breeding, known as *vaccaries* (Latin *vacca*, a cow), brought additional wealth to the Lord of the Manor. They were usually situated within his demesne and were worked by villeins.* Each farm was managed by an *Instaurator*, who looked after the stock and was responsible for the sale of cattle and the letting of pasture lands. There were several vaccaries in Sowerbyshire, including one at Mankinholes and a larger one at Baitings near Ripponden. The value of the "herbage of Mancanholemore in the year 1308, amounted to 13s. 4d.," and was duly entered in the Court Roll at Wakefield. Some instaurators were themselves wealthy tenants, as, for example, Gilbert of the Lea, mentioned above, who was chief instaurator of the Accrington vaccaries belonging to the Earl of Lincoln. His account of a single year's revenue (A.D. 1305) from the vaccaries of Blackburnshire shows how lucrative they proved. The sales were as follows:—

213 oxen - - - - -	£105 13s. 2d.
168 cows, 5 bulls and 2 calves -	£67 8s. 4d.
Hides and flesh - - -	£7 6s. 3½d.

After payment of expenses, Gilbert handed over the sum of £173 1s. 6d. to the Earl's receiver at Clitheroe. To this must be added £87, being the rent paid by the tenants of the vaccaries; making a total roughly equal to £5,000 of present-day money.

Large sums were paid for the right to pasture

*Villeins were tenant farmers who were known later as copyhold tenants (Chap. xi., p. 74).

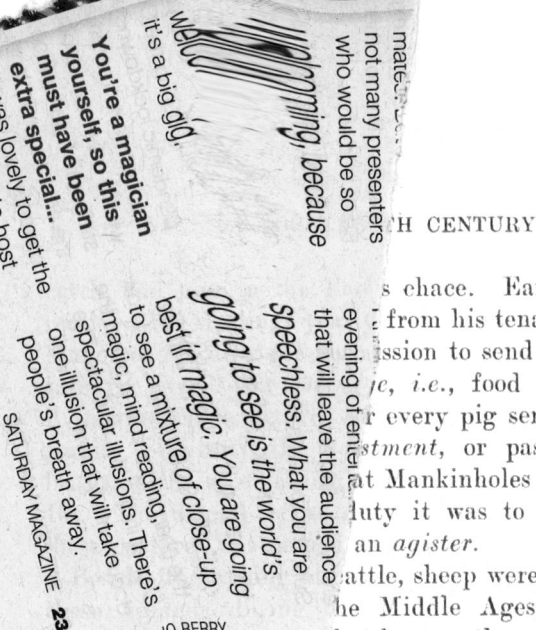

TH CENTURY   61

...s chace. Earl Warren
... from his tenants in the
...ission to send their pigs
...ic, i.e., food for swine.
...r every pig sent into the
...stment, or pasturage of
...at Mankinholes was worth
...luty it was to look after
...an *agister.*
...attle, sheep were reared on
...he Middle Ages, and the
...hat became the most impor-
...he manufacture of woollen
...oth. In the 14th century, the Priory of Lewes,
which owned large estates in Halifax parish (see
chap. xi.), received wool as rent from all parts of
the parish. Women carried the wool packs to
Halifax, where the Proctor or Prior's agent sold the
wool to cloth merchants. In the year 1366-7, for
example, 3 sacks or 78 stones of wool were sold for
£19. The wool from Heptonstall was brought by
three women who thereby earned 2d. each, besides
an allowance for ale.

In addition to wool growing, the manufacture of
cloth was already widespread. As early as 1275
William the *Fuller* served as surety to Thomas of
Langfield who was charged with trespassing in
Sowerby forest. A *fulling mill* was transferred
from Colne to *Wadsworth* about the middle of the
14th century, as Gamel Sutcliffe the owner had
married Ann Radcliffe of Stansfield. In the Poll
Tax returns for 1379 (chap. xii., p. 82) the names
occur of three *Walkers* or fullers in Wadsworth and

of one *Textor* or weaver in Midgley; whilst in the court records for 1380 is the name of William *Walker* of Stansfield. The manufacture of cloth, therefore, had become one of our local industries. Kersies were the articles most usually made, a material made up into smaller pieces than in the case of broad cloths.

III.—*Manorial Mills.*

These mills belonged to the Lord of the Manor. They were water corn mills, being built near running streams. Tenants were compelled to grind their own grain at the lord's mill, a twentieth of the grain being paid for the use of his mill. One of the earliest mills in this neighbourhood was in Stansfield, as before the close of the 13th century mention is made of "5 oxgangs of land in Stansfield, with the mill and 7 more oxgangs in the same town belonging thereto." Corn mills were erected at Burnley, Worsthorne, Cliviger, Heptonstall and Warley. In 1382 the mill at Heptonstall was rented by Ralph Milner for 6s. 8d. from the Priory of Lewes.

IV.—*Mining.*

The mineral wealth found in this neighbourhood provided further means of livelihood. There was an iron forge in Sowerby forest worth £9 12s. yearly, which it was thought might continue for ever. Many traces still remain of ancient iron forges or *bloomeries*, that were probably in existence at this period and continued as late as the 17th century. The most important was at Ruddle Scout in Cliviger, where several bands of iron stone occur and entrances into the mine may still be seen. Remains of slag occur in Walsden valley, near Waterstalls, in Birks Wood and up Ramsden Clough. The Ramsden reservoir covers the site of an old bloomery; during the construction of the reservoir, slag and pieces of iron were unearthed at a place formerly known as Furnace. The method of smelting was very simple. The ore was mixed with wood or charcoal and placed in a pile on the hill side, where plenty of draught secured the reduction of the ore to spongy iron, from which the slag was then hammered out. By this means only part of the iron was extracted from the ore, much being also left behind in the slag. The mine in Cliviger was possibly first worked in the year 1305, for in the Earl of Lincoln's accounts for that year this item occurs:—

Iron ore sold for 10 weeks - - 6s. 8d.

No mention of iron ore is to be found in the account for the year 1295, but a curious entry shows that coal was being obtained from Cliviger:—

Sea coal sold there - - - - 3d.

Wood cutting was of great importance in those days. Wood and charcoal were used in iron smelting;* wood or turf fires were general; houses were made of wood; whilst every enclosure of forest land involved the removal of trees and shrubs. A glimpse of the old method of building is afforded in a petition of Thomas of Luddenden (in 1364) " for a tree to repair his house with, he being poor."

The houses of the wealthy consisted of a central

---

* In the Earl of Lincoln's accounts, for the Blackburn Hundred (1305) is the following item: "cutting down and cutting up wood for burning iron ore, 7s. 5d."

hall that was open to the roof and served as a living room. On one side was a parlour with a chamber or bedroom above, approached by steps outside; at the other end was the merchant's warehouse or farmer's buttery. Outhouses and cottages were at the back, across a yard. The dwellings of the poor were low, damp, cheerless buildings.

The presence of wolves and wild boars in this district should not be forgotten, nor the dangers that accompanied them. Almost every year instaurators reported the loss of a calf or yearling strangled by a wolf, and among the items of expense (for 1305) we find 6s. 8d. for taking wild boars, and 17s. 8d. for "making folds for the Master Forester and cutting down branches for the wild animals."

Some particulars may be added of the wages paid and the prices current six centuries ago. The amounts given should, however, be multiplied by 20 before comparing them with present-day figures. An Earl's steward received a yearly salary of from £6 13s. 4d. to £13 6s. 8d.; the bailiff, £9 10s.; a forester or parker, £2 5s. 6d.; an instaurator, £2. With these amounts may be contrasted the yearly wages of a carter, viz., 6s., and of a herdsman, 3s. The possession of a cottage and plot of land, rent-free, may also be assumed, as well as rights of pasture. On the Lancashire estates of the Earl of Lincoln, reapers received 2d. a day; meadows were mown at the rate of 4d. an acre; oats cost 2s. a quarter; oxen, 9s.; cows, 7s.; whilst the price of horses varied from £1 to £3. Butter and cheese were sold at $5\frac{1}{2}$d. a stone; a pound of pepper cost 1s. 8d. to 2s.

The reader may now understand more clearly the

condition of the Todmorden district during the later Middle Ages. Within the compass of a few miles were to be found the Earl's forest and chace where wild beasts still roamed, his park with herds of deer, his demesne lands with cattle farms and pastures, his corn mills by the running streams. There were also tenants' farms with sheep pastures and crops of oats and barley, whilst spinning, weaving and fulling, iron smelting and coal mining were numbered among local industries. With such variety of labour the neighbourhood needed little help from the world outside. Special needs were met by means of fairs and markets. In 1286 a man is recorded to have travelled from Bradford to Manchester to fetch salt. Gradually markets were established in various manors and brought additional wealth to their lords. Edmund de Lacy, for instance, obtained Henry III.'s permission to hold a market and fair in Rochdale; and it is probable that not only in Burnley, but also within the shadow of the churches of Halifax and Heptonstall, markets were held before the close of the Middle Ages.

CHAPTER XI.

Mediæval Churches and Law-courts.

In the last chapter Norman earls were considered as great landowners, interested in the cultivation of their estates and in receiving whatever rents and services were due to them. Their influence will now be traced in religious affairs and in the administration of justice in the neighbourhood of Todmorden.

It is probable that the oldest memorial of religion in Todmorden is Mount Cross, near Stiperden (p. 39). It is impossible to say whether any rude churches were erected in the district before the Norman conquest. The early English were not famous builders, and their churches were often constructed of wood. The Normans, however, were a much more highly cultivated race, and when they came to England a great development took place in architecture. They were, moreover, sincerely religious, and churches as well as castles rose over the length and breadth of the land. The influence of this revival was felt locally. Both the Warrens and Lacies were typical Normans, and owing to their zeal churches were built at Halifax and Rochdale during the century after the Conquest. No change was made in the diocese to which each church belonged, but the first Norman Bishop of Lichfield removed the headquarters of the diocese from Lichfield to Chester. It is probable, however, that when the church at Halifax was built, the Halifax parish was carved out of the older parish of Dewsbury.

The Earls of Surrey and of Lincoln bestowed many valuable gifts upon the Church. The first Earl Warren, for example, in gratitude for the kind way in which he and his wife had been entertained by the monks of Cluny when they were travelling on the Continent, built the Priory of St. Pancras at Lewes in Sussex. This was the first Cluniac monastery erected in England. The family of Lacy founded the Abbey of Stanlaw in Cheshire (afterwards transplanted to Whalley) and also Kirkstall Abbey near Leeds.

Abbeys and priories were the homes of monks who cultivated the adjacent lands and gave themselves to a life of prayer. Norman earls were often anxious to secure the favour of these religious houses and sought to enrich them with gifts of lands from their numerous manors. There are several local examples of such bequests. The second Earl Warren, by a charter earlier than the year 1121, granted to the Priory of Lewes the Church of Halifax with all the lands and tenements belonging thereto, including estates in Stansfield, Heptonstall and Wadsworth. The church of Rochdale and part of the Forest of Rossendale were bequeathed by the Lacies to the Abbey of Stanlaw. Towards the close of the 13th century William de Haword granted a portion of his lands in Todmorden to the same abbey. The Abbot of Kirkstall Abbey had a carucate (120 acres) of land at Holme, in Cliviger, where there was a grange under the superintendence of a Cistercian monk.

In this way many estates in the Todmorden neighbourhood became the property of ecclesiastical absentee landlords, whose chief interest was in the revenues to be derived from them. The Halifax parish will serve as an example. In the year 1292 the annual value of church lands in the parish was about £110 (or £2,500 to-day). Of this sum, £16 was paid to the Vicar of Halifax, who was appointed by the monks of Lewes; the remainder (roughly equal to-day to £2,000), was poured into the coffers of the distant Priory. Although the vicar's stipend was a very liberal one for those days, it is obvious that most of the money raised by the Halifax church was diverted in order to add to the splendour of an already wealthy Priory, instead of being devoted to the religious needs of the parish. This is the probable reason why nearly two centuries elapsed after the Norman conquest before a chapel was built to the west of Halifax.

The first chapel erected was that of Heptonstall. It was dedicated to St. Thomas of Canterbury and was in existence before the year 1260. The site was well chosen, for perched on the cliff overlooking the northern bank of the Calder, the chapel was conveniently placed not only for its own township but also for the townships of Stansfield and Wadsworth. The chapelry of Heptonstall comprised the five townships of Wadsworth, Heptonstall, Stansfield, Langfield and Erringden (Fig. 23). The appointment of curate lay with the Vicar of Halifax, who was ordered by the monks of Lewes to pay him a salary of £4 a year. William, the Clerk of Langfield, was probably one of the earliest priests, but few names of curates have been preserved before the 15th century.

As big landowners, the monks of Lewes made their

influence felt within the Halifax parish. A proctor, appointed by the Prior, acted as bailiff in looking after the Priory estates, and held the Prior's Court at Halifax for the collection of rents and transfer of land. Occasionally the Court sought to exceed its proper duties. In 1307, for example, at the Sheriff's Court held in Halifax at the Moot Hall, the jury* complained that the Prior held his court four times a year, instead of twice; that he had appointed ale tasters and prevented some of the Earl's tenants from living in the township of Halifax: matters that belonged, not to the Prior's, but to the Earl's Manor, Court. The protest proved effective and the Prior ceased his illegal proceedings.

The legal powers entrusted to Earl Warren during this period may be best understood by a brief account of the courts that were held within his Manor of Wakefield. There were two separate courts, known as "The Court" and "The Turn." The Court was the more important. It was usually held every three weeks at Wakefield, but occasionally it met elsewhere, as at Halifax. Another name given to it was "Court Baron," *i.e.*, the court where the Baron as Lord of the Manor exercised jurisdiction over his tenants. It was the court more particularly of the freeholders, although villeins also attended for certain purposes. The business of the court was exceedingly varied, including not only the holding and transfer of lands, but the appointment of manorial officers, and the punishment of manorial offences. The Earl's steward usually presided,

* The names of the jurymen included John of Stodelay (Stoodley), Richard of Wadsworth, and Adam of Midgley.

attendance was compulsory, and heavy fines were levied for absence unless permission had been previously obtained.

Earl Warren held also the right to hold a second court, known as "The Turn," or "Court Leet." As a rule it was a criminal court, dealing with less important cases, and was held at the close of the Court Baron. The many-sided activity of these courts may be seen from the following examples. Interesting glimpses are also afforded of the different conditions that prevailed within the Halifax parish six centuries ago.

I.—*Cases of Theft.*

(*a*) November 22, 1274. Stephen the Waleys (or Foreigner) had a man, John of Asberne, who was charged with taking a stag in Sowerby Forest. A man named Hulle was with him, and it was stated that Adam, son of Thomas of Holgate, found them skinning it. For helping to eat the stag Adam was fined 40 shillings, or the price of four oxen; and John of Midgley, Adam of Wadsworth and Nalke of Heptonstall became sureties for his good behaviour. The chief culprits had escaped, but were to be arrested if found within the Earl's manor.

(*b*) Court of Wakefield, May 1, 1277. Richard, son of the smith of Stansfield, seized on suspicion of theft, gave 13s. 4d. to be under the surety of Alkoc of the Frith, Richard, son of Ralph of Stansfield, William the Carpenter of the same place and John the smith, until the Steward's Tourn at Halifax.

(*c*) Tourn at Halifax, June 5, 1307. John of Milnehouses, Robert, son of the Chaplain of Elland,

John of the Castell, John of Birton and William of
Birton broke into the house of William of Stodelay
(Stoodley) and stole goods worth £20. This charge
was presented by the townships of Stansfield, Langfield, Wadsworth, etc. The culprits were to be
arrested.

II.—*Cases of violence.*

(*a*) Tourn at Halifax, Nov. 22, 1284. " Nicholas of
Werloley (Warley) met Robert Feres in Werloley
wood and beat him till he gave him 1½d. Nicholas
gave 20s. to be quit."

(*b*) Tourn at Halifax, Dec. 6, 1308. "John of
Hertlay drew blood from William of Stanesfeld.
Fine 12d."

III.—*Manorial offences.*

(*a*) 1361. John of Horsfall of Langfeld was fined
for fishing in the Calder.

A statute passed in 1266 regulated the price of
bread according to the price of flour per quarter and
prohibited the selling of any ale, the quality of
which the Earl's ale-tasters had not approved.

(*b*) Tourn at Halifax, Nov. 22, 1284. Twelve
jurors, including Richard of Stansfield and Thomas
of Langfield, stated that the wife of John the Grave
sold ale contrary to the statute. She was fined 6d.

(*c*) Oct. 25, 1379. John, Clerk of Heptonstall,
was fined for selling bread contrary to the statute.

(*d*) 1376. The wife of John of Horsfall of Langfield was fined 6d. for brewing.

(*e*) *Incroaching on land.* Tourn at Halifax, Nov.
6, 1296. "Richard Lorimar' of Stansfield" incroached

on the highway with a hedge and ditch. The road had to be made up again and he was fined 6d.

(f) *Leave of absence from Court.* Court at Wakefield, 1285. Thomas of Langfield gave 4s. for respite of suit of court (or leave of absence from court) till Michaelmas.

IV.—*Wager of Law.*

If one party to a dispute demanded a jury, the request was granted on payment of a small fee. When a jury were unable to agree as to the truth of certain charges, the accused person was permitted to clear himself by a process known as ' wager of law.' A local example will explain what was the usual procedure.

At Halifax, Whitweek, 1275. William of the Hirst complained of an assault in the night-time by William, son of Adam of Wadsworth, and several others. He stated that his doors were broken open, himself dragged from bed and beaten, and that when he fled he was chased and pelted with stones. He claimed 39s. damages and 13s. 4d. compensation for the outrage he had suffered.

The accused pleaded not guilty, and as they bore good characters, and decisive evidence could not be obtained, they were ordered by the Court to wage their law and if possible establish their innocence. First, each of the defendants took an oath as follows :—"Hear this, sir, I am not guilty of this charge made against me by William de Hirst . . . . so help me God." Then in turn eleven neighbours of the accused avowed upon oath that they believed the defendants spoke the truth. Thereupon the charge was dismissed, and William of the Hirst was fined 5s. for having lodged an unjust complaint.

V.—*False charges.*

Great care was taken that complaints should be accurately lodged, and false accusations were not suffered to go unpunished.

(*a*) Court at Wakefield, Feb. 2, 1275. John Stel complains of Thomas, son of John of Langefeld, in a plea of robbery.

Thomas is imprisoned. The plaintiff says that Thomas took from him a bay horse (he knows not by what warrant or by whose order), also 15d. worth of cloth from his daughter, half a lump of iron, a saddle and a bit, but he does not name the price of anything except the iron. Thomas denies it, and craves judgment because John did not name his proper name, nor the day nor the hour; nor ought the charge to be tried in that Court.

Thomas therefore goes quit, and John must go to prison for his false complaint. He made fine of 6s. 8d.

(*b*) Court at Wakefield, Aug. 24, 1307. William, son of William of Mancanholes (Mankinholes), is fined 12d. for not prosecuting his suit against Adam of Kirkes-chawe for trespass.

VI.—*Transfer of lands.*

Manor Courts were of the utmost importance in the transference of manorial lands from one tenant to another. When a free tenant succeeded to an estate, he paid a sum of money or fine (known also as a *relief*) to the Lord of the Manor. A similar payment by a villein was called a *heriot*. In 1377 an incoming tenant paid the sum of 5s. on taking possession of "a messuage, croft, half-bovate, and six acres of royd land" in Woodhouse, Langfield. There was also a ceremony of *investiture*, when each tenant swore fealty to his lord and obedience to the laws and customs of the manor. In the Halifax parish a straw, fastened to the legal document, served as a symbol of the estate that was being transferred.

Villeins held their estates on servile tenure, and when a villein died, his heir had to appear before the Court to plead for permission to succeed to the estate. Strictly speaking, a villein's lands belonged to the Earl, who might dispose of them as he thought fit. But when a villein had made application for his lands and the Court had recognised his claim, his name was entered upon the copy of the Court Roll, with the conditions of tenure fully set forth. This entry was the only evidence a villein had of his right as a tenant, but the presence of other villeins at the Manor Court lessened the danger of injustice.

VII.—*An unjust steward.*

The following examples show what sometimes happened.

(*a*) In the year 1276. "They say that Richard de Haydon, Steward of Earl Warren, maliciously vexed Richard de Stansfield, and charged him with having harboured a certain felon and extorted 10 marks from him."

(*b*) A resolution of the Court at Wakefield, Jan. 30, 1359. "If any tenant in the lordship of Halifax be beheaded for theft or other cause, the heirs of the same tenant ought not to lose his inheritance," whatever may have been the action of the Earl's steward.

VIII.—*Right of gallows.*

The greatest privilege conferred on the Earls of Surrey by the king was the "right of gallows." When Edward I. demanded of John, fifth Earl Warren, by what right he exercised his privileges, the Earl replied that he "claimed gallows at Wakefield, and the power of doing what belonged to a gallows in all his lands," adding that he and all his ancestors had used the same from time immemorial. In other words Earl Warren had the right to execute thieves caught on his estates. Other Earls possessed the same privilege (the Earls of Lincoln, for example, had a gallows at Bradford), but this right was exercised in the manor of Wakefield for three centuries after it had been abolished in every other part of England; indeed for three hundred years after the family of Warren was extinct. In the parish of Halifax the right of gallows was comprised in the famous "Gibbet Law," which persisted until the year 1650, when public protests brought about its abolition. The law provided that any felon taken within the forest of Sowerby, including Wadsworth, Heptonstall, Rottenstall, Stansfield, Cross Stone, Langfield and Erringden, and having goods to the value of 1s. 1½d., or confessing to such theft, should be placed under the care of the bailiff at Halifax. The trial was held in the Court House before a jury of 16 men (four from each of four townships chosen by the bailiff), and if the accused was condemned, he was executed on the next principal market day

76   HISTORY OF TODMORDEN

to serve as a warning to evil doers. On any previous but less important days the culprit was exhibited in the stocks with the stolen goods in front of him. Old woodcuts still preserve the memory of the

Fig. 16. THE HALIFAX GIBBET.

actual gibbet, erected in Gibbet Lane, Halifax, and show us the method of execution (Fig. 16). "A Privy Chamber man extraordinary" who visited Halifax in 1639, on his way to York to attend

Charles I., has left an interesting description of the gibbet:—

"June 27. Thursday I came to Halifax, a pretty well built town of stone and consists much of clothiers, to encourage whose trade, was granted that privilege of beheading by their trade law any malefactor taken (as they say) hand napping, back bearing, or confessing the felony. Their beheading block is a little out of the town westward; it is raised upon a little forced ascent of some half a dozen steps, and is made in the form of a narrow gallows having two ribs down either side-post, and a great weighty block with riggalds (grooves) for these ribs to shoot in, in the bottom of which block is fastened a keen edged hatchet. Then the block is drawn up by means of a pulley and a cord to the cross on the top, and the malefactor lays his head on the block below; then they let run the stock with the hatchet in, and dispatch him immediately." Hence the Halifax gibbet was not unlike the guillotine used in Paris during the French Revolution. The axe is still preserved at the Manor Court, Wakefield, and is a relic of an age when swift and brutal vengeance was inflicted for theft.

On the hill above Scaitcliffe, and therefore outside the parish of Halifax, is a farm still known as Gibbet. This name also may point to the existence centuries ago of a gallows, within the jurisdiction of the Earls of Lincoln.

CHAPTER XII.

An Old Poll Tax Return.

Before completing the account of the Todmorden neighbourhood during the later Middle Ages, three questions may be briefly considered. First, how far back can the name of Todmorden be traced; second, were any noteworthy Todmorden families living in the district in mediæval times; and third, can an estimate be given of the population of Todmorden during the 14th century?

I. The name of Todmorden cannot be traced back as far as those of Stansfield and Langfield. The latter occur in Domesday Book, but the earliest references to Todmorden are met with in 13th and 14th century documents that relate to the transference of property. Two examples may be cited in illustration.

(*a*) "Court held at Wakefield, June 11, 1298. Sourby. Michael, son of Richard of *Todmereden* gave 2s. to take half of all the land at the Helm left unoccupied on the Earl's hands by Jordan Peule for ever. Pledge: Hugh of Lictheseles and Adam the Crouther."

(*b*) In the year 1318, certain lands in *Todmorden* were conveyed by charter to Henry of Haworth, together with a hunting lodge in Inchfeld and pasture belonging thereto.

In similar deeds the names occur of Walsden, Henshaw, Knowl, Gauxholme and Stones; places that are all within the present township of Todmorden and Walsden.

II. There are three families that were of considerable importance in this district for several centuries: the Stansfields, Radcliffes and Crossleys. Of these, priority is claimed by the Stansfields. Their legendary ancestor was Wyan Marions, a Norman knight in the service of Earl Warren, to whom it is said the Earl granted the sub-manor of Stansfield. Undoubtedly there was a mill in existence in this township at a very early date (p. 62); and it is probable that a mediæval building once stood where Stansfield Hall now stands. The Stansfields of Stansfield Hall left the district about the middle of the 17th century.

Members of the Radcliffe family acquired large estates in the hamlets of Todmorden and Walsden during the 15th century, and erected a timber built hall on the site of Todmorden Hall. Some of the oak beams of the earlier structure still form part of the present mansion. Several of the Radcliffes rose to distinction. The family severed their connection with this district in the 18th century. A genealogical table of the family is given in Appendix IV.

The earlier history of the Crossleys of Scaitcliffe is quite obscure. No assured pedigree can be traced before the 16th century, but members of the family are mentioned in 14th century documents. An inscription placed by one of the Crossleys at the head of several graves in St. Mary's churchyard reads as follows: "To perpetuate the memory of the Crossleys of Scaitcliffe in this Township. Adam de Croslegh and Matilda his wife; John de Croslegh,

Johanna his wife, William their son, Thomas de Croslegh and Richard his son, died between the years of our Lord 1307 and 1420." The Crossley family retained possession of Scaitcliffe Hall until a recent date.

III. It has been stated that not more than 150 persons lived on the uplands between Todmorden and Halifax in the days of William the Conqueror. Valuable information may be obtained as to the population of the same district during the 14th century from the poll tax returns in Richard II.'s reign. In the second year of his reign, Richard's council demanded a subsidy for the protection of the country from the ravages of the French and Scotch. All persons over 16 years of age, except priests and mendicants, had to contribute to this tax, and their names were entered on a series of rolls compiled for each county. A complete series of West Riding rolls still exists, which contain not only the names, but often also the residence or occupation of the taxpayers as well as the amount of money they contributed. The returns are entered separately for each wapentake, in sub-divisions according to the different townships. The details of local townships in the Halifax parish are found among the four rolls for the wapentake of Morley.

The total amount raised in the West Riding was £341 (perhaps equal to about £6,000 to-day), towards which Morley, one of eleven wapentakes, contributed £39 10s. 2d. It is interesting to observe which were the wealthiest places in the Riding, and to compare the list with a corresponding list to-day. In 1379, Doncaster came first, with a tax of £11 13s. 6d.;

Wakefield second, with £6 6s. 0d., and Leeds third with £4 15s. 8d. Then followed Mirfield, Elland and Bradford. In the following table several of the townships in the parish of Halifax are arranged in order of importance, according to the number of taxpayers, the amount paid and the estimated population of each township.

	No. of Taxpayers.	Tax paid.	Estimated Population.
Stansfield	43	15s. 8d.	128
Wadsworth	37	13s.	118
Sowerby and	28	9s. 4d.	151
Erringden	10	3s. 4d.	
Warley	24	8s.	101
Halifax	22	7s. 4d.	90
Langfield	22	7s. 4d.	67
Midgley	21	7s. 4d.	86
Heptonstall	16	5s. 4d.	55

The total number of taxpayers was 223, of whom 140 were described in the roll as married. The population, therefore, may be reckoned at about 800, of whom about 200 were in Stansfield and Langfield and upwards of 400 in the chapelry of Heptonstall.

Obviously there were no crowded cities in the West Riding in the 14th century. On the contrary the population was thinly scattered over broad green plains and uplands.

When the names of the taxpayers are examined there is much to arrest attention. Most of the names sound very familiar. In the list of taxpayers in Stansfield, for example, are the names of John of Shore, William of Stansfield, John of Eastwood,

D

Richard of Horsfall, Richard Greenhurst, William Spenser, Adam Wright, Thomas Crossley, Isabella Crosslee, Roger Turner, Johanna Harper, and William, son of Richard. Here are English surnames in the making; men and women with the same Christian name being distinguished by their occupation, dwelling-place or parents. In the list for Heptonstall occur the names of Richard of Greenwood, Richard Milner, Robert of Bryge (Bridge), John Clerk and Joan Harper. The following pursuits are indicated in the returns for the above townships: wright (wheelwright), turner, milner (miller), weaver, tailor, harper, clerk, walker (or fuller), shepherd or herdsman, smith, arrowsmith, fletcher (one who fledged arrows with feathers) and spenser (one who bought supplies for large households). All who paid the tax contributed fourpence with the exception of five persons. John of Dean, weaver, and John Midgley, both resident in Midgley, paid sixpence. Three persons were styled merchants and paid one shilling each. They were John of Shore, William of Stansfield (who have already been mentioned) and Robert of Wadsworth. In all probability they were wool merchants, but we cannot tell whether they were members of a gild. Further down the Calder there was a greater difference both in wealth and occupation. Elland, for example, contributed 45s. 4d., boasting of a knight, who paid 20s.; a franklin or merchant trading over sea, who paid 3s. 4d.; as well as two merchants, a tailor, smith, carpenter and three websters or female weavers. Although in the more remote parts of the parish of Halifax, wealthier traders had not settled, this old poll tax return confirms the conclusion reached in Chapter XI. that the manufacture of cloth was already carried on in this neighbourhood.

The origin of some of the most familiar surnames may be traced in these poll tax returns. Greenwood, the commonest name in Halifax parish, was at first a place name in Heptonstall township; Crossley was derived from Cross Lee; Stansfield and Wadsworth were also place names. To these may be added the names of Sutcliffe (from South Cliff, near Halifax), Barker (probably meaning tanner), Kershaw (from carr, hummocky ground, and shaw, a wood), and Holt (meaning wood).

It is unfortunate that no corresponding returns have been preserved of the various townships in the Hundred of Salford. In 1380, however, when a poll tax of three groats was levied, 146 persons contributed to it in the parish of Rochdale. Of these 53 were in the township of Hundersfield, but none of the names that have been deciphered can be referred to the hamlets of Todmorden and Walsden situated within the township.

CHAPTER XIII.

TODMORDEN DURING THE REFORMATION PERIOD.

The second half of the fifteenth century was marked in the Todmorden district by a rapid increase in population and a great development of the woollen industry. It was no less remarkable as a period of church building.

Fig. 17. HEPTONSTALL OLD CHURCH, LADY CHAPEL.

Heptonstall Chapel was rebuilt before the middle of the century. William del Brygge (of the Bridge) left money in 1440 towards making the bells; a bequest suggestive of the completion of the building. The chapel was built in the perpendicular style of architecture and was more than once enlarged. To-day the old church lies in ruins (Fig. 17), but it was

THE REFORMATION PERIOD

used for public worship until the middle of last century.

In Todmorden, St. Mary's chapel was built at some time between the years 1400 and 1476. No lovelier position could have been chosen. The chapel stands like a sentinel at the junction of three valleys and faces the sun rising. A grassy knoll lifted it above the floods, whilst a little to the south was Todmorden Hall, to which a private pathway led from the graveyard. At the bottom of the slope the Calder flowed, being partly hidden by a grove of trees, and then curved across the valley to the opposite hill where, on the lower slope, stood Stansfield Hall, with the corn mill nearer to the stream. Owing to its convenient situation Todmorden chapel was attended by the inhabitants of the adjacent townships of Stansfield and Langfield. "John Crosley of Kilnehurst" for example (in 1521), though he ordered his body to be buried at Heptonstall, bequeathed 8s. to the "chapell of Todmerden." But Heptonstall chapel was built for the Yorkshire townships, and for generations, families like the Stansfields worshipped there. On one of the windows of the chapel there used to be the arms of the Stansfields of Stansfield Hall with the date 1508 also inscribed.

According to an old local tradition Cross Stone Chapel was built by the Stansfields of Stansfield Hall. The first building must have been erected before 1537, since in that year Thomas Stansfield of Sowerby gave to the chapel 103s. 4d. for a chalice. The chapel was subordinate to Heptonstall Chapel, no right of either burial or baptism being granted until a much later date (1678). In Elizabeth's reign

Cross Stone Chapel appears to have been rebuilt, and a salary of £20 a year to have been guaranteed to the curate by the inhabitants of both Stansfield and Langfield—the two townships within the chapelry of Heptonstall that the chapel was intended to serve.

For many centuries the beliefs and rites of the Roman Catholic Church had been accepted by the English people. The Pope was regarded as the head of Christendom; monastic institutions, which were under his control, were numerous and powerful. The sacrifice of the mass, the adoration of the Virgin and saints, daily prayers and masses for the dead and a church service recited in Latin, were parts of a system that made the priest the centre of the religious life of the community.

In the Halifax parish these beliefs were accepted without hesitation up to the very eve of the Reformation. One of the duties, for example, often undertaken by a Catholic priest was to sing masses for the souls of the dead. Endowments either in land or money, and known as chantries, were founded for his support, and for the maintenance of the altar or chapel where a priest officiated. Two such chantries were established at Heptonstall. The first was dedicated to the Virgin Mary and was founded by many of the parishioners about the beginning of the 16th century. William Greenwood of Heptonstall, in 1506, desired his executors to purchase as much land as possible for 10 marks to maintain "one honest priest to sing within the chapel of our Lady."* The priest of this chantry had also to assist the

* Fig. 17 shows the "Lady Chapel" within the Old Church, where the chantry priest sang masses.

curate of the chapel to administer the sacraments and visit the sick. The second Heptonstall chantry was founded by William Greenwood in 1524, and was of the value of £5 per annum. Numerous bequests were made by persons who were anxious to secure the services of a priest. In 1531 Robert Sutcliffe of Mayroyd gave the sum of 7 marks in order that Sir Gilbert Stansfield, priest, might daily sing and pray for his soul and the soul of his wife and all their ancestors for two whole years after his death. Money was often bequeathed for new vestments, books of anthems, and for the repair of the building. Heptonstall Chapel, moreover, possessed an organ in the days before the Reformation. Hence no sign of discontent was visible among the inhabitants of the Heptonstall chapelry on the eve of the Reformation. On the contrary, the crosses that stood on the uplands at Stiperden, Cross Stone and Mankinholes, at Heptonstall and on Reaps Moor were still venerated symbols of religious faith.

It was not long before a storm cloud burst over the English Church. Henry VIII., intent on marrying Anne Boleyn, denied the Pope's authority, severed the English Church from Rome, and afterwards diverted much of her wealth into his own treasury. His vengeance fell first on the monasteries subject to the Pope. In 1536 he suppressed all monasteries with an annual rental of less than £200. Then during the next three years, he seized the greater abbeys and monasteries, and finally, the colleges and chantries for priests.

Important local consequences followed from each of these changes. First Lincolnshire and Yorkshire rose in revolt. On Sunday, October 8, 1536, while a rebellion was being planned in Lincoln Cathedral, "two men of Halifax" arrived with the news that their country was up and ready to aid Lincolnshire. This was the beginning of the Pilgrimage of Grace. In the parish of Halifax, the Vicar of Halifax, Dr. Haldesworthe, with the family of Savile, took the side of the king. Their enemy, the Tempests, with Sir Stephen Hamerton, lord of the township of Langfield, joined the insurgents. Sir Stephen suffered a traitor's death at Tyburn, and his estates were forfeited by the king. The Towneleys of Towneley Hall, though strong Catholics, held aloof from the rising.

Second, the Priory of Lewes, which had an annual revenue of £1,700, shared the fate of the larger monasteries. In February, 1537, Robert Croham, the last Prior, surrendered the Priory with all its dependent estates into the hands of the king. The Prior's bailiff held his last court on April 24, 1537. The ancient Priory thereby severed its connection with the parish of Halifax; a connection that had lasted for four centuries. Henry VIII. bestowed the Priory upon Thomas Cromwell, who thus became Lord of the Manor, Lay Rector of Halifax, and one of the biggest landowners in the neighbourhood.

Third, after the seizure of the monasteries, Henry VIII. turned his attention to chantries. Royal commissioners twice visited the Halifax parish in search of gain. On the first visit to Heptonstall (1546) they reported that the chapel was six miles distant from Halifax Church. There were two chantry priests, Robert Bentley and Richard

Mitchell. The latter also helped the curate to administer the sacrament to the parishioners, the population of the chapelry numbering 2,000. A third priest was maintained by the churchwardens from the proceeds of certain lands they had purchased.

Two years later (1548) Edward VI.'s commissioners appeared in the chapelry. The chapel was described as being in a "moorish country," four or five miles distant from Halifax. There were 1,600 communicants in the chapelry, and in addition to the curate, the chantry priests, Bentley and Mitchell, were again mentioned. Both priests were said to depend for a livelihood on the profits of the chantries, it being also added that Bentley was but "indifferently learned." On both occasions the commissioners found neither goods nor plate. Many chapels in the Halifax parish were closed, but Heptonstall Chapel was suffered to remain, so as to meet the needs of the large population within the chapelry.

During the interval between these two visits, what were considered the symbols of popery began to be destroyed. Churches were rifled of their images, stained glass windows were broken and walls were washed with lime to blot out the frescoes that adorned them. An English communion service for the people was added to the Latin mass, and not long afterwards the first English service book was introduced. Three years later (in 1552) a second and more Protestant prayer book was ordered to be used in the churches; altars were replaced by communion tables and priests had to appear in simple surplices instead of their usual vestments. Another commission was also appointed to seize any church property that had passed without warrant into the possession of laymen, and to confiscate unnecessary church ornaments. At Heptonstall several vestments and bells were found, but the organ (condemned as a relic of popery) had been taken to pieces and hidden in the church coffer and in one of the houses of the parishioners.

The Chapel of Todmorden appears to have been confiscated by the king at the earlier enquiry, but was bought back by the inhabitants for the sum of 6s. 8d. In 1552, when commissioners again visited the chapel nothing was found beyond a chalice, vestment and cross of copper and gilt. An important local change, however, had already followed the suppression of the monasteries. With a portion of the wealth obtained from abbey lands, Henry VIII created six new bishoprics. The immense diocese of Lichfield was divided into two parts, the northern half with the Archdeaconry of Richmond taken from the diocese of York, forming the new see of Chester. Hence the parish of Rochdale was included in the diocese of Chester (A.D. 1541) and was transferred from the province of Canterbury to that of York.

No records have been left of the influences that led men on these uplands to embrace the Protestant faith. It is probable, however, that contact with foreign traders in northern wool-markets; the Protestant preaching of John Bradford in the neighbourhood of Manchester; and the influence of Alexander Nowell, Dean of St. Paul's, whose mother was a Kay of Rochdale; all helped in this direction.

Bolton, Manchester and Rochdale were noted for their Protestant zeal. Moreover Queen Mary's persecutions must have roused a spirit of revolt among Halifax parishioners. Robert Ferrar, Bishop of St. David's, who was burnt at the stake at Carmarthen, was a native of the parish, having been born at Ewood Hall in the township of Midgley.

In Elizabeth's reign the unceasing efforts of Protestant vicars in both Rochdale and Halifax fostered the growth of Puritanism. From the township of Midgley came Richard Midgley, who was trained at Cambridge and adopted strongly Puritan opinions. He was appointed Vicar of Rochdale, and for more than 30 years was pre-eminent in piety and zeal. His fiery eloquence was instrumental in converting thousands of men and women. More than once he was summoned to Chester to explain why he wore neither surplice nor cope and refused to observe holy days. Along with other Puritans, he issued a declaration against popish festivals and practices, and all manner of rough sports. He was foremost in promoting education in his parish, granting a site and raising money for building the Rochdale Grammar School. Associated with him in this work was Charles Radcliffe of Todmorden Hall, whose son, Robert, was appointed the first headmaster of the school (Appendix IV).

In 1595 Richard Midgley was succeeded at Rochdale by his son, Joseph; also a Cambridge man and a Puritan of a still more unbending type. Christopher Ashburn, another Protestant vicar, was appointed Vicar of Halifax at the beginning of Elizabeth's reign. During the second rising of the

North on behalf of Romanism, Ashburn offered to raise three or four thousand men from his own parish in defence of the Queen. His zeal was specially commended by Archbishop Grindal, who declared that such a condition of things was the result of continued preaching that had made the men of that parish better instructed than the rest.

With Puritan vicars in Rochdale and Halifax, the curates appointed to Todmorden, Cross Stone and Heptonstall would also be Puritan in their beliefs. In 1590 Gilbert Astley, curate of Todmorden, was summoned before the Bishop of Chester for not observing holy day. The influence of such men must have been great, and the work of men like the Midgleys left its mark in a Puritan type of religion well suited to the independent spirit of clothiers and farmers living on the uplands.

Although the great majority of the inhabitants embraced the Protestant faith, the Towneleys of Towneley Hall kept unflinchingly to Roman Catholicism, enduring imprisonment and persecution rather than the abandonment of their principles. The record of Sir John Towneley's life during Elizabeth's reign is one long tribute to his stubborn fidelity.

"For professing the apostolical and Catholic Roman faith he was imprisoned first at Chester Castle, then sent to the Marshalsea, then to York Castle; then to the clockhouse in Hull, then to the Gatehouse in Westminster, then to Manchester, then to Broughton in Oxfordshire, then twice to Ely in Cambridgeshire and so now, 73 years old and blind, is bound to appear and keep within five miles of

Towneley, his house; who has since 1571 paid into the exchequer £20 a month and doth still, so that there is paid already above £5,000."

Fines were levied for absence from the Protestant service of the English Church. Roman Catholic services were illegal, and men met in secret to celebrate the mass and secure a priest's blessing. In the spacious kitchen chimney of Old Town Hall (built at the end of the 16th century) a door was concealed leading to a secret underground passage that emerged at a much lower level in Pecket Wood. There were chambers in the old hall at Holme to which priests resorted nearly a century later. Such devices tell their own story of days when Catholics secretly worshipped amid a people of alien beliefs. It also shows how plots for the assassination of Queen Elizabeth were hatched in the dark and suffered to grow into formidable conspiracies. So great was the fear inspired by them, that a Loyal Association for the preservation of the Queen's person was formed, consisting of the gentlemen of England. Many in Yorkshire were anxious to become members, the principal freeholders and clothiers about *Halifax*, Wakefield, and Bradford, more especially, "sueing to be accepted into that society."

A great change had been wrought in the religious beliefs of the people in both the Rochdale and Halifax parishes since the days of the Pilgrimage of Grace. Instead of chantry priests singing masses for the souls of the dead, Puritan clergymen were preaching the doctrines of Calvin to crowded congregations. Indeed in the reign of James I. the clothiers in the Halifax parish declared that " out of their zeal to God's holy religion, they did freely and voluntarily, out of their charges, maintain and give wages to ten preachers, over and above the duties belonging to the Vicar . . . . and that, by the special grace of God, there was not one Popish Recusant inhabiting in the said great and populous parish of Halifax."

CHAPTER XIV.

CAVALIERS AND ROUNDHEADS, OR DAYS OF STRIFE.

The Reformation taught Englishmen to set a higher value on their own personal beliefs and political privileges. In Elizabeth's reign, her parliaments became more independent and less willing to submit to a policy they considered wrong. But Elizabeth was a wise queen who knew when to yield to her parliaments and how to retain the affection of her people. She was followed, however, by kings who were much less wise, for they governed England without heeding the wishes of many of their subjects, and often rejected with scorn the counsel of parliaments that had been summoned to transact the business of the realm. There were two questions, more especially, on which James I. and Charles I. quarrelled with their parliaments. First came the question of religion. Parliament sympathised with the Puritans and wished for more latitude in the rules and ceremonies of the Church. Both king and bishops, however, were determined to enforce order in every diocese. The second question in dispute was still more important, viz., whether kings might justly levy taxes without consent of Parliament.

The Todmorden neighbourhood was strongly Puritan, and the policy of both James and Charles had important local consequences. Early in James I.'s reign, commissioners were sent into every diocese to put down Puritan irregularities. An enquiry was held at Rochdale when it was found that the vicar, Joseph Midgley, "refused to observe the order of communion, did not wear a surplice or a cloke with sleeves, did not use the cross in baptism or catechise." He was also accused of shortening the prayers in order to lengthen his own sermons. For these offences he was deprived of his office.

When Charles I. came to the throne he repeatedly quarrelled with his parliaments, and then for eleven years ruled alone. In consequence he had to raise money as best he could. Two of the methods adopted are of local interest. Every freeholder who owned land worth £40 a year was ordered to accept knighthood—an honour requiring the payment of heavy fees—or to pay a heavy fine. Local gentlemen chose the latter course. Savile Radcliffe of Todmorden Hall, whose estates were worth £134 a year, paid a fine of £25. Henry Cockcroft of Mayroyd was fined £15. A few years later ship-money was levied in every English county to equip ships for the royal navy. The inhabitants of Leeds and Halifax and their precincts were ordered to contribute with the inhabitants of the port of Hull towards three ships, to be at Portsmouth by a given date, furnished as men of war and victualled for four months. Thereupon these towns presented a petition to the Privy Council urging that the villages around them were wealthier and better able to bear the tax, from which they prayed to be freed. But equal objection was raised by rural townships. The constable at Sowerby could not collect the full amount demanded in 1635, and had to make up the deficit; the same difficulty was experienced each year the tax was levied.

The question at stake was whether Parliament could for ever be ignored by the king; Puritans, moreover, were deeply incensed at religious changes that seemed to them to savour of popery. But Englishmen were slow to rise in opposition to Charles. In Scotland, however, an attempt to introduce the English prayer book led to a national rebellion, and Charles was forced to raise an army to put it down. To the northern counties fell the duty of furnishing the necessary men. Local townships had to send men to Halifax, suitably clothed and armed, to be drilled and trained in companies for service on the Scotch Border. Items such as "knapsacks and bandoliers; caps, coats, doublets and breeches; gunpowder and yards of match" are duly recorded in constables' accounts, for the cost of these materials was borne by each township. In 1639, *e.g.*, Sowerby township paid £7 10s. for gunpowder; £33 10s. for soldiers' wages and training; and £24 for the repair of old, and purchase of new, arms; a total of £65.

The Scotch war soon ended with the king's defeat, and Charles was compelled to summon Parliament. For many months damaging blows were struck at the royal authority, until finally two parties stood opposed: one henceforth willing to trust the king and anxious to preserve the authority of the bishops; the other desirous of abolishing bishops and of making the power of Parliament still more complete. Hence arose the great struggle between the Cavaliers and Roundheads. It was no ordinary conflict. Friends were parted asunder, even parents were separated from their children, as both parties passionately insisted on the justice of their own cause and declared it to be for the honour of England herself.

On these uplands the pulse of political life beat firmly for the Parliament. In East Lancashire a revival of popery was greatly dreaded, and in the Rochdale parish, in March 1642, every eligible person signed a protestation, resolving to maintain religion against popish innovations, to protect king and parliament and the rights and liberties of the subject. Oddly enough, the name of the curate of Todmorden is not in the list, but probably the cure was then vacant.

Before the end of the year 1642 war broke out. At first East Lancashire and the West Riding of Yorkshire constituted one wide area for the Parliament. Manchester was the military centre of the Lancashire Roundheads. Leeds, Bradford and Halifax were equally zealous in furnishing men and money for the Parliamentary cause. The conflict, however, opened badly for the Parliament. In December, 1642, the Marquis of Newcastle drove Lord Fairfax, the leader of the Yorkshire Roundheads, from Tadcaster to Selby; then, occupying Pontefract, he cut off the towns in the West Riding from any hope of re-inforcements. Strafford's nephew, Sir W. Savile, seized Leeds and Wakefield; but on January 23, 1643, Sir Thomas Fairfax, with troopers from Halifax and Bradford, drove Savile out of Leeds and recaptured Wakefield.

In this engagement Todmorden men took part, for Jonathan Scholefield, curate of Cross Stone Chapel, was one of the chaplains of the Parliamentary troops and along with Lieutenant Horsfall, from Underbank, Eastwood, greatly distinguished himself. The following graphic account by an eye-witness refers to the storming of Leeds on Monday, January 23, 1643. Sir Thomas Fairfax had disposed his troops along both banks of the Aire to the west of the town. On the north side Serjeant Major Forbes with Lieutenant Horsfall, etc., and a company of Lancashire soldiers under Captain Chadwick gallantly attacked the Cavaliers in the 'great trenches.' Meanwhile soldiers on the south side of the river crossed the stream and dislodged the sentry, informing Major Forbes of their success by a great shout. Thereupon Major Forbes climbed to the top of the works ("Lieut. Horsfall lending him his shoulder") and " he most furiously and boldly entered the works single; him his said Lieutenant (wading through the river side below the work) next followed most resolutely. Then the rest followed, and Mr. Jonathan Scholefield (the minister at Croston chappell in Halifax Parish near Todmerden) in their company begun, and they sung the first verse of the 68th Psalm, ' Let God arise, and then his enemies shall be scattered and those that hate him flee before him.' And instantly after the great shout on the south side river, still informing of the enemy's flight from the upper and next sentry (where about 100 were) Serjeant Major entered that also, and Mr. Scholefield begun and they sung another like verse. So these works being gained, the enemy fled into the houses."

A fierce fight ensued, ending in the renewed flight of the enemy. Sir Wm. Savile attempted to marshall his troops, but in vain; " which he seeing, and that 12 musketeers, drawn on both sides that lane by Mr.

Scholefield had gained a cannon by killing the cannoneer . . . . he and the rest, perceiving the town lost, about an hour after the first sentry was entered, fled away."

It is no wonder that Sir Thomas Fairfax warmly praised the valiant behaviour of the men from Bradford and Halifax, although they were but raw levies.

A few months later, the Marquis of Newcastle took Leeds by storm; he defeated the Fairfaxes at Adwalton Moor, near Bradford (June 30), and the whole of the West Riding fell into his hands. The following month Halifax was occupied by the Royalists, and Heptonstall was left fronting the enemy, thus forming one of the advanced posts of the Northern Roundheads. In Rochdale there was a Parliamentary garrison of 1,200 men and the pass over Blackstone Edge was guarded by a troop of 800 soldiers with two guns. There was no thought of yielding, and when the Marquis of Newcastle summoned the town of Manchester to surrender, a large body of soldiers was massed near Rochdale on the Yorkshire road, and application was made to Parliament for 40 barrels of powder. A troop of Royalist horse-soldiers, attempting to force a passage over Blackstone Edge, was repulsed and the Marquis of Newcastle turned aside to engage in the siege of Hull. (Fig. 18.)

Meanwhile Royalist garrisons held the West Riding towns in subjection. At Halifax Sir Francis Mackworth had 2,000 men, with troops stationed on the Warley upland and at Sowerby Bridge to guard against attacks from Heptonstall

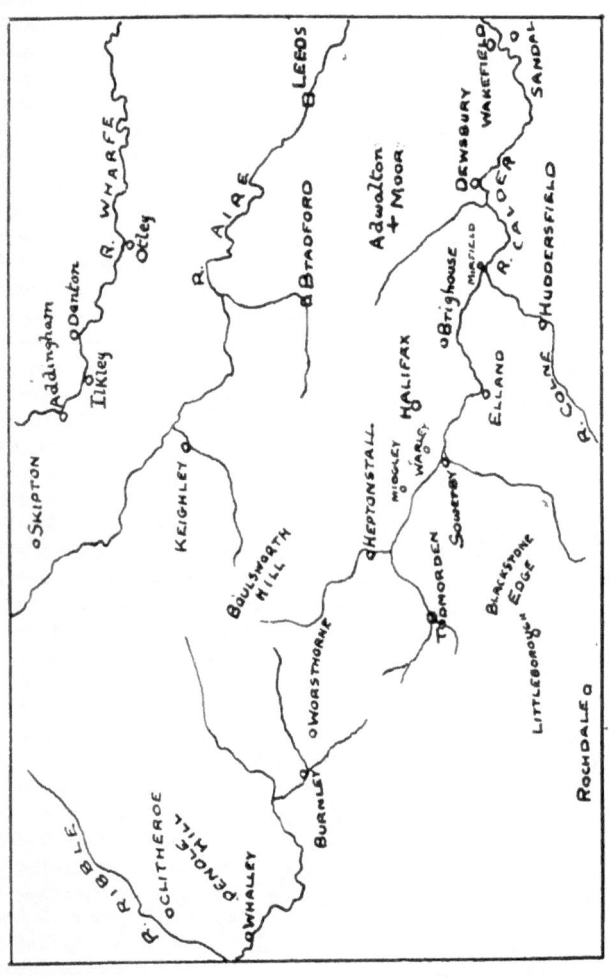

Fig. 18. Map to Illustrate Civil Wars.

and Blackstone Edge. The Parliamentary garrison at Heptonstall, under Col. Bradshaw, was greatly inferior in number, consisting of 280 musketeers, 60 horse-soldiers and a few hundred clubmen. Repeated sorties, however, were made against their enemies. On the night of October 23, after crossing the Hebden valley and advancing along the Midgley road, soldiers from Heptonstall assaulted the mansion at Hollins, taking it and capturing many prisoners. Sir Francis in return, on the morning of November 1st, amid a storm of wind and rain, attacked Heptonstall with a force of 800 cavalry and infantry, but the Cavaliers were driven back with much loss of life. The following January also the Royalist outpost at Sowerby Bridge was routed by the Roundheads. But quickly the fortune of war changed, for a few days later Sir Francis Mackworth advanced against Heptonstall with the whole of his troops and large reinforcements from Keighley. Thereupon the garrison retreated to Burnley, taking their prisoners with them, and left Heptonstall to be pillaged and burnt by the victorious Royalists. (Fig. 18.)

Relief, however, was at hand. A Scotch army was marching over the Border in support of the Parliament and the Marquis of Newcastle was again compelled to act on the defensive. Before the end of January, Sir Thomas Fairfax once more called on the men of the West Riding to fight against Irish soldiers whom Charles I. had brought over into Cheshire. All able bodied men between 16 and 60 years of age were ordered to repair to Mirfield, bringing with them four or five days' provisions and the best weapons they could procure, so that with the help of God they might drive out the enemy, establish peace and obtain free trading again to the comfortable support of poor and rich. Sir Thomas defeated the Irish at Nantwich and then despatched a Parliamentary force over Blackstone Edge to the relief of Halifax and the West Riding. The result was that Sir Francis Mackworth abandoned Halifax (within nine days after taking Heptonstall) and retired to York. In June Prince Rupert was sent from the Midlands with 20,000 men to the aid of the Marquis of Newcastle. Marching through Lancashire he stormed Bolton and crossed the Pennines in the neighbourhood of Burnley. (Fig. 18.) Parties of his soldiers passed through Worsthorne, plundering as they went and driving off the cattle of the farmers. The decisive struggle was at hand, and at the battle of Marston Moor men from this district fought on opposite sides. The Stansfields were Parliamentarians, but Charles Towneley of Towneley Hall, John Crossley of Scaitcliffe and Joshua Radcliffe of Todmorden Hall, were ardent Royalists. It may be that Joshua Radcliffe was clad in the white armour and coat of mail that had been his great-grandfather's; John Crossley's sword was long preserved at Scaitcliffe. There is a tradition that at Maiden Cross near Coppy, one of Towneley's men bid farewell to his sweetheart when leaving for the battle. He never returned and the woman, frantic in her grief, often resorted to this cross where last she had seen her lover. It is only a story, but it depicts a sorrow that was repeated a thousand times in those years of strife.

This neighbourhood, with its strong Puritanism, insisted on having clergy of similar beliefs. Dr. Marsh, the Royalist vicar of Halifax, was ousted from his office; Robert Bath, the Puritan vicar of Rochdale, continued at his post until the Restoration. After the abolition of Episcopacy, Parliament set about establishing Presbyterianism, and Lancashire was one of the counties where it was most fully established. Under the new system Lancashire was divided into nine ecclesiastical districts. Todmorden Chapel, in the parish of Rochdale, was included within the second division, known as the 'Bury classis." The district was under the control of a synod or committee of ten clergymen and twenty laymen, who met monthly for a period of ten years (1647–57). Its chief business was to ordain ministers to vacant cures and to prevent unlicensed preachers from spreading false doctrines. Presbyterians insisted on uniformity in religious belief quite as strongly as the bishops had insisted on uniformity in ceremonial, and they denounced the religious toleration favoured by Cromwell and the army. Todmorden curates seem to have been very troublesome. Robert Towne was suspended for heresy, and replaced by Mr. Hill; whilst Francis Core preached in Todmorden Chapel without permission of the synod and declined to appear before it when summoned to do so.

Presbyterianism had no sooner been established in Lancashire when a fresh Royalist revolt and the approach of a Scotch army threatened its very existence. Cromwell and his Ironsides hastened north after putting down a Welsh rising at Pembroke. Entering Yorkshire he marched from Knaresborough, through Otley, Addingham and Skipton (Fig. 18), and entered Lancashire on August 16, 1648. It was the duty of the northern townships to furnish provisions for his army on its march. The Sowerby constable, for example, on August 13, paid 10s. to three men who went with provisions to Addingham. On August 18, for " sixteen hundred of bread, bought in Halifax, and 20s. in money," he paid in all £17. Nathan Hoyle with seven men and ten horses then took the bread to Skipton at a cost of 18s., but as the army had already entered Lancashire, a further journey was necessary at a cost to the township of 11s.

Though the Lancashire Presbyterians distrusted Cromwell, they fought with the Ironsides against the Royalist troops under Marmaduke Langdale and the Scotch army under the Duke of Hamilton. At Preston Cromwell gained a decisive victory; a few months later Charles I. was executed and a Commonwealth was proclaimed. The clergy were ordered publicly to declare their allegiance to the new government. Those who refused—and there were many Lancashire Presbyterians among them—were deprived of their livings. Robert Bath of Rochdale, however, took the required oath.

The state of the Church occupied the attention of the leaders of the Commonwealth. Parliamentary commissioners twice visited this district (in 1650 and 1658) and recommended the formation of a separate Todmorden parish. On the second occasion it was reported that 117 families lived in the chapelry, the tithes being worth £21 10s. The chapel was well built and convenient to hold the inhabitants, having a chapel-yard, where time out of mind, the dead had been buried. This statement, however, was disputed, the chapel being described as almost a ruin, and the tithes assessed at not more than £14. In 1650, Francis Core, the curate, lived in a little house built by the parishioners, and received a yearly salary of 6s. 8d. Eight years later Thomas Somerton was minister. His presence provoked disputes among the inhabitants; he preached strange doctrines and sympathised with the Quakers, a fact worthy of note, as there was a large number of Quakers in this district a few years later.

It is evident, from the above account, that no settled order prevailed in the Church when the Presbyterians were in power. With the restoration of Charles II. to the throne, the Church again passed under the control of episcopalian clergy loyal to the accustomed form of worship. Henry Krabtree (chap. xvi) became curate of Todmorden; Robert Dewhirst, curate of Cross Stone, and Joseph Ferret, of Heptonstall. Since that time few incidents have occurred to mar the peace of the Church's existence.

Out of the strife and turmoil of the civil wars there came a change in men's attitude towards religion. The idea of religious toleration, although imperfectly understood, began to influence men's minds and to make it possible for men of different religious beliefs to live peaceably side by side. Religion became less national and more personal. The consequence was that when Parliament insisted on a rigid uniformity of belief and ceremonial within the English Church, men left it in order to worship in other ways. Hence there arose religious societies like those of the Quakers, Presbyterians and Baptists, all of whom found adherents in the Todmorden district before the close of the seventeenth century (chap. xvii).

CHAPTER XV.

THREE CENTURIES OF TRADE AND INDUSTRY.

In the account of local industries during the fourteenth century a description was given of the power and wealth of the Earls of Surrey and of Lincoln. The power of great manor lords, however, was considerably modified during the century preceding the Reformation. Villeins as a class disappeared and in their place arose small tenant farmers and a labouring class that demanded good wages. The older forest and demesne lands were let to various tenants, and many waste and common lands were enclosed. The park of Erringden, for example, was split up into separate estates in Henry VI.'s reign, whilst waste lands in both Wadsworth and Stansfield were appropriated by the Saviles and sold during the reign of Henry VIII.

The soil on the Todmorden uplands was poor in quality. In Elizabeth's reign Camden stated that the land in the Halifax parish was so barren that more than a bare livelihood could not be expected from it. Similarly in Charles II.'s reign, during a scarcity of corn, the constables of the various Halifax townships reported that their country was mountainous, and that not twenty, among twenty thousand persons, had more corn than was enough for sowing the little ground they had and maintaining their families. With regard to the mineral wealth in this neighbourhood, some coal must have been obtained, inasmuch as in the year 1580, coal mines in Todmorden were granted for 21 years to one John Blackway. Without steam power, however, it was impossible to get much coal.

The one hope of prosperity lay in the possession of sheep farms and the manufacture of woollen cloth. It is not surprising, therefore, that the great feature in this district of the three centuries under consideration (1450 to 1750) was the rapid development of the woollen industry. As early as the 14th century wool was of increasing importance, and before the close of the 15th century the manufacture of cloth was widespread. Halifax and Ripon were rivals for the foremost place in the West Riding for cloth manufacture. In the years 1473-5 Halifax stood first amongst Yorkshire towns with a sale of nearly 1,500 pieces of cloth. Leeds and Bradford sold only 320 and $178\frac{1}{2}$ pieces respectively. The woollen cloths sold at Halifax were brought from all parts of the parish, every upland or rather every farmstead being a centre of the woollen industry.

The system of industry was entirely different from that of the present day. Instead of the factory system, a *domestic* system of manufacture prevailed in this district until the close of the 18th century. Every farmer was interested in the woollen trade. Sheep pastures abounded in both the Halifax and Rochdale parishes, and every process, from the shearing of sheep and preparation of the fleece, to the dyeing and finishing of the cloth, might have been observed on these uplands. Wool cards, spinning wheels and webster's looms formed part of the ordinary equipment of every farmstead. There were "tenter crofts" outside each hamlet where the tenter or frame stood on which the woollen cloth was stretched and dried; fulling and dyeing mills were built in different parts of the parish, and the "cloth halls" at Heptonstall, Halifax and Rochdale were crowded every market day.

At first clothiers manufactured as well as sold woollen pieces. Gradually two different classes came into existence among those engaged in the woollen trade. There was a small class of merchant clothiers who bought raw wool and sold the finished cloth. A much larger class consisted of woolcombers, spinners, weavers and dyers whom the clothiers supplied with wool and paid for the various processes of manufacture. This neighbourhood was noted for the number of its clothiers. They made money rapidly and estates were constantly passing into their hands. One illustration may be given. In return for certain money payments, James I. surrendered all crown rights in Erringden to George Halstead, John Sunderland, William Sutcliffe and Henry Naylor, all of whom were *clothiers*.

During this period men did not believe in freedom of trade or of individual enterprise. In larger towns merchants and craftsmen were grouped into different associations or gilds for the regulation of their own trade or industry and the prevention of competition. On these uplands, however, the woollen industry was probably developed among the inhabitants without any such restrictions. Moreover, in the 15th century the power of the gilds greatly declined, and in their place kings and parliaments attempted to regulate every branch of trade. Not only was the price of bread and ale fixed by law (p. 71), but Parliament sought to regulate the quality and price of manufactured goods, and to prevent individual traders from disturbing the usual course of trade. This policy may be illustrated by a statute passed in the reign of Queen Mary (1553-58) referring to the parish of Halifax. The Act was intended to prevent rich merchants from "engrossing" or cornering raw wool in parishes such as Halifax, and the reasons set forth are of the greatest interest as they throw a clear light on the condition of this district at that time. The Act stated that the parish of Halifax was planted amid great wastes and moors, where neither corn nor good grass could be produced except in rare places and by great industry on the part of the inhabitants. The inhabitants lived entirely by cloth making, most of them neither growing corn nor keeping a horse to carry wool nor being able to buy much wool at once. In consequence they had to repair to Halifax market to buy from one to four stones of wool and carry it home as much as six miles on their heads and backs, so as to convert the wool into yarn or cloth and sell the same and so buy more wool. In a period of forty years (1515—1555) this industry had added to the parish 500 households that would be reduced to beggary if they could not obtain a regular supply of small quantities of wool.

Unfortunately the West Riding clothiers were notorious for making inferior cloth, and Henry VIII. sent down Commissioners to find out and punish such as used "flocks, chalk, flour and starch" in cloth making. As many as 181 offenders resided in the

Halifax parish, including 62 from Heptonstall. Royal officers known as *ulnagers* (Lat. ulna, an ell) were appointed to measure and seal the pieces of cloth that were manufactured and to receive the tax (ulnage) levied by the Crown on each piece. In James I.'s reign a dispute arose between the King's ulnagers and the clothiers of Halifax, Bradford, Bingley and Keighley, as to the amount of taxation. Instead of the old tax of one penny, a tax of five farthings and later of three halfpence was demanded on each piece. The clothiers protested, and the case was decided in their favour by the Exchequer Court. During the trial it was stated that 20,000 men, women and children were employed in this industry in the four parishes and that in the Halifax parish alone, £40 was contributed monthly to support more than 600 impotent, aged and poor people. Richard Horsfall of Stoodley, a clothier, aged 51 years, said that he had to go seven miles, and others a further distance, to fetch the seals for their goods, as the sealers had given up coming to their homes. He stated that kerseys and broad lists were most commonly made in the Halifax parish, the latter being usually of better wool. The price of a kersey varied from 20s. to 33s. 4d. a piece, or from 20d. to 2s. a yard. John Farrar of Brearley, gentleman, complained of intimidation by agents of the ulnagers, who sought to compel the payment of the higher rate of ulnage.

The inhabitants of Halifax, in their protest against the payment of ship money (p. 96), stated that "more cloth was made in the several and dispersed towns and villages than in Halifax itself." The fact is that each hamlet was filled with people who were busy with an unceasing round of duties. Young and old alike had their allotted tasks in carding and spinning, weaving and finishing woollen pieces or in attending to various duties on the farm, such as milking, churning, cheese-making or harvesting.

Defoe, in his book entitled "A Tour through the whole Island of Great Britain," gives a vivid picture of life on these uplands:—

"In the course of our road amongst the houses we found at every one of them a little rill of running water, and at every considerable house a manufactory. The sides of the hills, which were very steep everywhere, were spread with houses; for the land being divided into small enclosures, from two to six or seven acres each, seldom more, every three or four pieces of land had a house belonging to them. We could see at every house a tenter, and on almost every tenter a piece of cloth, kersey or shalloon, which are the three articles of this country's labour. Though we met few people without doors, yet within, we saw the houses full of lusty fellows, some at the dye-vat, some at the looms, others dressing the cloths; the women and children carding and spinning; all employed, from youngest to oldest; scarce anything above four years old, but its hands were sufficient for its own support."

The principal market for the sale of woollen pieces was at the Cloth Hall in Halifax, and at the beginning of the 18th century immense quantities of cloth were sold weekly. Saturday was the chief market day. In spring and summer, business began at 6 o'clock; during the rest of the year, at 8 o'clock.

Halifax was also a market for agricultural produce; corn, butter, cheese and sheep being supplied from surrounding counties. Enormous quantities of black cattle were sold in autumn for killing, salting and smoking. A clothier often bought two or three fat bullocks to meet the requirements of his large household during the winter.

Fulling mills, as well as corn mills, were built near running streams. There was a fulling mill at Gorpley in 1620; and early in the 18th century fulling mills had been erected at Scaitcliffe and Lob Mill, and a sizing mill stood at Beanhole Head. Some idea of a clothier's stock-in-trade may be obtained from the will (in 1706) of Anthony Crossley of Scaitcliffe Hall. He left 20 kersey pieces (£25 in value), 5 packs of fleece wool (£80), one pack of skin wool (£5), meal to the value of £12 in the " skilling " or outhouse, as well as a number of sheep.

The conditions of life just described have long since disappeared. To-day on the uplands from Shore to Blackshaw Head substantial farmsteads, such as Hartley Royd, stand almost deserted, and farmhouses lie in ruins. They remain as symbols of the old domestic system of manufacture that passed away with the invention of the spinning jenny, mule and power loom. But it is well to remember that for many generations men lived busy and prosperous lives, finding the means of livelihood within their own homes on the uplands, and seldom passing below the mist line into the valley beneath.

CHAPTER XVI.

SOCIAL LIFE AND SUPERSTITIONS AFTER THE REFORMATION.

In the last three chapters some account has been given of the religious and political struggles in which Todmordians took part during the 16th and 17th centuries, and of the way in which they gained a livelihood. The sketch thus given of life on these uplands may be further filled in by a description of some of their ideas and habits.

First, with regard to education. In those days scarcely any public provision was made for the education of children. There were no elementary schools. A Grammar School was built at Rochdale in the reign of Elizabeth, and in Charles I.'s reign a Grammar School was founded at Heptonstall (p. 138). These were entirely inadequate to meet the needs of the population, judged by modern standards. Even in the 16th century there were 1,600 persons in Heptonstall chapelry who were communicants of the Church, whilst in the parish of Rochdale there were 5,000 persons. Hence it is manifest that only a very small proportion of the people sent their children to school. Writing was a rare accomplishment; few people could read; books were scarce and not greatly esteemed by the majority of farmers and labourers on the uplands. Neither doctors nor lawyers resided in Todmorden. Clergymen often added to their duties those of a physician.

Joseph Midgley, when dismissed from his post as Vicar of Rochdale, practised as a doctor; during Charles II.'s reign Henry Krabtree, curate of Todmorden, "ventured to give physic to country people."

Under these circumstances children had little or no schooling. They were trained from their early years to follow their fathers' pursuits and to lead an active outdoor life. Such an upbringing fostered sturdiness of character, but left the mind a prey to all kinds of crude ideas and superstitions. A belief in witchcraft was all but universal. James I. wrote a treatise on the subject; simple folk dreaded the power of a witch's curse. In "Lancashire Witches," Harrison Ainsworth gives an account of witchcraft in Pendle Forest in James I.'s reign. The scene of one of the incidents is laid in Cliviger. Not far from Eagle Crag, Nance Redferne and Nicholas Assheton, mounted on a long hazel branch, "whisked through the air at a prodigious rate" to Malkin Tower in Pendle. The names of Devil's Rock in Stansfield and Dulesgate are relics of similar beliefs. Even to-day horseshoes hang over the doors of stables, cattle-sheds and barns. Whatever their use may be now, in old days they acted as charms to keep away witches. The following legend is connected with Bernshaw Tower, Eagle Crag and Cliviger.

Long ago a beautiful heiress, called Lady Sybil, lived at Bernshaw Tower. She was exceedingly gifted and took a keen delight in the beauty of Nature. One of her favourite walks was to Eagle Crag, where she would often stand and gaze into the wooded chasm beneath. It was then that Lady Sybil longed for the supernatural power of a witch. At last, unable to resist the temptation of the devil, she bartered her soul in return for this magical gift. With the aid of magic she could change her shape, and it was her delight to roam over her native hills in the form of a beautiful white doe.

One of Lady Sybil's admirers was Lord William of Hapton Tower, a younger member of the Towneley family. She rejected his suit, and in his despair, he sought the help of Mother Helston, a famous witch. She told him to go hunting in the gorge of Cliviger. He did so and there caught sight of a milk-white doe. After a long pursuit he captured it near Eagle Crag, with the help of Mother Helston who joined the hunt disguised as a hound. Lord William fastened an enchanted silken leash round the doe's neck and led her in triumph to Hapton Tower.

In the morning it was Lady Sybil who graced Hapton Tower with her presence. Soon afterwards, when she had renounced witchcraft, she was married to Lord William. But the old longing for magical experiences returned, and again she wandered, as of old, in some secret disguise. Once, when she was frolicking in Cliviger Mill as a beautiful white cat, the miller's man cut off one of her paws. Pale and wounded, for she had lost one of her hands, Lady Sybil returned home. She had to face the anger of Lord William, to whom the missing hand with its costly signet ring had been brought from Cliviger. Magic skill restored the hand, and Lady Sybil was reconciled to her husband. Her strength, however, was gone, and when her soul had been rescued from the powers of darkness, she died in peace. Bernshaw

Tower was left tenantless, but for many years on All Hallow's Eve a spectre huntsman with a hound and milk-white doe flitted past Eagle Crag.

The story of Henry Krabtree, curate of Todmorden, gives a further glimpse of the superstitious ideas of our forefathers. He was a schoolfellow of Tillotson, Archbishop of Canterbury. In 1662 he became curate of St. Mary's, retaining his position for about 30 years. He was a staunch Royalist, and believed that Charles I. was murdered by " a nest of religious cut-throats." A simple story illustrates his superstitious nature. On one occasion, when preaching at St. Mary's, a mouse ran across the Bible that lay open before him. Hastily closing the service, Mr. Krabtree hurried home to Stansfield Hall, and found that thieves had entered his study and disarranged his papers.

He was a man of some originality, and was noted as an astrologer and doctor. He was the first curate who kept a register of baptisms and burials at St. Mary's. He often added astrological details to the entries. For example:

"1685. Nov. 1. James, son of James Taylor of Todmorden. He was born 2nd Oct. near sun setting and also near a full moon, which is a sure sign of a short life."

In 1685 he published an almanack entitled 'Merlinus Rusticus.' Merlin was the wise seer at King Arthur's Court, who was able to predict the future, and Krabtree, although but a "country Merlin," had important news to tell about the future. After the pages devoted to the almanack, he sketched the past history of the Turks and discussed the fate of the Roman and Turkish Empires. He drew the following conclusions.

The Roman Empire, the greatest and most powerful that ever was or shall be, although at its lowest ebb, shall never be overthrown, but shall continue till the world is destroyed. The Turkish Empire, despite its success in war at that time, had reached the summit of its power. It would be confined to the three horns of Egypt, Asia and Greece, never being converted to the Christian faith nor ceasing to war against Christ until the world should come to an end.

Mr. Krabtree's shrewd common sense appears in his comments on the different months of the year.

May. " Rise early, walk in the fields, where every garden and hedgerow affords food and physic. Walk by running streams of water and feast thy lungs with the fresh air. For food, sage and sweet butter make an excellent breakfast. Clarified whey, with sage, scurvy grass, ale and wormwood beer, are now wholesome."

October. " The time now requires that you consult with your tailor as well as with your physician. Therefore a good suit of warm cloth is worth 2 purges and one vomit. Keep warm betimes, for cold creeps upon men insensibly and fogs ofttimes beget a whole winter's distemper."

November. "The best exercise is hunting or tracing hares, but be sure that the park or lordship be your own, and then you need not fear an indictment, nor a fine at the next sessions."

The reputation of the author of "Merlinus Rusticus" spread far beyond Todmorden, and an interesting instance has been preserved of his activity as a physician. In 1688 a youth called Richard Dugdale, who lived at Surey, near Whalley, was troubled with epileptic fits. The local doctors could not cure him, and his father sought the help of Dr. Krabtree. Both father and son came to Stansfield Hall and stayed a fortnight. The treatment was apparently successful, and the Dugdales returned home. But soon Richard was attacked more violently than ever and Dr. Krabtree was again consulted. The method of treatment, however, was too severe and also too expensive to please Mr. Dugdale. "Blood-letting" and "physic enough for six men at once" left Richard barely enough strength to walk across the house. His case was then considered by some dissenting ministers in the neighbourhood of Whalley. They believed that Richard was a demoniac under the influence of Satan, and they tried to throw discredit on the Curate of Todmorden as being a wizard, whose efforts had naturally been unavailing. The Rev. Zachary Taylor, Vicar of Croston, warmly defended Krabtree (who was then dead), showing that he used no unlawful means. He said that Mr. Krabtree was "no great scholar, but a blunt and honest man, who served at a poor place for about £12 a year, which he augmented by venturing to give physic to the country people."

In those days men did not understand the conditions necessary for health. Little attention was paid to drainage, the removal of refuse or the possession of a pure water supply. The result was that fever and plague often attacked the inhabitants on these uplands. In 1631 plague appeared in Erringden. In Heptonstall nearly 40 houses were infected and more

than 100 people perished. All business was at a standstill, so that the town gate (or village street) grew over with grass. A fresh outbreak of plague occurred in Halifax in August 1645, due partly to the large number of Scotch soldiers quartered there during the Civil War. In the 18th century fever and small-pox are frequently mentioned in the accounts of overseers and churchwardens. The township officials often contributed towards the support of fever-stricken persons, sometimes sending to Halifax for medical aid, at other times relying upon local amateurs. The following entries are taken from the records of the township of Stansfield:—
1752. To Ann Eastwood for fisak (physic) - 2s. 2d.
1753.   Do.   for surgery to John
        Stansfield   -   -   -   -   - 1s. 6d.

Despite the ignorance and superstition, the danger of disease and the rough and ready methods that prevailed on the uplands, it is possible that life was pleasanter in other respects for the majority of men and women than it often is to-day. There was less of mechanical routine two or three centuries ago. Work was arduous, no doubt; but it was carried on at home, and so long as it was done men might choose their own time for doing it.

After the Reformation the woollen trade brought prosperity to every homestead in this district, and with increasing wealth the timber-built houses of mediæval times were replaced by substantial mansions and farmsteads, built of stone. The architecture of the Elizabethan and Stuart periods is characterised by a picturesqueness that prevented bareness or ugliness of outline. Wings jutting from a central hall; gables and chimney-stacks; porches and oriel windows, formed a harmony of design that still testifies to the superior taste of our ancestors. The principal rooms had a southerly aspect, and the mullioned windows, deep set in the thick walls, were filled with diamond panes. Many such mansions were erected in this neighbourhood in the 17th century, of which Todmorden Hall is an excellent example. It

Fig. 19. CARR HOUSE FOLD.

was rebuilt by Savile Radcliffe about three centuries ago, but some of the timbers of the earlier mediæval building still remain. The walls of the drawing-room are of panelled oak, and there is a fine oak mantelpiece on which the arms of the Radcliffe family are carved. Over the central corridor a hiding chamber is concealed.

SOCIAL LIFE AND SUPERSTITIONS

This district contains many examples of farmhouses built during the same period; Hartley Royd, Ashes, Carr House Fold (Fig. 19) and Great House in Stansfield; Pasture Side in Walsden; as well as several houses in Mankinholes. On one of the walls of what is now the kitchen at Beanhole Head, in Stansfield, there is a well-preserved specimen of decorative plaster work that bears the date 1634 and includes the monogram of Charles I.

The rooms in the farmhouses were low and poorly lighted. The usual fuel was turf taken from the moors. In winter many of the farms and cottages must have been damp with the heavy rains. Oat bread (haver cake), cheese and home brewed ale formed the usual diet of the poorer people; wheat bread was a luxury reserved for the rich.

The usual mode of travelling was on foot or on horseback. Packhorse tracks crossed the uplands in all directions. The road from Burnley to Halifax has already been mentioned (p. 32) and along its course are the sites and fragments of early crosses from Stump Cross at Mereclough, and Maiden Cross to Duke's Cross and Mount Cross in Stiperden. There the road to Rochdale diverged, passing through Shore and Scaitcliffe. At the latter place the road again divided. The one to the right went up Stigget Gate by Sourhall, Cloughfoot and Gorpley across Inchfield Pasture to Ragby Bridge, and thence by Allescholes towards Rochdale. The road to the left crossed the breadth of the vale to Adam Royd, and mounted the Langfield Moor at Stackhills towards Heyhead. There it joined the packhorse road from Lumbutts that skirts the moorland above Swineshead and Knowl as far as Bottomley, and crosses the Walsden valley both at Allescholes and Reddishore. On the packhorse road, not far from Shurcrack, there is an old milestone, with the following inscription on three of its sides: To Rochdale, 6 miles; to Burnley, 7 miles; to Halifax 9 miles. The corresponding distances along the valleys are 8, 9 and 12 miles respectively. A mile was possibly a little longer in those days, but as regards the distance to Halifax, the difference is mainly due to the straighter route over hill and dale. The road went by Lumbutts and Long Stoop into Withens and Cragg Vale, mounting direct to Sowerby across the further upland. Another road kept nearer to the valley, passing through Stoodley, Horshold, Old Chamber and Midgley. On the northern slope the road from Stiperden continued by way of Heptonstall, crossing the Hebden at the bridge and ascending the Wadsworth upland to Mount Skip, Midgley and Luddenden. The most famous pass connecting Lancashire and Yorkshire was the one over Blackstone Edge, the importance of which during the Civil Wars has already been pointed out.

Less important lanes connected the farms on the uplands. To-day they are left uneven and deserted, for the valley has long since drawn into itself all the currents of life and industry that once circulated so freely over the uplands. Two or three centuries ago long trains of packhorses or galloways, with well-padded wooden saddles, wended slowly over the shoulders of the hills with burdens of lime from Clitheroe, or coal from Cliviger, or iron from Bradford. On the approach of market day, men and women traversed these lanes carrying the cloth they had woven to the " piece room " (th' takkin'-in room) in the house of the master clothier, or themselves trudged many miles to sell their own pieces at Heptonstall, Halifax or Rochdale.

It was under such circumstances that our forefathers lived, fully occupied for the most part in gaining a livelihood and seldom venturing beyond the bounds set by their business journeys. Hence they had but little intercourse with strangers, and it was only in times of national excitement, when the beacon fires on Pendle Hill, Thievely Pike and Blackstone Edge flashed their messages north and south, that the thoughts and interests of the inhabitants strayed far beyond the circle of hills within which they were born.

CHAPTER XVII.

THE BEGINNING OF NONCONFORMITY.

The first Dissenters of whom we have definite knowledge in Todmorden were the Friends or Quakers. In 1648 George Fox began his public work in Manchester. A few years later he gathered many staunch adherents in the neighbourhood of Halifax. William Dewsbury, " perhaps the sweetest and wisest of the early Friends," was at Newchurch in Rossendale in 1653 and very possibly preached about the same time in Todmorden. In any case there were Friends in this district in 1654, John Fielden of Inchfield and Joshua Fielden of Bottomley being among the earliest converts.

Fox taught that a man's first duty was to obey the promptings of God's spirit within him, and to guide his conduct by the Inner Light that is revealed to every sincere seeker after Truth. He denied the right of bishops, presbyters and magistrates to interfere in matters of conscience. Both he and his followers disregarded the observances of the Church and declined to obey laws they considered unjust. Hence they were continually in conflict with the Church and with the law. Nevertheless, although their gatherings were illegal, Friends on every hill side in this locality met at one another's houses for worship in the days of Charles II. The first recorded meetings were held at Mankinholes in the house of Joshua Laycock, and near by, on December 3, 1667, half a little croft called Tenter Croft was rented as a burial ground at a yearly rent of "one twopence of silver" for a term of 900 years. This plot of ground still forms part of one of the farms; on one of the outbuildings there is a gravestone with the inscription: "J. S. 1685." Other old burial grounds may be seen at Shore and Todmorden Edge. In addition to these places Quaker families lived at Stoodley and Straithey in Langfield; Rodhill Hey, Rodhill Head and Hartley Royd in Stansfield and at Edge End, Inchfield and Bottomley in the Rochdale parish.

Many penalties were imposed on Friends for their disobedience to the law. In 1665 John Fielden was fined for not attending church. As he declined to pay, a cheese was taken from him and sold for 4s. 6d. Three years later he suffered 31 weeks' imprisonment for non-attendance; whilst in the following year five of his oxen were seized and sold (at a value of £23), and he himself spent eight weeks in prison at Preston.

Henry Krabtree, curate of Todmorden, viewed the Friends with considerable disfavour. Accompanied by his servant, Simeon Smith, he surprised a number of Quakers from Walsden and Todmorden when met together for worship at the house of Daniel Sutcliffe of Rodhill Hey (May 3, 1684). A fine of 5s. was imposed on each person who was present and as the amount was not paid, distraints were made on their household goods. In other words township officers entered each house and took furniture, etc., equal in value to the fine imposed. A month later a meeting in Henry Kailey's house at Todmorden Edge was similarly disturbed by the priest, and goods to the value of £20, an ark of oatmeal, and one pack of wool, were taken by distraint. Todmorden must have been noted for the number of Friends, as when such as declined to pay for the repair of the church and school at Rochdale were summoned by the Rochdale churchwardens, it was stated that the majority of the offenders came from Todmorden, where "the Quakers were both numerous and troublesome."

The Toleration Act of 1689 stopped all active persecution of Dissenters, by recognising the legality of their public worship. Meeting houses were built and maintained by the contributions of the worshippers. The Friends erected the first meeting house in this locality at Shewbroad in 1694; though the business meetings held there were described as "Mankinholes meetings" for another century. The Todmorden Friends belonged at first to the Brighouse district, not being transferred to Marsden until 1807.

The passing of the Act of Uniformity (1662) led to the formation of Presbyterian congregations throughout the country. It was not, however, till about 20 years later that we first hear of Presbyterians in this neighbourhood. Their presence was probably due to the preaching of Oliver Heywood who, before the Act of Uniformity was passed, had been the minister of Coley Chapel near Halifax. On Whit-Tuesday, 1683, Heywood visited Cross Stone. He preached in a "very large and commodious house" (Great House) to a crowd of people who thronged the building and its approaches. But before the minister had finished his sermon, Major

Marshall, clerk to Mr. Robinson, the curate of Cross Stone, appeared with a warrant and brought the service to a close. Mr. Heywood, however, was allowed to leave without being molested. In November of the same year his Todmorden friends again sent for him. In order to escape from observation he went to a " wilderness place " in Stiperden, " a vale among the moors in the road to

Fig. 20. CHAPEL HOUSE.

Lancashire " where there were but two houses, in one of which he preached. "Abundance of people came many miles, though it was in the night and very dark and slippery." The length of a Puritan sermon peeps out in the confession that he struggled with them three hours till he was very tired and hoarse.

As a result of Oliver Heywood's preaching, a

congregation of Dissenters began to meet on the Cross Stone upland, and in the reign of William III. Great House was hired for regular services for a term of 21 years. During this period a settled ministry was established, and a chapel with accommodation for at least 200 persons was built at Bent Head " for the people called Presbyterians to meet in." To-day this building is known as " Chapel House " and consists of four cottages. (Fig. 20.)

The Particular Baptists or Anabaptists appeared in this neighbourhood towards the end of the 17th century. William Mitchell and David Crossley, by the earnestness of their preaching, founded as many as twenty preaching stations during the years 1685-95 in Lancashire and Yorkshire. At first these congregations could not be distinguished from those of Presbyterians. During a visit to London, Crossley came under the influence of John Bunyan, and became a convinced Baptist. On returning north he succeeded in persuading most of his congregations to adopt Baptist principles. During the earlier years of the movement, Baptists from Todmorden and Heptonstall were members of a church in Rossendale, but in 1704 a building erected at Rodhill End in Stansfield was used as a " chappell or meeting house for Protestant Dissenters called Baptists or Independents." Some years later the church was separated from the one in Rossendale, and was attended by members from Todmorden and Heptonstall.

About this time Francis Gastrell, Bishop of Chester, gave an interesting estimate of the number of Dissenters in his diocese. In the portion of Todmorden included within the Rochdale parish, there were said to be 50 Quakers, 30 Anabaptists and 20 Presbyterians. No corresponding numbers are available for the parish of Halifax, but the principal meeting house of the Quakers was at Shewbroad; of the Presbyterians at Bent Head and of the Anabaptists at Rodhill End, within the Yorkshire townships of Langfield and Stansfield.

Each of the dissenting communities established on the uplands resulted from the preaching of men who travelled far and wide to proclaim their doctrines. Methodism was similarly introduced into this locality by the zealous labours of three men, viz., William Darney, William Grimshaw and John Wesley himself. Darney was a Scotchman, who spoke the broadest Scotch, and was a member of Wesley's first band of preachers. He visited Todmorden in 1744, preaching in a barn at Gauksholme, and under his guidance the first Methodist society was established in Walsden. Other societies were formed at Todmorden Edge, Cross Stone, Shore and Heptonstall, and were frequently visited by Grimshaw and Wesley. The former had been curate of Todmorden for nearly 11 years (1731–41), and after removing to Haworth, Grimshaw joined Wesley in his work, more than once accompanying him to Todmorden. John Wesley paid his first visit to this district on May 1, 1747. At mid-day he preached at Shore "half-way down a huge mountain, to a loving, simple hearted people"; then climbing Todmorden Edge, on the brow of a long chain of mountains, he called a "serious people to repent and believe the gospel." The first recorded Quarterly Meeting ever held in Methodism took place the following year (October 18, 1748) at Chapel House, Todmorden Edge, under the chairmanship of William Grimshaw. Stewards were appointed to look after the business of the various societies, and contributions were received from 23 Methodist class meetings. Todmorden, with six classes, contributed £1 1s. 11½d.; Heptonstall with 10 classes, forwarded £2 3s. 9½d.

In his Journal, John Wesley frequently remarks on the beauty of our hills and valleys. Two references are of particular interest and may be quoted. "On April 25, 1755, about 10, I preached near Todmorden (probably at the bottom of Pexwood). The people stood, row above row, on the side of the mountain. They were rough enough in outward appearance, but their hearts were as melting wax. One can hardly conceive anything more delightful than the vale through which we rode from hence (Wesley was proceeding to Hebden Bridge). The river ran through the green meadows on the right, the fruitful hills and woods rose on either hand . . . . At three in the afternoon I preached at Heptonstall on the brow of the mountain."

Four years later after visiting the same scene with Grimshaw and preaching to a congregation at Gauxholme, who once more "on the side of an enormous mountain," "stood and sat, row above row, in a sylvan theatre," Wesley exclaims: "I believe nothing on the post-diluvian earth can be more pleasant than the road from hence, between huge, deep mountains clothed with wood to the top and watered at the bottom by a clear, winding stream. At 4, I preached to a very large congregation at Heptonstall and thence rode to Haworth."

This double testimony to the beauty of the landscape between Todmorden and Hebden Bridge is the more noteworthy as Wesley, in his Journal, makes but few references to natural scenery, although he travelled throughout the length and breadth of the land. In old age Wesley still visited this neighbourhood. Joseph Atkinson, curate of Todmorden, was sympathetic towards the Methodists, and Wesley preached at St. Mary's as well as in the Wesleyan Chapel erected in 1783 at Doghouse. The latter—the predecessor of York Street Chapel—was the first Methodist Chapel built in Todmorden, but at Heptonstall in Croft Field a chapel had been erected twenty years before (1764). Wesley's last visit took place on May 25, 1786, when he was 82 years old. He preached at Heptonstall Church in the morning and at St. Mary's in the afternoon. In his Journal he writes: " How changed are both place and people since I saw them first! Lo, the smiling fields are glad, and the human savages are tamed."

Methodism obtained many converts from other churches, and its rapid growth was accompanied by some decline among Quaker and Baptist congregations. The Friends' meeting house at Todmorden Edge passed into the hands of the Methodists, and Methodist services were established at Rodhill End, the Baptist chapel there being sold to the Wesleyans. Methodism, however, was indirectly responsible for an important development among the Baptists in this locality. Dan Taylor, who had been powerfully influenced by the Methodist movement, began preaching at Nook in Wadsworth, and in 1764 founded at Birchcliffe the first General Baptist Church in England. Impelled by missionary zeal he established a branch church at Shore in 1777, and from Shore Chapel, in turn, other General Baptist Churches have been derived.

Similarly, through the preaching of Grimshaw in Wadsworth, Richard Smith was converted and instead of joining the Wesleyans, he became the minister of a Particular Baptist Church at Wainsgate. This church, which now worships at Hope Chapel, Hebden Bridge, can claim the distinction of having had Dr. Fawcett as its minister for more than 50 years (1764—1817), and of having numbered among its members John Foster, the famous essayist. Dr. Fawcett was, in his day, a noted Nonconformist divine, being an excellent preacher, a man of sound learning and a voluminous writer. Despite invitations to more important work in London and Bristol, he remained faithful to his northern church. He added to the duties of pastor those of master of a Boarding School for the instruction of youth in "the English, Latin and Greek tongues," and also trained young men for the ministry. He had the good fortune to launch on their future careers both John Foster and William Ward, the companion of Carey, the great missionary to India.

Foster was born in 1770 at the small manor house in Wadsworth, where his father gained a livelihood by farming and handloom weaving. The son was a quiet, thoughtful and very imaginative boy. At the age of 17 he entered Dr. Fawcett's Academy at Brearley Hall and later became a Baptist minister. His fame, however, rests entirely on the essays he wrote, especially on a volume published in 1806, containing four essays of which the most famous is entitled "On Decision of Character."

CHAPTER XVIII.

TODMORDEN SCHOOLS AND CHURCHES DURING THE 18TH CENTURY.

On the threshold of the 18th century Todmorden was still a district of scattered farmsteads, with not a single factory or mill chimney, and with but few cottages in the bottom of the valley. Turnpike roads, canals and railways were unthought of, and places such as Gauxholme and Lobmill were as far away from each other for practical purposes as Todmorden and Burnley are to-day. This neighbourhood was a bit of rural England almost hidden amid hills and moors; not a hint had been given of the smoke and ugliness of 19th century towns with their factories and streets.

Some idea of the conditions that prevailed two centuries ago is obtained from Bishop Gastrell's description of the Todmorden chapelry. He stated that the curate of Todmorden had a small house worth £1 a year; he received £1 for a charity sermon on New Year's Day, and the inhabitants contributed £14 a year. Formerly the sum was £20, but "there were many Quakers who refused to pay." Instead of receiving wages the clerk of St. Mary's begged wool through the chapelry. As for the chapel itself, if the description given in 1650 was correct (p. 105), it must either have been rebuilt or repaired after the Restoration. A century later it again urgently needed repair, and in 1770 the inhabitants, led by Anthony Crossley of Scaitcliffe, set about its renovation. Many parishioners gave both materials and labour; £600 was raised by subscription and a rate was levied in Todmorden and Walsden. The chapel tower, which was not pulled down, is probably the only part of the present building that dates back to the beginning of the 17th century.

Todmorden's first school was built under the shadow of St. Mary's. Its founder was Richard Clegg, Vicar of Kirkham, grandson of Richard Clegg of Stonehouse, Walsden. Over the door of the barn at Stonehouse is a stone that bears the inscription : " R.C. 1678." The vicar in 1713 conveyed " the newly erected house in Todmorden, then used as a schoolroom," to trustees, including Henry Pigot, vicar of Rochdale, and John Crossley, Scaitcliffe, yeoman. Mr. Clegg collected £50 and himself added £100. The interest of this money was devoted to the repair of the school and the instruction of four children, one appointed by the owner of Stonehouse, one by the owner of Eastwood and two by the churchwardens of Todmorden and Walsden. The schoolmaster was to be elected by the majority of the freeholders of Todmorden and Walsden. The schoolhouse was in the parsonage garden and consisted of a schoolroom for 100 scholars with a master's dwelling house above. The children's playground was situated at the back of the church.

Within a few years of the founding of Clegg's Endowed School the inhabitants of Stansfield and Langfield not only built a school for their children but also rebuilt the chapel at Cross Stone. Fig. 21

shows what was the appearance of the older chapel in 1714, just before it was pulled down. Permission to rebuild was obtained in 1717, and two years later the pews on the north side of the new chapel were allotted to parishioners from Stansfield, those on the south side being reserved for Langfield. The stipend of the Cross Stone curate suffered (as in the Todmorden chapelry) from the presence of Quakers, the

Fig. 21. CROSS STONE CHAPEL.

£20 guaranteed in Elizabeth's reign being no longer forthcoming. The curate lived in a poor cottage worth 20s. per annum; he received 40s. for an annual sermon at Halifax, together with an annuity of 10s. Before the new chapel was built a school house had been erected on a plot of land near the east end of the chapel-yard. Six poor children, four from Stansfield and two from Langfield, were instructed free of charge. The interest on a sum of £60 subscribed by the inhabitants of both townships was paid to the schoolmaster for their instruction. He was at liberty to teach as many other children for wages as he might think proper. The school had accommodation for about fifty scholars.

The schools at St. Mary's and Cross Stone were elementary schools, but at Heptonstall a grammar school had been founded in Charles I.'s reign. In 1642 Charles Greenwood, Lord of the Manor of Heptonstall, and Rector of Thornhill, the tutor and life-long friend of the Earl of Strafford, built a school house to be used after his death as a Free Grammar School for the children of the inhabitants of the town and township of Heptonstall. The income derived from two farms in Colden was set aside for the maintenance of a schoolmaster, "who had well profited in learning." Free instruction was given in Latin and Greek, and other subjects were taught by an assistant master at a moderate charge. The building stands outside the churchyard adjoining the old church.

During the 18th century Heptonstall Church was further enlarged by the addition of two galleries, until it had accommodation for 1,100 persons. John Wesley in 1786 described the church as the ugliest he knew, and with its double nave and chancel it undoubtedly presented an unusual appearance.

In alluding to the repair of Todmorden Chapel, reference was made to a rate levied for that purpose in Todmorden and Walsden. The business of a church was in the hands of the vicar or curate and of certain officers, called *churchwardens,* who were appointed annually by the parishioners. They were responsible for the maintenance of church property, and with the consent of the inhabitants had power to levy a rate to defray the expense. Take for example, Heptonstall Chapel. For the upkeep of the building and payment of clerk, sexton, bellringers and dog whipper, an annual rate was levied on each township within the chapelry. The proportion contributed by each township was as follows: Wadsworth, one-third; Heptonstall and Stansfield, each two-ninths; Langfield and Erringden, each one-ninth, of the total cost. In addition to this contribution, the inhabitants of Stansfield and Langfield had to keep in repair Cross Stone Chapel, school and parsonage.

Accounts were kept by the churchwardens, giving full details of each year's income and expenditure. These records throw an interesting light on this district during the 18th century. In connection with Heptonstall Chapel, almost every year items occurred for mossing, slating, pointing or flagging some part of the church or yard; bell ropes were renewed; bell clappers pieced on once more, the clock was cleaned, the church swept or its vestries whitewashed, whilst occasionally heavier expense was incurred by re-seating part of the chapel or strengthening the steeple with beams. "Mossing" means filling the crevices between the slates with moss to prevent rain and snow being driven by the winter gales into the interior of the building.

The following entries are taken from the churchwardens' accounts for the townships of Stansfield (1726-58) and Erringden (1764—1840):—

"1730. Paid to John Horsfall for building the minister's house at Cross Stone - - - £5 7s. 2d.
1738, June. Paid to Mr. Grimshaw for seating, mossing and mending the schoolhouse at Cross Stone - - - - 11s. 4d.
1757. For making the clock face at Heptonstall fast when near blown off in great winds - 2s. 6d.
1792. Wage of Bellringer at Cross Stone - - - - 12s. 0d.
1799, Feb. For cleaning snow out of Heptonstall Church and steeple - - - - - 4s. 4½d."

In 1780-81 Cross Stone chapel-yard was repaired and enlarged at a cost of £66 4s. 8½d., £44 3s. 1½d. for Stansfield, and the remainder for Langfield.

The church was also a centre of charitable agencies. Frequently bequests were left to the poor and it was the duty of churchwardens to see that the intentions of the donors were carried out. Thus in 1608 Henry Pollard gave the sum of £2 7s. 0d. a year out of a farm in Stansfield, called Jumps Farm, of which £1 18s. was for the use of the poor in Stansfield. Also in 1705 John Greenwood of Hippings gave 20s. a year to the poor of Stansfield to be distributed in canvas cloth to those not having relief from the parish. On turning to the churchwardens' accounts for Stansfield we find how these legacies were distributed. During the year 1730, for example, £2 was distributed among 37 persons from Henry

Pollard's legacy; and under the heading of Hippings' Legacy there are the names of nine men to each of whom a shift (or shirt) had been given.

The following curious extract is taken from the account of an Erringden churchwarden for the year 1765. In the midst of the usual entries the reader suddenly comes upon the following unexpected paragraph : —

"Before you read any further, Please to peruse the Advertisement at the end of these Accompts (Accounts)."

On turning over the page there is a true copy of an advertisement, printed by P. Darby, Halifax : —

"Whereas on Monday night the 16th or Tuesday morning the 17th of December, 1765, the Vestry Room of the Church of Heptonstall was broke open and from thence was stolen out two silver Cups with these Inscriptions :

'This Pece of Plat bought in the year of our Lord 1681 by Richard Horsfall and John Bentley for the use of Heptonstall Church for ever.' On the other this Inscription : ' This peice of Plate was bought in the year of our Lord 1718 for the use of Heptonstall Church for ever ' . . . . . Also one Silver Salver, four Pewter ffllaggons and five Pewter Plates without any Inscriptions. The Person or Persons to whom these are offered to be sold or pawned, are desired to secure the Person or Persons so offering such to be sold, to whom a handsome Satisfaction or Gratuity will be given by the Reverend Tobit Sutcliffe, Curate of Heptonstall in the Vicarage of Halifax, or Mr.

William Cockcroft of Mayroyd nigh Heptonstall aforesaid.

If any silver come melted down, the Persons to whom it is offered are desired to take particular Notice of those who bring such to be disposed of."

The steps taken in search of the thief and his final transportation after trial at Wakefield, may be noted in the entries that follow the above statement: but the stolen vessels were never recovered. The following year two new silver cups and salver, suitably inscribed, with two new flagons and six inscribed pewter plates were purchased for the church at a cost to the chapelry of more than £20.

CHAPTER XIX.

THE MANAGEMENT OF LOCAL AFFAIRS IN THE 18TH CENTURY.

In the interval between the 14th and 18th centuries great changes had taken place in the management of local affairs. In the 14th century interest centred in the Manor of Wakefield and in Earl Warren's Manor Courts. But gradually the Manor lost its importance, and in its place each township within the Manor took a considerable part in managing its own local affairs. There were different officers appointed annually by the town's folk to look after different matters affecting the well-being of the township. They had no power, however, to judge or punish wrongdoers. Such power was vested in county magistrates, chosen from the landed gentry, and named Justices of the Peace. The Justices met four times a year at Quarter Sessions for the trial and punishment of offenders, who were not sent to the Assize Court. Justices of the Peace acted as legal referees in the township where they lived, supervising the administration of the law and giving authority to local officers.

The chief township officers, of whom there are old local records, were the constable, overseer of the poor, surveyor of highways and pinder.

I. The *constable* was the most important official during the 18th century. The mere recital of his duties will show the extent and variety of local business with which he was charged.

1. It was the constable's duty to keep the peace and arrest evildoers; to test weights and measures in the township and to keep the stocks and pinfold in repair.

2. The constable levied a rate to pay the expenses incurred during his year of office and to contribute towards the general county expenses such as the maintenance of prisons and repair of bridges. He also assisted in collecting the land tax, window tax and dog tax, when levied on the township.

3. The constable prepared lists of men liable to serve in the militia and on juries, or as constables, overseers and surveyors of highways; and presented such lists to the justices.

4. The constable, with four men from the township, attended coroners' inquests; he accompanied innkeepers to the justices for the renewal of their licences: and obtained from the justices the necessary warrants for the appointment of local officers.

The following items are taken from the yearly accounts of local constables in the 18th century:—

Stansfield Township.

"1778.	Paid for repairing pinfold -	2s.	0d.
1782.	Paid for weights and measures - - -	10s	1d.
1785.	Going through the town to try weights and measures	12s.	0d.
1796.	Numbering militia and list writing - - - -	10s.	0d.

	Journey to Bradford with Militia list - - -	3s. 0d.
	Journey to Bradford concerning Dog Tax - -	3s. 0d.
	Paid the Assessor of Dogs -	£1 18s. 0d.
1806.	To James Stansfield for Iron work for stocks -	4s. 2d."

A list is given of the articles in the possession of the Stansfield constables, and in addition to balances, weights and measures, the list includes one thumb screw, two pairs of handcuffs, a truncheon and a whip. The following entry shows that occasionally constables made merry and caroused at the expense of the township:—

"1807. Expenses of giving up the accounts last year as under.

To 15 Dinners at 1s. each - -	15s. 0d.
To 13 Quarts of ale at 6d. per quart	6s. 6d.
To 30 Glasses of Spirits at 6d. per glass - - - - -	15s. 0d."

The Hamlet of Todmorden.

"1750.	Repairing stocks at Todmorden	6s. 0d.
1756.	For attending His Majesty's Window Viewers through my Constabulary - - -	3s. 0d.
1757.	For conveying 4 vagrants, viz., a woman and three children passing from Leeds to Rossendale the place of their abode and charges of one night's lodging them - -	3s. 0d.

1760.	Paid at proclaiming the King at Rochdale	2s.	0½d.
1779.	For attending at Rochdale with the publicans for their licence	1s.	0d.
	For attending at Rochdale with surveyors to be chosen and for the warrant	5s.	0d.
	For attending the Deputy Lieutenant at Manchester when the militia men were sworn into the service	2s.	6d.
1780.	For making search by warrant in Rochdale for pickpockets	1s.	0d."

A fair was held annually in Todmorden, and each year the constable cleaned his truncheon in readiness for the occasion (at a charge of 8d. to the hamlet). He also received one shilling for "walking the fair." When evildoers were caught, men were paid to watch them and prevent their escape, as no "lock-up" was then built. As late as 1805 the constable of Stansfield fined one man 1s. for not going to Divine worship; another man 1s. for swearing, and three others 3s. 4d. each for Sabbath breaking.

An account will be given later of the additional work that fell to constables in time of war (chap. xxii).

II.—*Overseer of the poor.*

In the 16th century the problem of poverty compelled the serious attention of Parliament. At first an attempt was made to cope with the evil by charitable gifts from the wealthy. But the plan failed, and in Elizabeth's reign (in the year 1601) an important Poor Law was passed which rejected voluntary methods and imposed on every township the duty of providing for its own poor. Township officials, known as Overseers of the Poor, were chosen by the inhabitants with the approval of the Justices and were empowered to levy a rate in order to obtain money for the relief of paupers. They were also empowered to distribute the money raised as they thought fit. This Act remained in force for more than 200 years (until 1834). Detailed information as to how the poor were treated in the 18th century can be obtained from overseers' accounts that have been preserved.

In the first place townships were very anxious not to relieve strangers. Before a person in poor circumstances was allowed to settle in another township, an agreement was entered into by the overseers of his own district that they would attend to his relief should poverty overtake him in his new home. These agreements were called "Certificates of Settlement." A batch of certificates relating to the township of Hundersfield (in which Todmorden and Walsden were situated) is in the possession of the Assistant Overseer. They embrace a period of over 150 years (1677—1833). If a stranger became a pauper, he was at once sent back to his native township for relief. Disputes were continually arising as to the settlement of paupers and large sums of money were spent on law-suits.

Paupers legally settled within a township were treated as the law directed. On the right shoulder of every pauper was a badge of red or blue cloth consisting of the letter P and the first letter of the township. For example :—

Stansfield Township.

"1752. Cloth to badge the poor and to Wm. Dearden for badging them 10d."

Money was given every month to the aged and infirm. Those who were sick received whatever help the overseers thought suitable. In some cases money was given; in others, clothing was supplied or doctor's bills, funeral expenses, rent or even furniture were paid for out of township funds. Sometimes goods were lent, and remained the property of the township. The following examples are taken from the Stansfield Overseers' Accounts :—

"1744. Burial of George Crowther - 10s. 0d. (This was the usual price of a pauper funeral.)
1728. For a Bedstead for John Drapper 3s. 0d. For two blankets and 1 rug and chaff bed for John Drapper - 8s. 3d.
1750. To Wm. Sutcliffe for helping to "flit" Widow Sutcliffe 2 times 1s. 4d.
1753. For Ellen Drapper. Rent - 8s. 0d.
1757. Bought of Robert Barker goods as follows and lent them to John Marshall: 2 pair Bedstocks, 4 Bed Blankets, 1 Caddow (quilt) - - - - 18s. 0d. 2 Bolsters, 2 Chaffbeds 4s.; 3 wheels and 2 pair Cards, 4s; Fire Iorn 5s.; 2 Jorn Pans and Hooks 3s."

Overseers provided work for unemployed paupers and repeated references occur to handlooms, cards, wheels and spindles, supplied to various persons in the township:—

"1742. To a pair of looms for John
Lord - - - - - 18s. 0d.
1749. One wheel and spindle for Jno.
Earnshaw - - - - 6s. 0d."

It was an overseer's duty to apprentice pauper children to some trade or employment. He had power to compel suitable persons to take paupers as apprentices, or to impose a fine for refusal. The usual age of apprenticeship was seven years, and farmers on the uplands often availed themselves of pauper labour. An agreement or indenture was drawn up between the master and the overseer, whereby the master promised suitably to feed, clothe and train the pauper child, a sum of 10s. being paid by the township towards his outfit:—

"1745. To Widow Sutcliffe for maintaining a Boy till he was placed apprentice - - - 1s. 0d.
To a pair of indentures and for filling them up - - - 2s. 4d.
To William Barker with the same apprentice - - - 10s. 0d.
To the Justices for signing the indentures - - - - 4s. 6d."

Early in the 18th century (1722) an Act of Parliament gave power to townships to purchase or hire houses for the accommodation of the poor. In consequence poorhouses came into existence in this neighbourhood. About the year 1738 the experiment was tried in Stansfield, but after two years was given up, probably because the new system proved to be very expensive. Later, however, poorhouses were to be found in both Stansfield, Langfield and Todmorden. In the case of Langfield a poorhouse was built at Croft Carr Green in 1786-7 at a cost of £164; in Stansfield and Todmorden there were poorhouses at Blackshaw Head and at Gauxholme. Detailed accounts have been preserved of poorhouse management that give particulars not only of the rent and the treatment of the poor, but also of the price of various articles in the 18th century. The following entries are typical of many more:—

"Stansfield, 1739. '27 pound a
Beef' for workhouse		4s. 4d.
A load of meal (240 lbs.)	£1	0s. 0d.
One load of malt		18s. 0d.
5 load of coals		3s. 6½d.
One stone and a half of potatoes		7½d.
9 lbs. of cheese		1s. 8d.
½ stone butter		2s. 4d.
½ lb. tobacco		5½d."

Many of the paupers were too old to engage in any work, but such as could work were employed in spinning worsted and broad woof, and in the production of bocking and shalloon warps.* The money

---

* Bocking was a coarse woollen fabric used for floor cloths, etc.; shalloon was a light woollen stuff, chiefly used for linings of coats.

received from the sale of the goods they made, helped to defray the expenses of maintenance. In the year 1739, for example, £5 16s. 0d. was obtained for goods sold at the workhouse in Stansfield.

During the greater part of the 18th century there seems to have been no qualified doctor in this neighbourhood (chap. xvi), but in 1791, Dr. Heyworth Heyworth served as medical officer for Langfield. For attendance on the paupers of Langfield Town, Sept. 1791—Jan. 1792, Dr. Heyworth's bill amounted to 12s. 10½d. During that time he had administered 3 Blister plasters at 1s. each; 3 Large Stimulating Mixtures at 1s. 3d.; 2 Pots of Digestive Liniment at 6d.; as well as a Rubbing Bottle, 6d., and some Healing Salve for 4d.

III.—*Surveyor of Highways.*

This office was instituted by Parliament in 1554. Surveyors were responsible for the repair and construction of roads within a township. They were authorised to call on the inhabitants to help in the work; or, with the consent of the ratepayers, they might levy a rate and pay labourers to do what was necessary. Surveyors' Accounts still exist referring to our local townships in the 18th and early 19th centuries. A record was kept of the number of days' labour spent on the roads; of the tools bought or mended or other work done. Occasionally the surveyors succeeded in getting the work done without the imposition of a lay or rate. The following entries may be quoted in illustration:—

Todmorden.

"1739. John Dawson and Edward Lacy, Surveyors.

Received by one Lay at 6d. per pound	£9	3s. 10d.
Disburst	£9	1s. 10d.
Balance		2s. 0d.
Paid to Wm. Crowther for 41 days work at 12d. per day	£2	1s. 0d.
Paid to Job Halliwell for 54½ days work at 12d. per day	£2	14s. 6d.
Paid to Jno. Tattersall for Smith's work in sharpening and repairing tools for the use of the Todmorden Highways		5s. 10d.
Paid for the use of Job Halliwell's spade		6d.
Paid to Simeon Lord for one Maul and 3 Wedges for the use of the Town hereafter for ever		10s. 0d."

Stansfield Township.

"1784, Jan. 5th. 'Paid to myself, shooling (shovelling) snow'	1s.	6d.
Jan. 11th. Do.	2s.	0d.

1790. John Dawson, Overseer.
    Paid for himself and his sons,
        April 30th to Oct. 30th, on
        the road between Moss
        Hall, Stiperden, Kebcote,
        Lanehead and Mytholm - £13 0s. 0d."

Todmorden.

" 1763. This year the roads were repaired by day works of the inhabitants, without any lay or assessment, so these accounts may be settled without either pen, ink or paper."

IV.—*Pinder.*

In rural townships there was an enclosure, called a Pinfold or Pound, where stray cattle were kept. It was in the charge of a local official known as the Pinder. In the year 1705, John Crowther of Heyhead was appointed " Pinder or Herdsman for the outpasture of Langfield, so long as he shall behave himself well and civilly in his office." He was empowered " to impound or put all manner of cattle trespassing or offending in the outpasture, in the pinfold situate in Langfield." The Langfield pinfold was in Lumbutts, near Lee Farm. In 1814 Samuel Fielden obtained permission to remove it elsewhere, so that he might construct a reservoir for the spinning mill at Lumbutts built by himself and his brothers. At a meeting held in the Dog and Partridge Inn, Lumbutts (1827), the Freeholders of Langfield resolved: " that the Pinder have a new hat and girdle, new coat and collar and a pair of new shoes."

CHAPTER XX.

THE INDUSTRIAL REVOLUTION AND THE STORY OF MR. JOHN FIELDEN, M.P.

A great industrial revolution took place in England during the latter half of the 18th century. Within a space of about fifty years greater changes were produced in this district than five previous centuries had been able to effect. Turnpike roads along the valleys took the place of packhorse roads over the uplands; the Rochdale canal joined the Calder and Hebble Navigation in Yorkshire with the Duke of Bridgewater's canal in Lancashire; and the invention of new machinery completely changed the older methods of spinning and weaving and led to the manufacture of both cotton and woollen goods on a much larger scale. It will be convenient to deal first with the improvements made in the means of transit, and then to trace the steps that led to the establishment of the modern factory system.

Improvements in transit.

Early in the 18th century loud complaints were made as to the condition of the highways. The old system, described in the last chapter, whereby surveyors were responsible for the repair of the roads in each township had proved unsuccessful. Ratepayers declined to spend much money on roads; the surveyors were poorly paid and had no power to compel men to work as they directed. An important road like the one over Blackstone Edge was sometimes impassable even in summer. Defoe, who travelled over it in August, 1724, described it as being " very frightful, narrow and deep, with a hollow precipice on the right " that made it very dangerous. Moreover, merchants, farmers and clothiers travelled many miles on business, and as trade expanded the need of better roads was felt more keenly. This demand led to the establishment of turnpike trusts or companies, who obtained the consent of Parliament to build turnpike roads and tollhouses, and to recoup themselves for the capital invested by levying tolls on all traffic passing over the roads.

The first turnpike road in this district was over Blackstone Edge (1734). Twenty years later an Act of Parliament was passed for "diverting, altering, widening, repairing and amending the roads " from the town of Halifax and from Sowerby Bridge by Todmorden to Burnley and Littleborough. In the first paragraph of the Act the roads are described as being, in some places, extremely rough and incommodious; in others, ruinous and dangerous, often leading over hills so steep and high as to be almost impassable for wheel carriages. The Act therefore recommends deviations in the roads so as to avoid the hills, and the widening of them with a view to securing a " much more easy, extensive and advantageous communication through that populous and trading country." Trustees, including Anthony Crossley of Scaitcliffe and John Sutcliffe of Stansfield Hall, were appointed to carry out the provisions of the Act. Roads were built, toll-houses and milestones were erected, the rate of the toll was fixed and township surveyors were ordered to furnish lists of persons liable to give two days' work a year for repairing the roads. The rate fixed for tolls in 1776 was as follows:—

"For every horse or other beast drawing any coach, waggon, cart, 2s. or 1s. 6d. according to breadth of wheel.

For every horse, etc., laden or unladen and not drawing, 6d.

For every drove of oxen or other neat cattle, at the rate of 2s. 6d. per score, and every drove of calves, sheep, swine or lambs, at 10d. per score."

The establishment of turnpike roads was the first step in a process that gradually left the uplands almost desolate. Inns such as those at Sourhall and Whirlaw were deserted in favour of rival inns in the valley at Spring Gardens (now Queen Hotel) and Castle Street. With the development of new machinery, neither packhorses nor waggons could keep pace with the growing requirements of trade and a project for the construction of a canal through this district took definite shape.

The first attempt (in 1765) was abandoned on account of the opposition of Lancashire merchants. In 1790, however, a committee of Hebden Bridge and Rochdale gentlemen promoted a scheme for a canal from Sowerby Bridge to Manchester. Four years later the scheme obtained Parliamentary sanction. The length of the canal was 33 miles, and during its construction (1794—1802) the reservoirs at

Blackstone Edge and Whiteholme as well as Hollingworth Lake were built.*

The Act of Parliament gives a list of streams where only surplus water was available for the Company, so as not to interfere with the existing water supplies of manufacturers and property owners. These streams are almost all in this district, beginning at Warland Clough, and including Midgelden Brook, Lumbutts Stream and Stoodley Clough. "At the Call or Weir next above Todmorden belonging to Joshua Fielden," water might be turned into the canal " when the stream shall flow over such Call or Weir more than $2\frac{7}{12}$ inches mean depth and 30 ft. broad." In the first scale of rates levied by the Canal Company, 2d. a mile was charged for every ton of merchandise, when a lock was passed through; otherwise the charge was $1\frac{1}{2}$d. a mile. The canal was navigable as far as Todmorden in August, 1798, and was finally completed four years later. Hence the 19th century opened with a double line of communication running at the foot of the hills, canal barges being used instead of waggons for carrying cotton and woollen goods over long distances.

Introduction of the Factory System.

. In the beginning of the 18th century the uplands were parcelled out into small farms, where men worked, not only as farmers, but as manufacturers of woollen shalloons, kerseys and bockings for the Halifax market. Gradually a change was brought about through the development of the cotton industry in Lancashire. Large quantities of cotton weft and

* The Gaddens reservoirs were constructed about 25 years later

linen yarn were produced in the neighbourhood of Bolton and Manchester. As trade increased merchants began to distribute warp and raw cotton in the surrounding villages, to be spun and woven into cloth. In consequence men on the Lancashire uplands (as in Yorkshire) became both small farmers and manufacturers. They worked, however, in cotton instead of wool. The rate of production was very slow. It took a fortnight to weave one cotton piece containing 12 lbs. of weft. And yet to keep a handloom weaver busy, six or eight persons were continually occupied in carding, roving and spinning.

The system of "putting out" warps and weft reached Todmorden soon after 1790. Messrs. Travis and Milne, of High Crompton, near Shaw, brought these materials to Gauxholme Fold every week, and received back the finished cotton pieces. The old domestic system was thus applied to the manufacture of cotton instead of woollen goods.

The next stage was reached when hand cards and spinning wheels could no longer keep pace with the hand loom, owing to improvements in weaving. The necessary speed was then obtained by the invention of the carding machine, spinning jenny and spinning frame. In this way elaborate machinery became indispensable and the old domestic system of manufacture was doomed to decay. The first cotton mill in this district was erected in 1786, by John Fielden, son of Samuel Fielden, of Swineshead Farm in Langfield. Removing to Walsden, he built on the Clough Farm estate, a small mill three storeys high containing carding and spinning machinery driven by a water-wheel. "Fielden and Travis," of Clough

Mill, thus became a centre for the distribution of warps and weft to weavers on the uplands. Other mills were soon erected, but in the story of one of them, viz., that of Joshua Fielden, of Laneside, the rise and progress of the cotton industry may be traced, whereby the old domestic system of manufacture was changed into the highly organised factory system of to-day.

Joshua Fielden was brought up at Edge End Farm as a farmer and woollen manufacturer. His father came from Bottomley, in Walsden. Still earlier the family had lived at Inchfield (Appendix IV). Joshua Fielden was a man of robust character. He was a Friend and worshipped at Shewbroad, where also he was buried. He pursued his business with untiring zeal. Every week he walked to Halifax market (a distance to and fro of 24 miles), carrying the woollen piece he had woven. But perceiving a possibility of greater success in the cotton industry, he left Edge End (1782), and established himself at Laneside. There he began the work of cotton spinning and weaving in three small cottages. Soon the building was enlarged and a spinning jenny replaced the spinning wheel. Next carding machines were added, and the first step was taken towards founding the future Waterside Mill. At first Joshua Fielden brought his weekly supply of cotton from Manchester in a cart, and for many years with his third son John (the future member for Oldham) he attended Manchester market every Thursday to deliver the finished cloth. Winter and summer alike they left home at four in the morning, arriving back at midnight. Joshua's five sons were all trained for the business. At the age of ten each began working in the mill. The work was arduous, but there was no danger at Laneside Mill of witnessing the cruelties that were inflicted on thousands of children during the earlier years of the factory system. On the contrary, the Fieldens were honourably distinguished by their opposition to such cruelty, and fuller reference must be made to the work they accomplished on behalf of factory workers.

The factory system was the result of individual enterprise and grew up at first without any kind of external control. The output of cotton pieces increased enormously, and manufacturers became eager to make large fortunes. " Factories were built on the sides of streams capable of turning the waterwheel. Thousands of hands were suddenly required in these places remote from towns. . . . . The small and nimble fingers of little children, being by very far the most in request, the custom instantly sprang up of procuring apprentices from the different parish workhouses of London, Birmingham and elsewhere. Many, many thousands of these little hapless creatures were sent down into the north, being from the age of seven to the age of thirteen or fourteen years old." *

The greatest cruelties were practised. Children not more than 7 years of age were compelled to work 14 or 15 hours a day, being often flogged to their work and kept without wholesome food. At this very time, however (towards the close of the 18th century), the hours of labour at Laneside Mill did not exceed ten per day during both winter and summer.

The following resolution, passed by the Todmorden

" The Curse of the Factory System," p. 9, by John Fielden, M.P.

and Walsden churchwardens in 1801, shows only too plainly that pauper children were employed in mills and that excessive hours and night-shifts were not unknown:—

"Agreed by the laypayers here present that Mr. Hudson shall have a number of children apprenticed out of the workhouse on condition that they are to work the usual hours and that at the usual time, not in the night."

At last (1802) Parliament intervened and limited the hours of work for parish apprentices to 12 a day. An unforeseen result followed, for masters sought to obtain labour from the children of parents on the spot. Moreover, the introduction of the steam engine enabled factories to be built in towns where the population was dense, and where poverty made parents more willing to secure a child's scanty earnings. In Todmorden the first "steam factory" was built by Henry Ramsbottom in Salford, but the Fieldens soon followed his example. Mechanical improvements, however, did not improve the lot of the workers. On the contrary, increasing competition compelled Fielden Brothers (as the firm was called after Joshua Fielden's death in 1811) to raise the hours of labour to 12 on five days a week, with 11 hours on Saturday, a total of 71 hours per week, since other manufacturers insisted on 77 and even 84 hours per week. In 1819 Parliament again interfered. Children under 9 were excluded from cotton mills; whilst those under 16 might not work more than 72 hours a week. At Laneside Mill the number was then reduced to 69, at which figure it remained until further legislation was passed in 1833.

All the mills hitherto erected had been spinning mills. The power loom had been invented, but as late as 1817 there were not more than 1,000 power looms in the whole of Lancashire. Hence in this neighbourhood spinners still depended on handloom weavers; and it has been said that at one time Fielden Brothers employed as many as 3,000 handloom weavers. The wages paid did not exceed 10s. a week, and when power looms were established they sank as low as 3s. or 4s. Children at this time (1820—1835) often learnt at home to weave the warp and weft brought from the spinning mills in the valley; but before manhood was reached the handloom was abandoned and the domestic weaver had become a factory operative. In 1829 Fielden Brothers erected a large weaving shed for 800 looms, and Laneside Mill was merged in Waterside. Later a larger shed was added containing 1,000 looms. Weavers with two ordinary looms earned 8s. a week; with looms for sheetings, 12s.; tacklers received from 18s. to 20s. On the uplands poverty was widespread. The average weekly wage of the inhabitants in outlying districts in 1833 was 4s. 3d. a head, or 10s. 3d. per family. Corn was dear, and oatmeal, skimmed milk and hard cheese formed the main diet of the working classes.

The hardships experienced were often attributed to the effect of new machinery, and riots broke out in Rochdale among the handloom weavers in 1808 and again in 1829; power looms were broken in Rossendale in 1832, whilst ten years later an agitation arose that reached this district and is still remembered by the oldest inhabitants. It was a time of acute distress;

trade was bad and higher wages were demanded by the operatives. In August, 1842, there was a general stoppage of work throughout South-east Lancashire, and those on strike determined to stop others also from working. Early on Friday morning, August 12, men and women from Rochdale and Bacup, armed with thick hedgestakes and crowbars, marched into Todmorden. Every mill was visited; fires were raked out and boilers emptied, and shopkeepers and innkeepers were forced to give up their bread and ale. The agitators or "Plugdrawers" visited Waterside Mill, where the operatives were actually receiving higher wages than the plugdrawers themselves demanded. No opposition was offered, as John Fielden had declined assistance, stating that the arms of his people were his protection, and when that ceased he hoped he should cease to live. Special constables were sworn in, and Hussars from Burnley were quartered in Buckley's Mill at Ridgefoot. The plugdrawers decided to march to Halifax, where on the following Monday, to the number of 6,000, they joined an immense contingent from Bradford. There were conflicts with the police, and many men were arrested, including several from Todmorden. Nothing came of the agitation, but such distress was one of the chief causes of the Chartist Movement (chap. xxii).

Meanwhile in 1833 John Fielden, of Dawson Weir, had become M.P. for Oldham, and was devoting his energies to bettering the condition of the working classes. In his election address he declared that "nothing but an anxious solicitude to see the people restored to their just rights, and especially the labouring portion of society greatly improved could have induced him" to enter Parliament. He was an advanced Radical, in favour of the abolition of the Corn Laws and a believer in annual Parliaments and vote by ballot. His plainness of speech and the disinterested spirit that actuated his public work are well illustrated in the first speech he delivered in the House of Commons (1833) on the subject of the cause of distress in the country :—

"The Chancellor of the Exchequer admits that there is very severe distress among the handloom weavers, and says it is caused by competition with power looms, and cannot be removed. . . . Are my poor distressed handloom weavers to rest satisfied with this explanation? If I thought power looms were the cause of the distress (I and my partners have nearly a thousand of them) and if it can be shown that they cause the distress, I should like to see them broken to pieces to-morrow. But this is not the cause, for anything calculated, as machinery is, to facilitate and increase production, is a blessing to any people, if the things produced were properly distributed, and it is the duty of the Legislature to cause such a distribution to be made; and if I were of opinion that the relief of the distress could not be effected by the Legislature, I would take my hat and walk away and not come within the walls of St. Stephen's again. The labouring people are in deep distress, there is a cause for it, and if the King's servants cannot find a remedy for it they are not fit to fill the benches they occupy in this House. . . . My training has been at the spinning jenny and the loom, and not at the college and the courts." And he bluntly declared that distress was caused by " taking away in taxes from those who labour and giving to those who do not labour."

John Fielden's entrance into political life was mainly due to his determination to help in every possible way to improve the lot of the working classes. As early as 1816 he had opposed the cruel treatment of women and children in factories, and he was of opinion that the only cure for these evils was the adoption of a Ten Hours' System. About 1830, a huge procession of factory workers passed through the streets of Manchester in favour of a Ten Hours' Bill. Hundreds of factory cripples headed the procession that was preceded by a black banner bearing in silver letters the words, " Behold and weep." This pitiful spectacle strengthened the resolve of John Fielden, Richard Oastler and Michael Thomas Sadler never to rest until the reform of the factory system had been achieved.

A scathing letter written by Oastler in the *Leeds Mercury* (Sept. 29, 1830), directed public attention to the subject. Sadler was successful in having introduced into Parliament in 1832 a bill for limiting the hours of labour in mills to 58 per week for persons under 18 years of age. The following year at a great public meeting in London, addressed by John Fielden, Lord Ashley for the first time associated himself with the cause of factory reform. That year, moreover, an Act was passed limiting the work of children between 9 and 13 years of age to eight hours a day and insisting on two hours' instruction (chap. xxiii).

Manufacturers at once raised an outcry against reform. In 1836 the master spinners and manufacturers of Oldham petitioned the Government, praying that all persons under 21 years of age might be employed for 69 hours a week. They requested the members of the Borough to support their application. In reply John Fielden stated that to allow young children between 11 and 13 years to work 69 hours instead of 48 was revolting to his feelings, and he advocated "eight hours' work per day in factories" as being long enough for either children or adults. In support of his opinions he published a pamphlet entitled "The Curse of the Factory System," wherein he showed that the workpeople had been and were cruelly treated and that they had not idly asked for protection. Further he avowed that he would "cast manufactures to the winds rather than see the workpeople enslaved, maimed, vitiated and broken in constitution and in heart," as his pamphlet proved only too clearly to be the case.

The little book contains an outspoken indictment of the factory system, but to us there is the additional interest of allusions to his own early life and the conduct of his firm.

"I well remember being set to work in my father's mill when I was little more than ten years old; my associates, too, in the labour and in recreation are fresh in my memory. Only a few of them are now alive; some dying very young but many of those who lived have died off before they attained the age of fifty years, having the appearance of being much older, a premature appearance of age which I verily believe was caused by the nature of the employment in which they had been brought up."

He then alludes to the hours of work at Waterside (facts already quoted), and to the fatigue he felt when the day's work was done; and describes how, when Nathaniel Gould of Manchester began to work for factory reform, a petition was presented to the House of Commons from Fielden Brothers and their operatives, urging shorter hours of labour for both children and adults.

John Fielden's persistent advocacy won the respect of the House of Commons. He promoted immense petitions in favour of reform and finally took charge of the Ten Hours' Bill when it passed into law. The bill provided that no person under 18, or woman above 18, should work for more than 10 hours in one day, or 58 hours in any one week. Its effect was to limit by the same amount the hours of work of all adult operatives. The second reading of the bill was carried on February 10, 1847, by a majority of 63 votes (151 to 88); and the measure was finally placed on the statute book, June 8, 1847. Lord Ashley testified to the valuable help that had been given by John Fielden owing to his experience, weight and disinterestedness.

The efforts of John Fielden had been crowned with success, and after his death those for whom he had fought realised the debt they owed to him, and desired in some practical way to show the public esteem in which he was held. In 1859 at a public meeting in the Oddfellows' Hall, Todmorden, it was decided to erect a public monument to John Fielden and to ask for the support of factory workers in Lancashire and the West Riding. There was an immediate response; more than £1,000 was raised by subscription, and Foley, the sculptor, was commissioned to carve a full length bronze statue, standing on a pedestal. On April 3, 1875, when the present Town Hall was opened, the statue thus erected in honour of John Fielden was unveiled by Lord John Manners. An immense concourse of both young and old assembled and, despite torrents of rain, all remained to do honour to the dead. More recently the statue was removed to its present position in Fielden Square. In the person of John Fielden, Todmorden may claim to possess a citizen, who on the wider field of public service, won by his devotion to the principles of justice and philanthropy the esteem of his contemporaries and the gratitude of countless thousands of men, women and children.

CHAPTER XXI.

TODMORDEN ON THE EVE OF THE RAILWAY SYSTEM.

Few persons now living can remember Todmorden as it was before the construction of the railway, and an effort of the imagination is needed to realise what Todmorden was like seventy years ago. The appearance of the landscape remained for the most part unchanged during the 18th century. The hamlets on the uplands were still to all appearance hives of industry, but the looms in the cottages were increasingly idle and men and women went down into the valleys to work. Mills had been built in almost every clough and there were rows of cottages along the turnpike roads. The greatest change had taken place at the centre in the rapidly growing village of Todmorden.

Let us in imagination walk along the streets of the village, beginning at Todmorden Hall. In front of the Hall a garden sloped almost to the open stream, whilst at the back were orchards filled with shrubs and fruit trees. Behind St. Mary's Church, Spring Gardens Inn stood in well cultivated gardens. It was tenanted by Thomas Hartley, and was much more frequented since the withdrawal of traffic from the uplands. Further up the hill side Hallwood covered the slope. Its name was derived from the Hall in the valley below. Fields belonging to the Hall farm extended along either side of the canal as far as Dobroyd. The land between the canal and road is still known as Hall Ings or Meadows. A century ago sizing mills, machinists' shops and dye works already occupied part of these fields. It was here that Henry Ramsbottom's " Steam Factory " was situated. Behind these workshops there was a reservoir which carried water by an artificial channel or " goit " through the grounds behind Todmorden Hall to Buckley's Mill at Ridgefoot. Dawson Weir, at Dobroyd, was the residence of John Fielden. The spinning mills and weaving sheds of Messrs. Fielden Brothers were at Waterside, on the farther side of both road and river. The latter, however, had been arched over for some distance near the mill. The additional buildings between the road and canal had not yet been built. Canal barges brought raw cotton to within a stone's throw of the mill, and took away calicoes, fustians and velveteens. At this time 60,000 lbs. of cotton yarn were spun in Todmorden every week and 7,000 pieces of calico were manufactured.

The oldest part of the village stood near the rising ground at Cockpit and Bank Top. A triangular block of property, consisting of timber yards and sawing mills, occupied what is now Fielden Square. Golden Lion Inn and several older houses were on the opposite side of the street which turned up Hanging Ditch, and branched along King Street towards Honey Hole. At Bank Top was the Friends' Meeting House and Burial Ground, built in 1808, after the meeting house at Shewbroad had been taken down. Nearer Hanging Ditch, on Cockpit Hill, stood the Unitarian Chapel, erected in 1824, of which John Fielden was one of the original trustees.

From this point of vantage the vale of Todmorden might be seen extending north-west and east towards the Burnley and Eastwood valleys. The canal, as it turned eastward, separated industrial Todmorden from the broader expanse of fields beyond, where flowed the branches of the Calder. The river ran open to the sky from Waterside until it dipped under the canal. It then proceeded beyond the present railway arch before changing its direction, and met the Burnley valley stream at Dam Scout in Stansfield Hall meadows. Four bridges crossed the river. The first at Cheapside was known as Pickles Bridge (near the present Post Office); " Neddy Brigg" crossed the canal; at the top of Water Street (then Shop Lane) was Royal Bridge, and County Bridge was situated at the junction of the turnpike roads near the Endowed School. The part of the river between the canal and Royal Bridge was arched over in 1836 by Mrs. Ann Taylor of Todmorden Hall. Before this was done the road crossed the river at Royal Bridge into Church Street (then the most important in the village), whilst Shop Lane (now Water Street) continued on the right hand of the river. Shop Lane was named from a grocer's shop, built in 1730, and called the Old Shop. Shop Lane Meadows stretched across Roomfield Lane as far as the bend of the river. Meadow Lane, that connects Dale Street and Halifax Road, is still an indication of its position. In those days both Church Street and Shop Lane were on a level with the river.

Beyond County Bridge, North Street continued on the left of the Calder. Below the bridge and opposite North Street (where the Town Hall now stands) a building had been erected by public subscription, which the Wesleyans used as a school.

Roomfield Lane went eastward, with hawthorn hedges on either side. The most conspicuous buildings were York Tavern on the right and the Wesleyan Chapel on the left. There were a few cottages, and below the chapel the Rev. Joseph Atkinson, curate of St. Mary's, lived in a house to which a small farm was attached (on the site of Roomfield House). The rest of the land between the river and canal as far as Stansfield Mill consisted of meadows that belonged to the Stansfield Hall and Kilnhurst estates. Todmorden's first cricket field was situated in Old Shop meadows, and three days' matches were played there before the railway had been built. During heavy winter rains the river often overflowed its banks and the fields were flooded.

Beyond the river, past the cottages and inns in North Street, stood Buckley's Mill, which was built by Anthony Crossley about the year 1796. Patmos comprised scarcely more than a dozen cottages. Cobden was Buckley's Hollow (often flooded in those days to a depth of six feet), and above, on a level with Dog House was Buckley Wood. Stepping stones across the river led from the high road to Pinhall Lane (now Wellington Road), which mounted the slope towards Stansfield Hall with its adjacent cottages. West Lodge was built in 1834 by Mr. Hammerton of Burnley, who was the first solicitor to reside in Todmorden. The New Connexion Methodists had built a chapel at Patmos, and an Inghamite* chapel stood at Ferney Lee. There was also a cluster of cottages at Toad Carr, but the rural

* Rev. Benj. Ingham (1712—1772) of Ossett, a disciple of Wesley, founded 60 "Inghamite Societies" in Yorkshire.

character of the scenery was still unimpaired. Further up the valley Thomas Ramsbotham lived in the mansion he had built at Centre Vale, whilst John Crossley at Scaitcliffe Hall lived where for many generations his family had resided. The hill slopes were well wooded; in the cloughs primroses, violets and wild hyacinths still grew in profusion, and kingfishers with bright plumage hovered over pools and streams.

A small mill built on the hill side above Hole Bottom marked the beginning of a firm destined to rival that of Fielden Brothers in importance. Lawrence Wilson began the manufacture of bobbins in a building, the ruins of which may still be seen at Hough Stones. He had been a journeyman bobbin turner in Halifax. With his savings and a sum of £50 lent by John Fielden of Dawson Weir, he started business in 1823 on his own account. Two years later he removed to Pudsey, but as the water supply was insufficient in summer, he built a new mill in the bottom of the valley, giving it the name of Cornholme. In this way the present works of Wilsons Ltd. arose, although the period of greatest expansion did not take place till many years later.

From the above description it is obvious how small the village of Todmorden was so late as seventy years ago. It consisted of a straggling line of houses, shops and inns crossing and recrossing the river from Patmos to Pickles Bridge with an industrial tract of land at Salford and Waterside. Nevertheless the number of inhabitants was rapidly increasing. The population of the township of Todmorden and Walsden increased nearly threefold from 1801 to 1841 (2,515 to 7,311), and for the three townships (including Langfield and Stansfield) the population during the same period was more than doubled (8,453 to 19,044).

This growth in numbers made itself felt in several ways. In 1802 the Todmorden and Walsden parishioners, at a meeting held at Gauxholme, decided to establish a market on Thursdays for the benefit of manufacturers and tradesmen. Later two markets were established, one on Thursday for corn and provisions, and one on Saturday for meat, fish and greengroceries. A cattle market was also held on the first Thursday in each month. The market place was at White Hart (Eccles') Fold, near St. Mary's Church. Often on Sunday after morning service, the parish clerk acted as town crier and at the gate of the churchyard announced which local farmer or butcher would kill a cow or sheep that week, so that fresh meat might be obtained.

Animated scenes were witnessed in Church Street on Saturday nights when farmers and their wives came into the town to market. Two annual fairs for cattle and general trade were held on the Thursday before Easter and on Michaelmas Day (September 27), when it is said that more business was done than at most fairs in the North of England, considering the size of the town.

Changes of great importance also took place in the religious life of the district. Owing to "the great increase of inhabitants" the Todmorden churchwardens resolved in 1801 to enlarge the graveyard at St. Mary's, and a few years later, to have service "both in the forenoon and afternoon on

EVE OF RAILWAY SYSTEM

Sundays." In 1824 a new parsonage house was erected at Ridgebottom. A little later a Sunday School was built on land belonging to White Hart Farm that had been obtained as a burial ground. These changes culminated, through the influence of the Rev. Joseph Cowell, in the erection of a new and larger church near the site already secured for a cemetery and parsonage. Many of the older inhabitants regretted the abandonment of St. Mary's. All opposition, however, was overborne, in 1832 Christ Church was opened, and for many years St. Mary's was deserted. Further, the church at Cross Stone, built in 1717, was pulled down and in 1835 the present church was opened for public worship.

Meanwhile the number of Nonconformist chapels had been rapidly increasing. Allusion has been made to the Friends' Meeting House at Bank Top and the Unitarian Chapel on Cockpit Hill. In 1808 Rodhill End Chapel was sold to the Wesleyans, as the Baptists then worshipped in the valley at Rehoboth in Millwood. A Baptist congregation was formed at Lineholme (in 1816) as an offshoot from Shore Chapel, whilst in the same year the chapel at Patmos was built (p. 172). Nor was the chapel at Dog House large enough for the Wesleyans at the centre. About 1820 the building already mentioned as occupying the site of the present Town Hall was used by the Wesleyans as a Sunday School, and in 1827 York Street Chapel was built. About this time also a Primitive Methodist church was established at Knowlwood through the influence of preachers from Halifax. Also before the railway viaduct was constructed, the first chapel belonging to the Methodist

Association in Todmorden was built on the land where Bridge Street Chapel now stands.

A few words may be added descriptive of the general life of the people. Dr. Heyworth Heyworth was for many years the only doctor. He lived in Water Street and his garden extended across what is now York Place. Later Dr. Hardman resided in York Street and was the local factory surgeon. Many of the inhabitants, however, still resorted to witch doctors at Charlestown, Cragg or Halifax, either to cure ailing children or ward off ill luck in farming. Even the members of the Baptist Chapel at Shore thought fit to discuss the subject of witchcraft at one of their church-meetings. In the minutes for March 2, 1825, the following entry occurs: "All present, with the exception of three who were neuters (neutral), thought it was sinful for Christians to apply to witches to remove some malady out of their own or their children's bodies or on any other account." This resolution does not imply any disbelief in witchcraft. Superstitions, indeed, still lingered; on every farm-door horseshoes were fastened; men carried boxes containing charms to keep them safe from ill luck or disease, or slept with knives hung above their pillows to keep off nightmares.

With regard to facilities for travelling, in 1820 a movement was set on foot by John Crossley of Scaitcliffe to raise £500 in order to induce one of the mail coach proprietors from Halifax to Rochdale to run a coach through Todmorden instead of over Blackstone Edge. The following year a coach service was secured, at first twice a week and then daily. The place of call was the Golden Lion Inn, where the first regular post office was also established. There were two coaches, the " Shuttle " and " Perseverance," and the district was still sufficiently rural in character for an observer on the Canal Bridge to watch the progress of the coach from Castle Lodge on its way to Todmorden. Letters were carried by coach. The postage of a single sheet cost from 4d. to 1s. 3d. according to distance. Travelling also was expensive. Children had few holidays and seldom went more than a few miles from home. Money was scarce and earned only by long days of toil. As for pastimes, cock fighting (the name of Cockpit is suggestive), rabbit coursing and rat catching were indulged in, and even bull-baiting had not disappeared from Worsthorne, as late as 1834. The gentry engaged in shooting, or in hunting hares and rabbits or a stray fox with a pack of harriers. Within quite recent times a pack of hounds was kept at Stoneyroyd and " Hare and Hounds Inn " still reminds us of this cross country sport.

This chapter may conveniently be closed with a brief account of the construction of the railway. In 1825 a company was formed to promote the building of a railway from Manchester to Leeds. Five years later a survey of the district was made by George Stephenson. After repeated efforts the company obtained Parliamentary sanction to establish a railway from Manchester via Todmorden and Dewsbury to Normanton and thence to Leeds. The work began in August 1837. Two years later the line was open for traffic from St. George's Fields, Manchester, to

Littleborough. The following year the portion from Normanton to Hebden Bridge was also available. The people of this district exhibited the greatest interest in the opening of the railway. The hill sides were lined with thousands of spectators, and at Sowerby Bridge the first train was boarded by eager passengers who stood upright on the tops of the carriages, stooping as they passed under bridges. The accompanying diagram, kindly furnished by the chief engineer of the Lancashire and Yorkshire Railway Company, gives some idea of the appearance of the carriages. (Fig. 22.)

The last portion of the line to be completed was that between Todmorden and Littleborough, where the greatest difficulties had to be surmounted in the construction of Summit Tunnel and the spanning of our own valleys. The Todmorden viaduct consists of nine arches, seven having a span of 60 ft. and a height above the road of $54\frac{1}{2}$ ft. Difficulties were also met with at Charlestown where a tunnel was partially bored and then abandoned owing to the loose nature of the rocks. The present railway curve in consequence follows the winding of the valley. The railway was finally completed on March 1, 1841, and this district was brought into still closer communication with more distant places. At a later date the older roundabout way to Leeds was replaced by the present line which passes through Halifax and Lowmoor, and thence branches to both Bradford and Leeds.

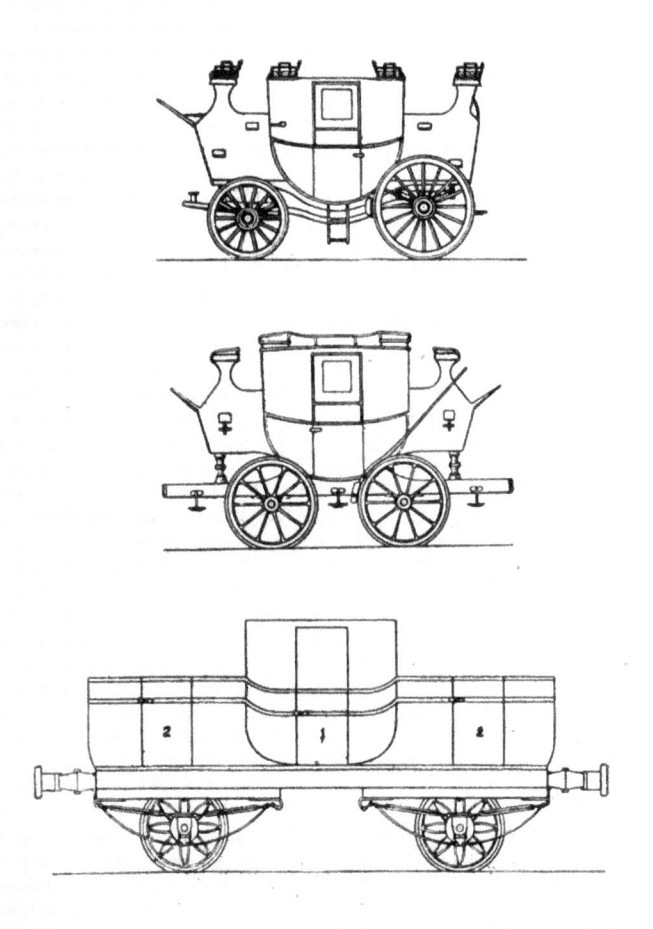

Fig. 22. FIRST CARRIAGES USED ON LANCASHIRE AND YORKSHIRE RAILWAY.

CHAPTER XXII.

Local Politics in the Nineteenth Century.

In the days of the Reformation and the Civil Wars men were compelled to fight out, as well as to reason out, the problems of civil and religious liberty. In the eighteenth century local officials had to work out in detail, as best they could, great national problems such as the treatment of the poor. During the first half of the nineteenth century there were several questions that aroused a keen interest in Todmorden. Taking them in the order in which they came, these were first, matters connected with the struggle against Napoleon; second, the Reform agitation and the Chartist movement; third, the introduction of the Poor Law of 1834; and fourth, the establishment of county police.

I.—*The Napoleonic Wars.*

During the war with France (1793—1815) men from the local militia were drafted into the ranks of the regular troops. It was the duty of each township to furnish a certain number of men. They were chosen by ballot, but there was often the greatest unwillingness to serve, and heavy fines were paid in order to escape from doing so. What were known as militia clubs were formed in many townships. Members paid an annual subscription, and the funds of the club were used to hire a substitute in place of any member chosen by ballot. In 1807 a club in Erringden had 33 members, the subscription being £1 1s. 0d. Men who were not members of a club paid as much as ten guineas to be relieved from service. Constables, on the other hand, paid large sums or *bounties* to induce men to enlist, and on these occasions drink flowed plentifully. For example, in the same year, 1807, the Erringden constable paid as follows:—

"James Haworth, Bounty, Luddenden £27 0 0
List Money - - - - - 0 1 0
Paid for meat and drink at Luddenden when he hired into the militia - - - - - 0 11 3"

To fill the gaps in the regular troops constables often went recruiting. The Stansfield constable was busy in 1803 searching for recruits at Todmorden, Bradford, Worsthorne and Heptonstall, money being freely spent on ale at each place. Several entries show that the pressgang was not unknown in this district. Usually vagrants were drugged with drink and then carried off to the wars. The following entries occur during the American War of Independence:—

"Langfield, April 1779. Spent at James Howarth's at Todmorden, when we impressed men - - - - 9s. 0d.
Erringden 1779. Going through the Town for men to assist in pressing 1s. 0d.
Spent when we were on the search - 4s. 6d."

Traces of the volunteer movement may also be found in these local records. One of Napoleon's ambitions was to invade England, and from 1803-5 a French army near Boulogne waited for a favourable opportunity to cross the Channel. In that time of peril a scheme of national defence was organised, and 300,000 volunteers offered themselves for service. The following entries occur in the Erringden Constable's Account for the year 1803:—

"Aug. 31. My journey one day
noticing volunteers - - 2s. 6d.
Oct. 25. To expenses when raising volunteers - - - £4 5s. 2d.
Nov. 26. To Mark Uttley for collecting first and second calls of Volunteer subscription money - - - - 4s. 0d."

The sum of £4 5s. 2d. was paid to the constable, showing that the expenses incurred had been defrayed by private subscription.

Napoleon's overthrow in 1814 was commemorated in this neighbourhood by the erection of Stoodley Pike. A meeting was held on 22nd September, 1814, at Mr. David Cawthorn's (Golden Lion Inn), when it was resolved "that Messrs. Samuel Greenwood,[*] Thomas Sutcliffe and Richard Ingham, having this day applied to the Landowners of Langfield for their consent to erect a Pillar on the ancient site of Stoodley Pike to commemorate the peace which Great Britain by her perseverance, wisdom and valour has so gloriously achieved for the nations of Europe, and for this purpose to grant them 123

[*] Samuel Greenwood, of Stones, was a member of the Society of Friends.

square yards of land (for the use of this public monument and for no other purpose whatever) the meeting do agree that the said Samuel Greenwood, Thomas Sutcliffe and Richard Ingham shall be Trustees of the said Pillar and Land and shall take hold and enjoy for the purpose aforementioned the said 123 yards of land, they and their heirs for ever."

The following November William Sutcliffe of Stoodley and John Arthur Ingham of Shaw were appointed as additional trustees " for preserving the 123 yards of land and maintaining the Pillar *now building thereon* at Stoodley Pike." The monument, which was rather like a mill chimney, was built on a place where previously there had been a cairn of stones. The cost of erection was met by subscription. By a curious coincidence, this memorial of Peace fell to the ground on the day the Russian ambassador left London (February 8, 1854) at the beginning of the Crimean War. After the war, at a meeting held at the Golden Lion Inn in June, 1856, it was decided to erect the present monument.

II.—*The Reform Agitation and the Chartist Movement.*

The period that followed the Battle of Waterloo was one of acute distress in this country. War had interfered with trade; the price of corn was high and there was a succession of bad harvests. Among the working classes discontent grew rapidly and an urgent demand arose for Parliamentary reform, so that the House of Commons might reflect more accurately the wishes of the people. The inhabitants of Todmorden were keenly interested in this subject.

As early as June, 1819 (two months before the "Peterloo Massacre"), a meeting in favour of reform was held in Todmorden. Eleven years later, at the request of 52 inhabitants of Langfield, the Constable, John Veevers of Kilnhurst, summoned a public meeting. It was held at Lumbutts, and the chief speakers were John Fielden of Dawson Weir and Dr. Hardman.* Resolutions were passed and petitions were drawn up in favour of the reform of the House of Commons, of annual parliaments, universal male suffrage, vote by ballot, reduction of taxation and the repeal of the corn tax. These petitions were forwarded to the Earl of Radnor and Mr. Hunt, M.P. for Preston, for presentation to both Houses of Parliament.

The following month, January, 1831, at a meeting held at the White Hart Inn, Todmorden, under the chairmanship of John Fielden, it was resolved to form a Society, to be called the Todmorden Political Union, with the following clearly defined objects:—

" To endeavour to obtain by legal means, and these only, a radical reform in the constitution of the Commons House of Parliament. To prepare petitions and addresses (and remonstrances if necessary) to the King and to the two Houses of Parliament respecting the preservation and restoration of national rights; to procure . . . the repeal of all taxes which affect the Press, and prevent the dissemination of knowledge. To

* See the "Voice of the People" for January 15, 1831; a small eight page newspaper in favour of reform, and published in Manchester. Price 7d.

endeavour to obtain the abolition of every species
of slavery throughout His Majesty's Dominions
.... To take cognizance of all real local abuses
and to prevent as far as practicable all public
wrongs and oppressions."

The members of the Union took politics seriously.
Three days after the introduction of the first Reform
Bill into the House of Commons (March 1, 1831), the
Council of the Union sent an address of thanks to
the Ministers, which was duly acknowledged by Earl
Grey. The same year a General Election took place
and Earl Grey was returned to power with a large
majority. A Reform Bill passed through the House
of Commons, and the country waited in suspense to
see what action the House of Lords would take. A
public meeting was then held in Todmorden and
petitions were forwarded to the Peers, urging them
to pass the Bill and denying that there was any
uncertainty as to the wish of the people to see the
Bill become law. When the Lords had rejected the
Bill, addresses were sent to the King urging him to
dissolve Parliament and to the Government as well
as to the people of Todmorden, bidding them not
to despair as success was assured, and rebutting the
slander that the advocates of Reform were the
enemies of the King and Constitution. Intense
excitement prevailed throughout the country and
riots broke out in many large towns. The Bill went
through the House of Commons a second time and
was sent to the Peers. They no longer dared to
reject the measure outright but hoped to alter many
of its provisions. Whereupon the Todmorden

Political Union again addressed His Majesty's Ministers, solemnly warning them that any serious alteration in the Bill " would inevitably produce great dissatisfaction in the manufacturing districts, and consequences might follow which it is awful to contemplate." The address then proceeded as follows :—" That our opinion may be properly appreciated, permit us to say that our Union consists of merchants, manufacturers, tradesmen, mechanics, artisans, etc., residing in the neighbourhood, so that our information on their opinions and sufferings may be relied on.

" We form part of an extensive manufacturing district, the people of which have been long suffering from the pressure of the times, and thousands of families among the operatives are absolutely in a state of starvation, who, though in full employment, cannot obtain 3d. a head per day to subsist on; and they have borne this in the most patient manner, and have evinced a moral principle beyond all praise.

" They wish for peaceful relief, they have hoped that the Reform Measure would lead to an amelioration of their condition, and they now await in awful silence the results of the proceedings in the House of Lords."

When finally the opposition of the Peers was overcome and the Bill received the Royal Assent, the Union decided publicly to celebrate the occasion. The function took place on August 4, 1832, and began with a banquet in the open air for 350 guests, under the presidency of John Fielden. A grand procession was then formed, including the Society of Whitesmiths, Independent Order of Oddfellows,

Royal Foresters, Druids, Mechanics' Trades Society and the Loyal Free Mechanics. Each Society had its own band and banners; the Hebden Bridge Band was also present. The Union had a special flag designed, bearing the words "The Members of the Todmorden Political Union. Union has conquered and will conquer."

It was expected by thousands of working men that the reform of the House of Commons would result in immediate and widespread benefits to the wage earning classes. Intense disappointment ensued when food did not become cheaper, nor wages higher nor work more plentiful. Hence there arose a new movement, known as the Chartist movement, that for ten years (1838-48) attracted great attention throughout the country and found many earnest supporters in this district. In order to secure a House of Commons sympathetic towards wage-earners, Chartists advocated the following reforms: manhood suffrage, annual parliaments, vote by ballot, payment of members of parliament (poor men also to be eligible for election), and representation in parliament to be proportional to population. The six points of the Charter correspond very closely with the reforms advocated at the public meeting at Lumbutts in 1830 (p. 184), and it is not surprising that Chartism had many local supporters. Meetings were frequently held on the moors, where thousands of persons assembled to hear the Chartist leaders, Feargus O'Connor and Ernest Jones.

One section of the Chartists proposed methods of "physical force," and it is said that men secretly collected pikes and engaged in drill exercises on the

Todmorden uplands. Some agitators wished for a universal strike among working men. Among those responsible for the rising of the plugdrawers were some who belonged to this section. In that month (August, 1842) a Chartist meeting was held at Basons Stone, when a thousand persons were present. Robert Brooke, a lame schoolmaster, urged that men should cease working till the Charter was obtained; that the overseers should be asked for relief or some other means be adopted to obtain it. For this speech Brooke was arrested and tried at Lancaster with more than fifty other Chartists, who were also charged with uttering seditious speeches. All, however, were acquitted. Many leading Chartists were imprisoned for inciting men to use force rather than to rely on argument. Their friends raised money for their support. A meeting was held, for example, at Pike Holes, near Stoodley Pike, attended by 2,000 persons, to protest against the non-representation of working men in Parliament, and the sum of £1 13 6 was collected " to help to freedom, Ernest Jones."

The Chartist movement did not continue beyond the year 1848. Cheaper bread, better trade and reduced taxation eased the lot of working people and made men content to wait more patiently for further reforms.

In Appendix III. an account is given of the changes made in the Parliamentary representation of this district by the Reform Bills of 1832, 1867 and 1885.

III.—*Introduction of the Poor Law.*

Within a few years of the passing of the Reform

Bill, Parliament dealt successfully with several important questions. By the Poor Law Amendment Act of 1834 the older system of township relief as administered by overseers came to an end. In its place, larger areas, called Poor Law Unions, were taken, and within each Union the relief of the poor was vested in a committee elected by the inhabitants and known as a *Board of Guardians*. It was the duty of each Board to obey the instructions of Poor Law Commissioners appointed by the Government to assist in carrying out the law. An overseer's duty was confined to levying a rate and collecting the money required by the Guardians; he took no part in its distribution. The new Act restricted outdoor relief within much narrower limits. Able-bodied persons who needed relief could only receive it in workhouses, erected within each Union.

The new system aroused great opposition. Townships disliked the control exercised by the Commissioners; a workhouse was regarded as a prison and given the name of Bastille,* and the treatment of the poor was considered harsh and degrading. The opposition in this neighbourhood was more persistent than in any other part of England, and a disgraceful riot occurred when an attempt was made to enforce some of the provisions of the Act. A brief sketch of the introduction of the new system into this district will explain how this came about.

An order of the Poor Law Commissioners, dated January 28, 1837, declared the townships of Todmorden and Walsden, Stansfield, Wadsworth, Hep-

* A famous prison in Paris that was destroyed during the French Revolution.

tonstall, Langfield and Erringden to be a united district, known as the Todmorden Union. The Board of Guardians was to consist of 18 members, viz., 4 each from Todmorden and Walsden and Stansfield; 3 each from Wadsworth and Heptonstall, and 2 each from Erringden and Langfield. The following month, when the first election of Guardians took place, it was found that Todmorden and Walsden and Langfield declined to appoint any representatives at all. The first Board, therefore, comprised only twelve members. It elected James Stansfield, solicitor, as clerk; and the Union was divided into a Todmorden and Hebden Bridge section for the registration of births and deaths. A fresh election then took place, and about a year later precise instructions were received from the Commissioners as to the duties of the Board and its officials, wherein it was stated that on and after July 6, 1838, the Guardians would be held responsible for the proper discharge of their duties.

Meanwhile opposition to these changes was steadily growing. John Fielden was most uncompromising in his hostility to the new Act, and many of his fellow townspeople did not scruple to threaten violence. It was determined to hold a great anti-poor law meeting at Wood Mill, Eastwood, on July 6, at the very time and place appointed for the meeting of the Guardians. In consequence, at a special meeting held at the White Hart Inn on the preceding day, the Guardians decided to postpone their meeting. They expressed their willingness to bring the new Act into operation if adequate civil and military protection were granted, but declared that it could not be successfully introduced unless the local influence and opposition of Mr. Fielden could by some means be overcome by the Government.

The Guardians made their first demand for money on July 27, 1838. The sum of £50 was required from Todmorden and Walsden, and £20 each from Langfield and Erringden. The townships declined to pay, and the overseers of Langfield and Erringden were summoned before the Halifax magistrates. William Ingham of Mankinholes, acting on the instructions of the Langfield ratepayers, still declined payment and was fined £5. As he refused to pay the fine, two constables, Messrs. Feather and King, were sent from Halifax to make a distraint on Mr. Ingham's household goods. Their arrival was anxiously awaited, and when, on Friday afternoon, November 16, they reached Mankinholes with a horse and cart, an alarm bell was rung, and from all sides hundreds of angry men and women hurried to the village. A terrible scene ensued. The horse and cart were thrown violently down, with one of the constables on the top. The cart was smashed and burnt. The two constables, after seeking refuge in the overseer's house, were compelled by the mob to come out and swear never to engage in the like business again. Being let go, they raced along the road to Stoodley, pursued by an infuriated crowd who repeatedly assaulted them, until at last they found shelter near Eastwood.

The following Wednesday, a rumour spread through the district that the constables were coming with a company of soldiers. This false report led to a still more serious riot. Hundreds of men, armed with clubs, assembled in Mankinholes and then proceeded to visit the homes of the Guardians or of prominent supporters of the new Act, and to break windows, doors and furniture. Royston Oliver, Multure Hall; Samuel Oliver, Wood Mill (where Constable Feather had found protection); Mr. Ormerod; Stones Wood; Mr. Greenwood, Watty Place; Dr. James Taylor, Todmorden Hall, Chairman of the Board of Guardians; and Mr. Greenwood, Hare Hill, were among those on whom the rioters wreaked vengeance. At Todmorden Hall, damage to the extent of £1,000 was inflicted. This wanton violence was met by energetic action on the part of the magistrates. Special constables were sworn in, and soldiers, both horse and foot, were quartered in the town. A raid was made on the mill of Fielden Brothers at Lumbutts and about 40 men were taken into custody. Some were conveyed to York Castle and after trial were found guilty, but the Judge dismissed them with a caution. One person, tried at Lancaster, was sentenced to nine months' imprisonment.

Several years later the townships of Todmorden and Walsden and Langfield still declined to contribute towards Poor Law relief, but the magistrates refused to grant distress warrants unless the Poor Law Commissioners would secure them against any damage that might be caused. Moreover the Guardians themselves, in a petition to the Government, expressed their decided opinion that the Act had not led to an improvement in the condition of the poor, or a diminution of pauperism, or a saving in the poor rate. They asserted that an " honest, industrious poor man who stood in absolute need of relief . . . was an object of compassion, but that the new Poor Law . . . by denying all out-door relief to able-bodied labourers, however meritorious, punishes poverty as a crime," a proceeding they regarded as unchristian in its severity and certain to produce distressing and appalling results in manufacturing districts.

The Guardians continued to rent buildings as poor houses in each township, but no steps were taken to build a workhouse for the Union. The Fieldens of Waterside proposed to build three cottage hospitals in different parts of the Union for the aged and infirm. At different periods deputations went up to London to gain the consent of the Central Board, but without success. Finally, after 40 years had elapsed (1877) the central authority threatened to break up the Todmorden Union, including one part in the Rochdale, and another part in the Halifax, Union, unless a workhouse was built; and all opposition ceased.

IV.—*County Police.*

Dislike of outside interference was also shown in the days when Sir Robert Peel's new system of police organisation was brought into this district. By this Act a township ceased to control the constable. The magistrates might appoint constables without any regard to the wishes of the inhabitants, and the cost of police was met out of the county rate. Some such action on the part of the magistrates in this neighbourhood led to a crowded meeting being held in Oddfellows' Hall, Todmorden (1853), when Joshua Fielden of Stansfield Hall took the chair. In the speeches delivered, the main objection raised was that the police formed an additional standing army and were a menace to the liberties of Englishmen. Local jealousies, however, were powerless to prevent the adoption of newer methods, and opposition died away.

Sixty years ago a spirit of independence was dominant in this neighbourhood. Men were eager to gain greater political privileges, but were anxious to preserve the older powers of local administration, and were jealous of outside interference. The spirit of independence and thrift among the working classes is also apparent in the story of the rise of the Co-operative movement in this district, to which brief allusion may now be made.

The beginning of the Co-operative movement in Todmorden dates from 1847, when a few men combined together to buy flour and meal and then sold these articles to each other at cost price. It was a small beginning. Each week the particulars of every purchase were written on a blackboard for the inspection of members. The following year a subscription of £1 was paid by each member, the society began to accumulate capital, and goods were sold at a profit so as to provide interest on the members' deposits. A general grocery department was also established, and in April 1848, the society was registered under the name of " James Hindle & Co." Cash payment was insisted on from the start, and at first members of the committee of management served in turn as shopmen. In 1850, owing to an increasing membership, a separate shop was established in Shade, under the control of the Shade members. Next year the two branches dissolved partnership, and in this way there were founded the two oldest local Co-operative societies, viz., the Todmorden and Bridge End Societies. The immense expansion in business and in wealth of these societies during the last fifty years shows how widespread is the support that has been given to the principles of co-operation among the industrial classes in this neighbourhood.

CHAPTER XXIII.

EDUCATIONAL PROGRESS IN TODMORDEN IN THE 19TH CENTURY.

A century ago there were only a few schools in this neighbourhood. Heptonstall Grammar School, Clegg's Endowed School in Todmorden and Cross Stone School, with various private "academies" and schools, supplied the needs of the middle classes. The Grammar School at Heptonstall had 50 pupils; seventeen of them received free instruction in Latin, the remainder paid fees for instruction in English subjects by an assistant master. Clegg's Endowed School had 40 fee-paying pupils.

Working-class children had no such opportunities of education during the earlier part of the 19th century. Their only chance of education lay in attendance at Sunday Schools. In 1801 the ratepayers of Todmorden and Walsden employed Ellis Hartley, Schoolmaster, to teach reading to " little children *who were not otherwise employed.*" Five years later the ratepayers of the same township passed a resolution declaring, " That Sunday Schools are a laudable institution, and that a charity sermon or sermons be recommended to be preached, and a subscription be opened; and, in case people come forward in a generous manner, that twenty guineas be allowed out of the poor rate to support the same for one year." It was further resolved that the most convenient places for schools in this district would be at Todmorden, Sourhall, Gauksholme and Square, in Walsden.

What measure of success attended these resolutions is uncertain. Ten years later, however, a meeting was held in the vestry of the Methodist Chapel, Doghouse, attended by Mr. Atkinson, curate of St. Mary's, and Mr. Gloyne, Wesleyan minister, when it was decided to establish a Todmorden Sunday School in premises where the Town Hall now stands. The movement received very hearty support, and within a few months a room was fitted up for Sunday School work. Some idea of the cost of equipment may be gathered from the following items:—

"July 8, 1816. Fitting up School by Jno. Holt.

150 ft. 3 inch Petersb^g Deals in forms at 10d.	£6 5s. 0d.
Sawing in Do.	8s. 0d.
Nails and screws for Do.	9s. 6d.
Making and fixing up	£2 16s. 0d.
48 Reading Boards at 5d. each	£1 0s. 0d.
Writing Desk and Footboard for Superintendent	14s. 0d.
Pointers for Monitors	6d."

Nearly £15 was spent on furniture. The preliminary outlay on letters and alphabets, spelling books, Catechisms, Testaments and Bibles, paper, quills and candles brought the total cost to more than £50.

The following year a branch school was opened at Cloughfoot. At a general meeting of subscribers and teachers held on April 26th, 1818, the report stated that owing to the depressed state of trade, and consequent diminution of wages, a great number of parents were unable to provide their children learning by any other means than that of Sunday Schools. Upwards of 400 children attended the Sunday School at Dog House; there were 150 children in the Union School and the same number at Cloughfoot. Great progress had been made in reading and writing, and there was an evident improvement in behaviour. Several boys and girls at Cloughfoot who scarcely knew a letter in the alphabet when the school was first established, after a year could read well in the Bible.

The Todmorden Union School was worked for the most part by Wesleyan Methodists, and in a few years seems definitely to have been associated with them. The character of the instruction given may be illustrated from the minutes of the Teachers' Meetings (1820—1828). The School was held every Sunday morning, from 9 to 11 o'clock, and in the afternoon, from 1-30 to 3-30. After singing and prayer, 40 minutes were devoted to reading, 10 minutes to spelling and 35 minutes to religious instruction. Markham's Spelling Books, for the older scholars, were bought from Mr. Hartley, of Rochdale, at 9s. 6d. a dozen; children in the alphabet and easy reading classes were supplied with sheets. In 1828 evening classes for writing were held twice a week. Juvenile teachers were employed in teaching infants, and as a reward for their valuable services were themselves taught writing on Saturday evenings.

Other Sunday Schools were established in various parts of the district. In 1818 a school was built by

EDUCATIONAL PROGRESS

public subscription at Lanebottom, Walsden, "to consist of 4 dwelling-houses on the ground floor, with a chamber above to be used from time to time as a school for teaching the children of poor and indigent parents to read and write and the common rules of arithmetic upon each Sunday." The Unitarians established (in 1825) a " free school for 100 children of all denominations from the age of four years to the time of going to the factory." Three years later a Todmorden Friendly School taught " knitting, sewing, reading, writing and arithmetic and other useful arts." In 1830 a schoolroom was erected at Cloughfoot, "to be used as a Sunday and day school for the education of youths of both sexes and of all denominations." There was also a school for 100 girls in connection with St. Mary's Church.

Factory schools came into existence in 1833, and to these schools factory children were compelled to go. A school had already been established at Waterside by Fielden Brothers, one of the office clerks serving as schoolmaster. There were more than 100 children in attendance in 1837. At that time Mr. Cooke was the master, in whose opinion a halfpenny a day was a reasonable sum for each child to pay for instruction. An inspector's report (dated 1848) commented on the small number of children who could write, and directed that certificates should be refused to such as " ought to write and did not." Only a very small proportion of men and women could write; three out of four persons might know how to read, but not one in ten could sign their own names.

On the uplands similar educational methods were

gradually adopted. At Shore Sunday School, for example, a teachers' meeting was held in 1845 to consider how best to introduce writing into the school. Some years later a free night school was instituted for the scholars. The minister was appointed teacher and was paid ninepence per night for his services. The scholars, however, were ordered to pay " a halfpenny per month towards light."

The efforts on behalf of education hitherto described were due mainly to the zeal of local religious organisations. The beginning of a national system of education was made in 1833, when Parliament first gave grants in aid of day schools built by various churches. The Todmorden National School was the first school in this neighbourhood to satisfy Government requirements and to receive Government grants. It was stated by the promoters that with the exception of Sunday Schools, there were no schools in this locality for the children of the poor. The cost of the school was estimated at £1,599; £600 had been raised by subscription, £300 had been received from the National Society, and a further grant of £500 was paid by the Government. Among the principal supporters of the school were James Taylor, of Todmorden Hall; Mr. Hammerton, solicitor, and John Crossley, of Scaitcliffe, who laid the corner-stone of the porch (May, 1844). Other Church schools were built at Priestwell, Walsden, Harley Wood and Shade. Hence with the undenominational and factory schools already in existence, day schools gradually took the place of Sunday schools in the education of the poor.

The day schools that had been established proved

insufficient for the needs of the population, and in 1874 the Education Act of 1870 came into operation in this locality. By this Act the district included within the Todmorden Poor Law Union was converted into a School Board area, known as the United District of Todmorden. The ratepayers were empowered to elect a board of thirteen members, whose duty it was to provide elementary education for the whole of the children in the district. A preliminary enquiry by the Education Department in London revealed the fact that, whereas there was school accommodation for 2,250 children, additional accommodation was needed for 2,760 children.

The first School Board for the United District was elected in August, 1874. The first Chairman was H. W. Horsfall, of Hebden Bridge; its most distinguished member was Mrs. Samuel Fielden, of Centre Vale. Mrs. Fielden had devoted many years to the study of educational methods for younger children. She was anxious also to do something towards training more efficient elementary school teachers, and herself engaged for many years in the actual work of a school. At first in unpretentious buildings in Cobden, and later in her own school at Centre Vale, Mrs. Fielden engaged in educational work along lines she herself had sketched out and practically tested. Centre Vale School continued in existence until 1896, and had an excellent reputation. The standard attained by Mrs. Fielden's pupils in reading was particularly noteworthy.

Mrs. Fielden's educational interests were not confined to her school or to her work on the Todmorden School Board. In the University of Manchester she founded the Fielden Chair of Education, and later established the Fielden Practising School in connection with the Education Department of the University. Her valuable services to the cause of education were recognised by Manchester University when the Honorary Degree of Doctor of Literature was conferred upon her (1906).

Under the management of the United District School Board many new schools known as Board Schools (now Council Schools) were built both in Todmorden and Hebden Bridge. The Board also were anxious to develop the work of the upper standards in the Roomfield School, Todmorden, and the Central Schools, Hebden Bridge. In 1893 Organised Science Classes were established at Roomfield, from which after many changes the present Todmorden Secondary School was developed.

The United District of Todmorden and Hebden Bridge was divided in 1896 into separate areas, each town coming under the control of a separate School Board. In 1903, the Todmorden Borough Council became the Education Authority of the Borough. Through its Education Committee it exercised full control over elementary education, but shared with the West Riding County Council the management of secondary, technical and evening schools. In the same year the schools in Hebden Bridge passed under the control of the West Riding County Council, and a Secondary School has since been established to meet the needs of the older pupils in the locality.

Such in brief outline is the story of schools in the Todmorden district during the 19th century.

As regards the means of mental improvement

among men and women, it should be remembered that two generations ago books and newspapers were dear (the first number of the "Todmorden Advertiser" cost 4d.), and hence those who were anxious to gain increased knowledge were interested in the promotion of libraries, and such organisations as Mechanics' Institutes. The Todmorden Old Library was founded as early as 1798; its members met on each " Monday before full moon." In 1836 a Mechanics' Institute was established, and for a time had a vigorous existence. A well-used library, and classes for the study of various sciences, grammar, elocution and music were included in its activities. Then for a time it declined, to be revived later through the influence of lectures by men like Henry Vincent and Thomas Cooper. In 1869 the Mechanics' Institute was affiliated to the Yorkshire Union of Mechanics' Institutes, and the first Government Science Classes ever held in this district were organised. Joshua Fielden, M.P., was President of the Institute, Alderman Bracewell, Mayor of Todmorden (1908-9), and James Whitehead, Clerk to the Education Committee, were the first joint secretaries. Examinations were held in May, 1870, in Practical, Plane and Solid Geometry, Machine Construction and Building Construction. Among the successful students was the late Alderman Crossley, Mayor of Todmorden (1905-8). The work thus inaugurated, remained for many years under the management of a local committee; it then passed under the control of the School Board, and finally of the Todmorden Education Committee. Through every change for a period of more than 40 years, Mr. Whitehead has faithfully served the highest interests of this neighbourhood by his work as Secretary. To-day the three classes of the year 1870 have grown into the Technical School at Waterside, several Branch Evening Schools and the Fielden School of Art.

Several men in this neighbourhood have achieved distinction by their ardent pursuit of knowledge in one or other of its branches. John Nowell, of Springs, Harley Wood (1802-67), became a noted specialist in mosses, and in conjunction with Abraham Stansfield, founded the Todmorden Botanical Society. When a young man Mr. Nowell attended a grammar class held at Shore Sunday School; his first teacher of botany was Edmund Holt, of Lumbutts. Mr. Nowell and Mr. Stansfield began the compilation of a Flora of Todmorden, including flowering plants, ferns and mosses.* A monument was erected in St. Mary's Churchyard in honour of Mr. Nowell, who, despite his scientific distinction, was content to earn his livelihood as a " twister-in."

Samuel Gibson, of Hebden Bridge, ranks with John Nowell and Abraham Stansfield as an enthusiastic nature student. Interested more particularly in geology, he discovered among beds of shale in Horsebridge Clough, a new species of fossil-shell that has been named after him, Goniatites gibsonii, or Gibson's goniatite.

Robert Law, of Walsden (1840—1907), was another local geologist. He became a successful teacher of geology, and by persistent work in this neighbour-

---

* See Appendix II. Recently a Book on the Flora of Todmorden has been published, which was written by Mr. Abraham Stansfield of Kersal Moor, Manchester.

hood, Derbyshire, East Yorkshire, the Isle of Man, and also in Switzerland and Canada, gathered together a valuable collection of Carboniferous fossils and of flint implements. He was elected a Fellow of the Geological Society (1886). To-day the " Law Collection of Carboniferous Limestone Fossils " may be seen in the South Kensington Museum. His memory will also be perpetuated by the Law Medal, awarded annually by the Geological Society for the best research work in practical geology.

In mechanical science John Ramsbottom was preeminent among local men. His inventive faculty and power of hard work raised him to the position of chief engineer of the London and North-Western Railway.

The Todmorden Scientific Society came into existence soon after the establishment of science classes in the early seventies, and lived for about twenty years. In 1893 a local Reading Circle developed into the Todmorden Literary Society, and for a few years flourished vigorously, before being dissolved. The name of James Standing should not be omitted from any list of local writers. His verses in dialect, notably, " Women's wark is nivvir done," are well known, and entitle him to a place among Lancashire writers with Edwin Waugh and Ben Brierley. His early death prevented the full development of his literary gifts.

In the world of art, Todmorden has had one distinguished representative in Alfred W. Bayes (1831—1909), who left his home in Lumbutts in early life for London in order to develop his artistic gifts. As a painter and etcher Mr. Bayes achieved considerable repute, and for a great number of years his pictures were exhibited in the Royal Academy and the chief art galleries in London and the provinces. He frequently visited this neighbourhood, and his pictures of local scenery and pictures illustrative of old Puritan customs and ways of life are to be found in the homes of many Todmordians.

CHAPTER XXIV.

TODMORDEN IN RECENT DAYS. HOW TODMORDEN BECAME A BOROUGH.

The changes that remain to be described may be conveniently grouped under three heads: first, trade and population; second, ecclesiastical changes; third, local government.

I.—*Trade and Population.*

During the earlier half of the 19th century the firm of Fielden Brothers overshadowed all others in this neighbourhood. To-day "Fielden Brothers, Ltd." is still the premier firm, with 100,000 spindles and 1,600 looms. There are other firms, however, of great importance, especially that of Mr. Caleb Hoyle, J.P., of Derdale and Walsden, with 60,000 spindles and 1,600 looms. Mention may be made of the mills belonging to Mr. Joshua Smith, of Cornholme (1,760 looms), and to Messrs. Luke Barker and Sons (1,406 looms, and 7,500 spindles), and also of Ridgefoot Mill that for a long time was in the possession of Ormerod Brothers. In Cornholme the bobbin works founded by Mr. Lawrence Wilson continued to prosper, and to-day the buildings at Cornholme and Garston cover $15\frac{1}{2}$ acres. In other departments of enterprise the firm of Lord Brothers, Canal Street Works, founded by Mr. Edward Lord, has been long noted for the manufacture of cotton spinning machinery, a very large quantity being sent abroad.

The population of Todmorden has increased but slowly during the last forty years, rising from about 20,000 in 1861 to 25,400 in 1901: an increase of 25 per cent. In Hebden Bridge the population has grown much more rapidly, the increase in thirty years (from 1861 to 1891) being as much as 45 per cent. (10,800 to 15,700). Hebden Bridge is one of the chief centres in England for the manufacture of fustians and ready-made clothing. To-day the hillsides are lined with rows of cottages and dotted with new houses that indicate the prosperity of the district.

II.—*Ecclesiastical Changes.*

Not long after the erection of Christ Church, Walsden became a separate parish, and St. Peter's Church was built (1847). A large number of the worshippers at St. Mary's Church came from Walsden, and after the "Old Church" was closed another church was needed by Anglicans in Walsden. Similarly Harley Wood Church was built (1859) for the village of Lydgate, and a few years ago, through the generosity of Mrs. Masters-Whitaker, of Holme, a church has been erected in Cornholme. An Act of Parliament, passed in 1866, constituted Christ Church the parish church of Todmorden (as distinct from those of Cross Stone, Walsden and Harley Wood), St. Mary's Church being associated with it as a chapel of ease. Hence the old church of St. Mary's has never attained to the dignity of a parish church.*

---

* In earlier days St. Mary's Church was strictly a chapel of ease in the Parish of Rochdale. The clergyman in charge was "curate of the chapel of Todmorden."

IN RECENT DAYS

Most of the Nonconformist chapels on the hillsides were abandoned and replaced by larger buildings in the valleys below. The Presbyterian Meeting House at Chapel House was replaced by Eastwood Congregational Chapel; the Wesleyan Chapel at Rodhill End by Springside Chapel; the Baptists long ago moved from Rehoboth to Roomfield Chapel, whilst from Shore Baptist Chapel sprang the churches at Wellington Road, Vale and Lineholme. Larger upland villages, however, such as Mankinholes, Lumbutts and Blackshaw Head, still retain their Methodist chapels. The present Unitarian Church was built by the three sons of John Fielden, M.P. In excellence of workmanship and beauty of design it is unique among the churches and chapels in this district. In the Hebden Bridge district the most noteworthy change was the erection of the new church at Heptonstall and abandonment of the "Old Church." Mytholm Church (1844) stands at the foot of the cliff on which Heptonstall is built. St. Michael's Church, Mytholmroyd, as well as many Nonconformist chapels that have been built, indicate the populous condition of the valley as compared with what it was a century ago. On the uplands there are still large chapels at Heptonstall, Wainsgate and Midgley.

III.—*Local Government.*

In the 18th century churchwardens and vestry meetings of parishioners were of great importance in local government. Last century, however, local administration was almost entirely taken out of the hands of religious bodies. Paupers are no longer relieved by churchwardens, but by Boards of Guardians (chap xxii.); education is under the control of committees of County and Borough Councils (chap. xxiii.). This change, whereby local affairs are managed by specially elected local committees, responsible both to the ratepayers and to central departments in London, has now to be traced in other directions.

About sixty years ago a demand arose for greater local control in housing and sanitation. Various Public Health Acts were passed (especially from 1848 to 1875) which enabled different localities to be formed into sanitary districts controlled by local committees elected by the ratepayers. The administration of more populous or *urban* districts was vested in Local Boards whose duty it was to look after sewerage, water supply, highways and lighting, and to deal with infectious diseases and nuisances. In this district there were many matters urgently needing attention, for the roads were "badly paved, badly lighted and badly sewered." In 1860, at a meeting held in Oddfellows' Hall, Todmorden, under the chairmanship of John Fielden, of Ashenhurst, it was decided to take the necessary steps for putting the Public Health Act of 1858 into operation. The Todmorden Urban Sanitary District was thus constituted, extending along the three valleys as far as Knotts Road, Lobmill and Inchfield Fold. The population of the district was 11,840; its rateable value, £31,156.

The district was divided into four wards: Todmorden, Walsden, Langfield and Stansfield, each being part of the corresponding township. The election of the first Todmorden Local Board took place in July, 1861. Each ward sent four members, among whom were Messrs. John Fielden (Chairman), Edmund Whitaker, Joseph Knowles, Peter Ormerod, William Sutcliffe (Lowerlaithe) and William Barker.* A few years later (1868) Hebden Bridge and Cornholme were formed into urban sanitary districts, but in 1875 Cornholme was merged in the Todmorden district, outlying parts of Langfield and a large part of the township of Stansfield being also added.

Hence there were the following sanitary districts in this neighbourhood : —

1. The Todmorden Local Board District, comprising the townships of Todmorden and Walsden, Langfield, the two upper thirds of Stansfield, a part of the lowest third and a small part of Cliviger.

2. The Hebden Bridge Local Board District, comprising parts of the townships of Wadsworth, Erringden and Heptonstall and another part of the lowest third of Stansfield.

3. The Todmorden Rural Sanitary District, comprising the remaining and more upland portions of Heptonstall, Erringden, Wadsworth and Stansfield.

The Rural District was administered by the Board of Guardians until 1894, when, by the Parish Councils Act, Rural District Councils became the sanitary authority.

The area of the Todmorden Local Board District was a little larger than that of the present Borough. The business transacted by the Board was similar, in many respects, to that of the Town Council. A clerk,

* Wm. Barker was father of Dr. J. H. Barker, Chairman of the Todmorden School Board and Education Committee, 1896—1906.

treasurer, surveyor, medical officer and sanitary inspector had charge of different departments of public business. During the period in which Todmorden was under the control of the Local Board, footpaths were laid along the main roads, main drains were constructed and streets were lighted; the Market Hall was built, the Infectious Diseases Hospital at Sourhall was opened, and a fire engine was purchased. The supplies of gas and water, however, were in the hands of private companies or of property owners. Fielden Brothers had constructed a gasworks at Waterside as early as 1830, and supplied gas far beyond their own premises. There was also a gasworks at Wilson Brothers, Cornholme. Later the Todmorden Gas Company was formed, and the works at Millwood were erected. In 1892 these various gasworks were purchased by the Todmorden Local Board for £110,000, as it was believed that gas might be supplied to the inhabitants more cheaply if under public management; a belief that experience has since justified.

With regard to water supply, Todmorden had long been dependent on small reservoirs or on springs gushing from the hillsides. No storage existed that ensured the inhabitants against drought in a dry season. Hence to meet the ever-increasing needs of the population the reservoir above Ramsden Clough was constructed by the Todmorden Waterworks Company. Further, in 1892, Mr. John Ashton Fielden carried out the wishes of the late Samuel Fielden, of Centre Vale, by building at Leebottom, and presenting to the town, a large and well-equipped hospital, known as the Fielden Hospital. In like manner the Town Hall, built in 1875, at a cost of £54,000, by the three sons of John Fielden, M.P., in honour of his memory, was handed over for the use of the town.

These were the principal changes that took place whilst Todmorden was under the control of the Local Board. In 1894, by the operation of the Local Government Act, the Local Board became an Urban District Council. Two years later the final change was made in the constitution of the Local Authority when Todmorden received a Charter of Incorporation and became a Borough. To many persons this may appear to have been only a change in name. But the grant of a charter meant more than a change in name, or the additional dignity that is associated with a mayor, aldermen, and councillors. When Todmorden became a Borough, she gained additional powers of self-government and her name was added to the long list of towns and cities to whom already such increased powers had been granted. As a non-county borough, for example, Todmorden has full control over her elementary schools and has escaped absorption in the wider area of the West Riding.

The first steps towards incorporation were taken in 1885, but opposition during a lengthy public enquiry led to the rejection of the scheme. Nearly ten years later the project was revived, no serious objection was raised, and on June 2nd, 1896, a Charter of Incorporation was granted by the Privy Council. Two months later, on Charter Day, (August 2nd, 1896), the event was celebrated by a public procession through the streets gay with bunting, and by a banquet in the Town Hall. The Todmorden Co-operative Society, however, celebrated the occasion most notably, inasmuch as on Charter Day the foundation stones of the Todmorden Free Library were laid by Alderman William Jackson, J.P., then President of the Society, and the late A. G. Eastwood, Provisional Mayor of Todmorden. The members of the Co-operative Society, in honour of their own jubilee, decided to build and present to the town a public library and to hand over their own admirable collection of 8,000 volumes. The Library now contains about 14,000 volumes and is administered under the provisions of the Public Libraries' Act.

The first Mayor of Todmorden was Mr. Caleb Hoyle, J.P. (1896-9). His successors have been Ald. William Ormerod, J.P. (1899—1902), Ald. William Jackson, J.P. (1902-5); the late Ald. Abraham Crossley (1905-8); Ald. James Bracewell (1908-9); Ald. Edward Lord (1909-11) and Ald. Robert Jackson (1911). During the period covered by these years of office many important enterprises have been undertaken by the Council. The purchase of Ramsden Waterworks by the Rochdale Corporation necessitated the construction of Gorpley Reservoir (1900–5), whereby a pure and adequate water supply has been secured for the Borough. A scheme of sewerage was completed by the establishment of sewage disposal works at Eastwood (1901–8). Centre Vale School was conveyed to the Borough by Mr. John Ashton Fielden (1897) and converted into an Art School, known as the Fielden School of Art. Buildings at Waterside were also bought and adapted for the purpose of a Technical School, and also of a Fire Station. The Electricity Works were erected at Millwood (1905), and a convenient system of motor 'buses has also been established (1907). After considerable delay the new premises of the Secondary School have been built on the Stile estate (1910–12).

In 1909 Messrs. John and Hawksworth Barker bought upwards of three acres of land at Inchfield, Walsden, and presented it to the Corporation for a cricket field and recreation ground. After the death of Mrs. Fielden, of Centre Vale, Mr. John Ashton Fielden permitted the Todmorden Town Council to acquire the whole of Centre Vale estate for the nominal sum of £10,000. This transfer was effected during the Mayoralty of Ald. Edward Lord, who acted as intermediary, and the estate has been handed over to the town for the purpose of a public park. Buckley Wood, that clothes the hillside above Centre Vale, has also been presented to the town by Mrs. Greenwood, of Glen View. The first year of the Mayoralty of Ald. Robert Jackson has been rendered noteworthy by the formal opening, on March 30, 1912, of the Park at Centre Vale and of the Secondary School.

CHAPTER XXV.

To the Reader.

The story outlined in the preceding chapters began with the formation of the hills and the appearance of primitive man in this neighbourhood. It ended with the inclusion of Todmorden in the long list of English boroughs.

In the last chapter the reader was brought face to face with the actual government of Todmorden at the present day. The mere enumeration of such questions as education, the relief of the poor, sanitation and disease, or the supply of gas, water and electricity, shows how important the work of local administration has become. It also suggests how much the town owes to the men who, during the last forty years, served as members of the Board of Guardians, Local Board, School Board and Borough Council.

The improvements brought about during this period have involved great expense. The following table shows, in round numbers, what the cost of the most important public undertakings has been, with the charge on the rates during the year 1911–12:—

	Outlay. £	Amount Repaid. £	Amount Unpaid. £	Rate. s. d.
Education (Council Schools)	49,000	18,000	31,000	1 5
Water	96,000	13,000	83,000	5
Sewerage and Sewage Disposal	106,000	12,000	94,000	1 7½
Electricity	21,000	5,000	16,000	¼
Gas*	165,000	33,000	132,000	—

* The accumulated surplus of gas profits amounts to £12,000.

The heavy municipal debt thus incurred is due to the fact that many necessary public enterprises have been undertaken within a comparatively few years. Moreover, with the exception of gas production, there is not one which yields any surplus revenue. Despite these facts, no one would wish to go back to local conditions forty years ago, as sketched in preceding chapters. The actual cost of the advantages enjoyed, so far as the great majority of ratepayers are concerned, may be easily calculated. The total rate for the year 1911–12 was 7s. 9d. A householder in a cottage rated at £6 paid 46s. 6d. in rates, or less than a shilling a week; a £10 householder paid 1s. 6d. a week. Thirty years ago schoolpence in a single family often cost more than a shilling a week. To-day, for the same money, in addition to greater educational facilities, elementary, secondary and technical, with the possession of a Free Public Library, immense improvements have taken place in cleanliness, sanitation and lighting; an ample water supply has been guaranteed; electricity is available and a motor 'bus service has rendered communication within the Borough much easier.

The present generation in Todmorden is reaping the advantages derived from the public-spirited zeal of former generations. It is hoped that the account which has been given of Todmorden's past history will strengthen the reader's determination to make Todmorden increasingly capable of producing healthy, intelligent and public-spirited citizens. The reader is invited to look forward to the future, to consider in what ways Todmorden may be improved, and then loyally to work for the realisation of a high ideal.

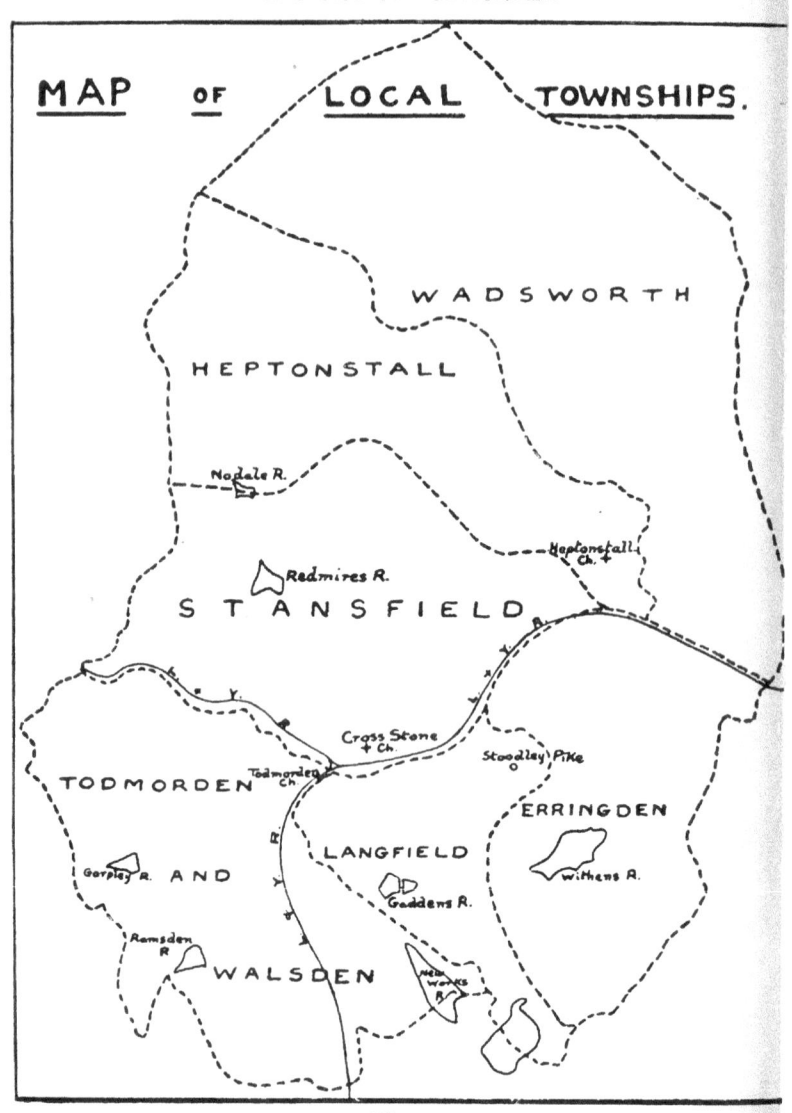

Fig. 23.

APPENDIX I.

Todmorden of To-Day.

1. *Municipal*.

Todmorden is a non-county borough, situated within the West Riding of Yorkshire; population (1911), 25,455. The Borough Council consists of 6 Aldermen and 18 Councillors, presided over by the Mayor. The Borough is divided into six wards; the names and population (1901) of each are as follows:

Stansfield	4,440	Central	4,134
Langfield	4,109	Todmorden	3,922
Walsden	3,500	Cornholme	5,313

Each ward is represented on the Council by one Alderman and three Councillors. Each year six Councillors are elected, viz., one from each ward. Three Aldermen are elected by the Council every three years.

2. *Township Divisions*.

These divisions are much older than the wards just mentioned. The latter were created in 1896, when Todmorden became a Borough. The former came into existence, in some instances, many centuries ago.

(*a*) Stansfield and Langfield. These townships are situated wholly in Yorkshire. The whole of Langfield is included within the Borough, but part of Stansfield is within the Hebden Bridge Urban District and the Rural Parish of Blackshaw.

(b) Todmorden and Walsden. This township is situated in Lancashire, and was created in 1801 by the union of the older hamlets of Todmorden and Walsden.

(c) A small portion of the township of Cliviger (also in Lancashire) is included within the Borough.

3. *Ecclesiastical Divisions.*

(a) The parishes of Cross Stone, Harley Wood and Cornholme are included within the Yorkshire diocese of Wakefield.

(b) The parishes of Todmorden and Walsden are included within the Lancashire diocese of Manchester.

The areas covered by these parishes do not correspond to any of the older township divisions or the municipal wards of the same names.

4. *Parliamentary Divisions.*

Todmorden is included within the following constituencies, the number of inhabitants within the Borough being also given:

(a) Sowerby Division of the West Riding of Yorkshire (population, 1901, 15,571).

(b) Middleton Division of South-east Lancashire (population, 1901, 9,086).

(c) Clitheroe Division of North-east Lancashire (population, 1901, 753).

5. *Poor Law Administration.*

The Todmorden Union consists of two sub-districts, viz.:

(a) Todmorden, or the civil parish of Todmorden

(coterminous with the present borough), and comprising the townships of Langfield, Todmorden and Walsden, part of Stansfield and a small part of Cliviger.

(b) Hebden Bridge, including the civil parishes of (1) Hebden Bridge (part of the townships of Erringden, Heptonstall and Wadsworth); (2) Blackshaw (part of Stansfield); (3) Mytholmroyd (part of Erringden, Wadsworth, Sowerby and Midgley).

The Board of Guardians consists of 23 members, 16 being elected by the civil parish of Todmorden, 4 by Hebden Bridge and 3 by Mytholmroyd.

6. *Climate.*

Prevailing winds: westerly, with north-east to east winds, especially in spring.

Rainfall: At Sourhall Hospital, the average rainfall during the years 1898—1911 = 51·9 inches, varying from 43·5 ins. (1905) to 66·2 ins. (1903).

The valleys are particularly liable to mist and fog.

7. *Death Rate.*

The average death rate during the same period (1898—1911) = 16·4 per 1,000, varying from 20·8 (1898) to 13·9 (1910).

8 *Table of Principal Elevations.*

(1) *Valleys.* The valleys descend from the Portsmouth boundary (702 ft.) and Walsden boundary at Steanor Bottom (605 ft.), via the Town Hall (423 ft.) to Sandbed (361 ft.).

(2) *Uplands.*

Fielden Hospital	640 ft.
Mankinholes	725 ft.
Cross Stone Church	750 ft.
Sourhall Hospital	1,025 ft.

(3) *Moorlands.*

Whirlaw	1,200 ft.
Stoodley Pike	1,307 ft.
Bride Stones	1,400 ft.
Trough Edge	1,491 ft.
Blackstone Edge	1,559 ft.
Hough Stones (above Stiperden)	1,574 ft.

APPENDIX II.

FLOWERS AND ANIMALS IN TODMORDEN.

(By Rev. John Naylor.)

(A) FLOWERS.

The plants of this locality were long ago diligently studied by the members of the Botanical Society. Two members, Abraham Stansfield and John Nowell, were among the most distinguished botanists in the North of England. The former was almost unrivalled as an authority on ferns; the latter attained fame as a student of mosses. These men knew every plant that grew in the valley or on the hills, and they noticed that at a few places the underlying rock was indicated by the kind of plants growing thereon. They found in certain spots plants which flourish where there is lime, and this led to the discovery of lime in some of the Millstone Grit beds.

Of late years botany has become more and more a study of plants in relation to soil and climate. From this modern point of view, plants which grow together under like conditions are named "*associations*." In this district there are several of these more or less clearly marked off from each other. A few such associations, with their commonest representatives, are given below.

HEATHER MOOR. Where peat abounds as soil *bilberry, ling, crowberry,* and *whin* are met with;

but in boggy places *cranberry, sundew, sedges,* and *bog asphodel* are found.

GRASS MOOR. In the drier places occur the *mat grass, sheep's fescue grass, wavy hair grass, tormentilla, ladies' bedstraw*; whilst in the damper spots are found the *purple molinia grass*, several species of *rush, cotton grass*, and the *four-leaved heath*.

PASTURE. Descending to the hill pastures just below the moors we find the *field wood-rush, quaking grass, yellow violet, gentian, milkwort, eyebright, adders-tongue fern*, and many a common grass.

WOODLAND. Where the *beech* trees are numerous and the shade and humus somewhat thick, little will grow besides the *broad shield fern, anemone, lesser celandine, woodruff* and *wood sorrel*. But beneath the lighter shade and on the better soil of the *oak* and *birch* woods thrive *dogrose, raspberry, ivy, bramble, honeysuckle, cow-wheat, lady fern, male fern, soft grass* and *golden rod*. In damp portions of the woodland, *coltsfoot, lesser celandine, wood anemone, stitchwort, bluebell, garlic, ragged robin* greet us in spring; while *bracken* and *cow parsnip* flourish in summer. Loving the dampness, we find the *oak, sycamore* and *wych elm* abundant, and *ash, hazel, alder* and *elder, willow* and *mountain ash* by no means rare. Among these trees flourish *wood-rush, sweet-cicely, wood-sorrel, woundwort* and *dock*.

CLOUGH STREAM. Where the water oozes lazily across swampy patches or drips over rocks we may expect to find *horsetails, marsh pennywort, golden saxifrage, brooklime, herb Robert, bitter cress, wall lettuce* with many a sedge and rush.

STAGNANT POOLS. Floating here is the *duckweed,*

anchored to the bottom is the *pondweed*, fringing the edges is the tall upright *glyceria* (so common by the canal side) or the floating *glyceria*, and in the sodden ground around *spearwort*, *marsh marigold*, *willow herb*, *spiræa* and *marsh thistle* mingle with other thirsty plants.

Let the student follow out this method of grouping the local flora, and let him not only find out what plants live together, and in what conditions; but enquire into the reason why associations grow where they do grow and not elsewhere.

(B) ANIMALS.

I. MAMMALS.

Common are the *mole, common shrew, water shrew, weasel, stoat, long-tailed mouse, common mouse, brown rat* (which has killed off the black rat), *water vole* (often miscalled water rat), *field vole, hedgehog,* and *rabbit.* Rare are the *long-eared bat*, the very hairy *natterer's bat, fox,* and *hare*: and extinction has become the fate of the once common *marten, polecat, otter, badger,* and *deer.*

II. REPTILES, AMPHIBIANS AND FISHES.

Of the three English snakes the only one that occasionally occurs here is the harmless *grass* or *ringed snake*. The venomous adder or viper and the smooth snake are absent. Sometimes the *common lizard* is seen on the moors; now and then a *blind worm*—a lizard which has lost its legs but not its eyes, basks in our sun. Newts are very rare, but at intervals the *smooth newt* appears. The *common frog* is everywhere, but the *edible frog* nowhere, to be seen; nor is the *toad* often to be met with.

In former days before the pollution of the streams *perch, carp, roach* and other fishes rewarded the angler's patience; but now he is not only patient but lucky if he catches a *trout, loach* or *gold carp* in our neighbourhood. The three-spined *stickleback* is the brave little representative of finned tribes which have left our streams and ponds—perhaps for ever.

III. BIRDS.

Although birds are the most changeful creatures we know in respect of habitation, it will best meet the needs of the reader of this book if we deal with them in the same way as with the plants. This can only be done in rough outline, but even this treatment of them will help to easier identification and study of them. Rare birds are omitted.

MOORLANDS AND GRASSY UPLANDS. Most of the following occur at special seasons but a few all the year round: *redwing, fieldfare, starling, ringousel, wheatear, hedge warbler, yellow-hammer, chaffinch, skylark, whinchat, twite, greenfinch, redstart, meadow pipit, night-jar, cuckoo, short-eared owl, kestrel, red-grouse, corncrake, golden plover, curlew, lapwing, Jack snipe.* On the reservoirs and swamps are to be frequently seen the *mallard, moorhen,* and *black-headed gull.* Several sea birds occur there at intervals.

WOODS. Here are the *song thrush, missel thrush, blackbird, redbreast, blackcap* (our best songster in the woods), *magpie, rook, great tit, blue tit, wren, sparrow-hawk, woodcock,* and *great spotted wood-pecker.*

STREAMS. The home of the *dipper* is here. Three

wagtails—the *pied, grey* and *yellow*—forage and play here, and occasionally the *kingfisher* flashes past them.

The *house sparrow, swallow, house martin,* and from time to time, the *swift* are met with among houses and around farms. The three latter love open spaces most. Their flight is not suitable to woodlands. The sparrow, like the Anglo-Saxon, is everywhere.

APPENDIX III.

Parliamentary Representation of Todmorden during the 19th Century.

The township of Todmorden and Walsden has always been included in a Lancashire constituency; the townships of Stansfield and Langfield have formed part of a Yorkshire constituency.

The Reform Bills of 1832, 1867 and 1885 brought about great changes, 1st, in the number of persons entitled to vote, and, 2nd, in the size of the constituencies in which the two parts of Todmorden were included. With regard to the number of electors, it is sufficiently accurate to say that the right to vote was gained, in 1832, by the middle classes; in 1867, by the working classes in towns; and in 1885, by the agricultural labourers in the rural districts. The changes produced in the size of the constituencies may be briefly indicated.

I. Before 1832 the County of Lancashire returned two members to Parliament, and in this immense constituency the local township of Todmorden and Walsden was included. The remaining portion of Todmorden was comprised within the County of Yorkshire, which at first sent two, and after 1826, four members to Parliament. The Reform Bills above mentioned brought about the following changes.

II. Lancashire was first divided (in 1832) into two divisions, North and South, each with two members; then (1867) into four divisions, N., N.E., S.E. and

S.W., also with two members each; and, finally
(1885), into 23 divisions, each returning one member.
Within South-east Lancashire there were eight
constituencies, of which the Middleton Division was
one. Corresponding to these changes, the township
of Todmorden and Walsden was successively comprised within South Lancashire (1832), South-east
Lancashire (1867) and the Middleton Division of
South-east Lancashire (1885). Since 1885 a small
portion of the township of Cliviger has been included
in the Clitheroe Division of North-east Lancashire.

III. Yorkshire underwent a similar process of subdivision. By the Act of 1832, each riding returned
two members. Later the West Riding was divided,
first (1861) into two divisions (North and South);
then (1867) into three divisions (North, South and
East), each division in each case returning two
members; and, lastly, (1885), the North Division of
the West Riding was subdivided into five constituencies, including the Sowerby Division, each constituency returning one member. During these changes
the Yorkshire portion of Todmorden was successively
included within the West Riding (1832); the two
North Divisions (1861 and 1867), and, finally (1885),
the Sowerby Division of the Northern portion of the
West Riding.

The political views of the inhabitants of this
district, both in Lancashire and Yorkshire, seem to
have been uniformly Liberal. In old days, before
the passing of the Ballot Act, when votes were
publicly recorded, a majority of votes was given to
the Liberal candidate in Todmorden, even when a
Conservative was returned by the whole division.

The most noted Yorkshire representative was Lord Frederick Cavendish. He represented the North Division of the West Riding from 1865, until his assassination in 1882 in Phœnix Park, Dublin. For many years the Middleton Division of South-east Lancashire was represented in the Conservative interest by Mr. Thomas Fielden and Mr. Edward B. Fielden, both grandsons of John Fielden, M.P.

APPENDIX IV.

The Genealogies of the Radcliffe and Fielden Families.

I. The Family of Radcliffe.

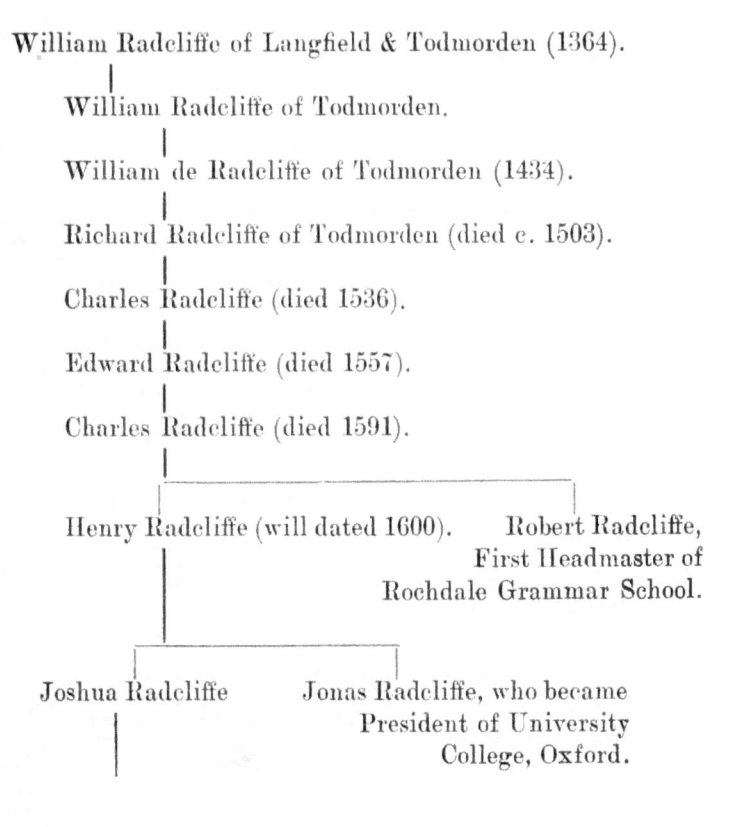

William Radcliffe of Langfield & Todmorden (1364).

William Radcliffe of Todmorden.

William de Radcliffe of Todmorden (1434).

Richard Radcliffe of Todmorden (died c. 1503).

Charles Radcliffe (died 1536).

Edward Radcliffe (died 1557).

Charles Radcliffe (died 1591).

Henry Radcliffe (will dated 1600).   Robert Radcliffe, First Headmaster of Rochdale Grammar School.

Joshua Radcliffe   Jonas Radcliffe, who became President of University College, Oxford.

Savile Radcliffe (b. 1583; d. 1652), who re-built Todmorden Hall in 1603.

Thomas Radcliffe.   Joshua Radcliffe (died 1676).

Elizabeth Radcliffe m. Roger Mainwaring of Kerincham, Cheshire.

James Mainwaring.

Roger Mainwaring.

In 1717 Roger Mainwaring sold Todmorden Hall to John Fielden, fifth son of Joshua Fielden, Bottomley, Walsden.

II. THE FAMILY OF FIELDEN.

William ffeilden of Leventhorpe, near Bradford.
 (His will was proved in 1573).
Nicholas ffeilden of Inchfield, Walsden.

Abraham Fielden of Inchfield, Walsden
 (Will proved 1644).
Joshua Fielden of Bottomley (d. 1693).

Joshua Fielden of Bottomley (d. 1715).

Joshua Fielden of Bottomley and Edge End, Todmorden (1701—1781).

APPENDIX IV

Joshua Fielden of Edge End and Waterside (1748—1811).

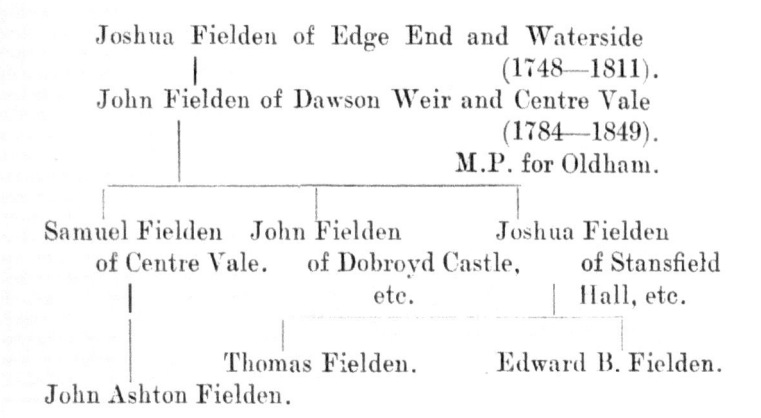

John Fielden of Dawson Weir and Centre Vale (1784—1849). M.P. for Oldham.

- Samuel Fielden of Centre Vale.
  - John Ashton Fielden.
- John Fielden of Dobroyd Castle, etc.
  - Thomas Fielden.
- Joshua Fielden of Stansfield Hall, etc.
  - Edward B. Fielden.

APPENDIX V.

Local Maps and Records.

I. *Maps*.

Ordnance Survey Maps. England and Wales.
One Inch to the Mile. Nos. 76 and 77.
Both maps are required for the whole neighbourhood.
Six Inches to the Mile.
Todmorden.   229 N.W., N.E., S.W., S.E. (4 maps).
229A. N.E., 214 S.W.
244 N.W., N.E.
Hebden Bridge. 230 N.W., S.W., N.E., 229 N.E.
215 S.W., N.W.
214 S.E., N.E.
Geological Survey Maps. England and Wales.
One Inch to the Mile. No. 88 N.W. (Original 1 inch Survey).
Four Miles to the Inch, including most of Yorkshire and part of Lancashire. No. 7.

II. *Township Records*.
(a) In the possession of the Assistant Overseer.
1. Certificates of Settlement. Township of Hundersfield (1677—1833).
2. Ledger of accounts of churchwardens of the Township of Stansfield (1726—1758).
3. Accounts of churchwardens, overseers, constables and surveyors of highways. Township of Langfield (1700—1832).

4. Extracts from an Old Minute Book of the Langfield Freeholders.
5. Minute Books. Todmorden and Walsden (from the year 1801).

(b) In the possession of the Clerk to the Board of Guardians.
1. Accounts of churchwardens, constables and surveyors for Erringden (1764—1840).
2. Minute Books of meetings of Board of Guardians (from the year 1837).

III. *Reference Department of Todmorden Free Library.*

This Department contains a large number of valuable books, papers and documents dealing with local history and local affairs. See Catalogue.

INDEX.

Agistment, 61
Ale Taster, 69, 71
Ashburn, Christopher, 91
Astley, Gilbert, 92
Atkinson, Joseph, 133

Baptists, 107
—— Particular, 130, 131, 133, 134
—— General, 133, 134, 175
Bayes, Alfred W., 205
Beacons, 125
Berewicks, 47, 48, 49
Bloomeries, 63
Bobbin mill at Hough Stones and Cornholme, 173
Bordars, 47, 48, 49, 52, 53
Bride Stones, 28
Brigantes, 29, 32
Bronze age, 27
Brooke, Robert, 188
Buckley's mill, 163, 170, 172
Buckley Wood, 215

Calder, bridges over, 171, 172
Camden, 108
Canals, the first, 156
—— scale of charges, 157
Carboniferous limestone, 7, 13, 14
Carr House Fold, 122, 123
Carucate, 48
Celtic graveyard, Butt Stones, 25–27
Celts, Brythonic, 29, 35
—— Goidelic, 27, 28

Centre Vale, 173, 201, 215
—— school, 201, 214
"Certificates of Settlement," 147
Chautries, Heptonstall, 86–89
Chapel house in Stansfield, 129, 130, 131, 209
Charter day, 213
Chartist movement, 163, 187–188
Children in mills, hours of, 160, 161
Christ Church, school and parsonage, 175, 208
Christianity, introduction of, 38
Churchwardens' accounts, 139–142
Civil wars in West Riding, 98–103, 104, 105
Clegg, Richard, 136
Cloth halls, at Halifax, 110, 113, 125
—— at Heptonstall, 110, 125
—— at Rochdale, 110, 125
Coal Measures, 10, 15
—— fossils in, 11, 17
Constables' accounts, 144–146, 181, 182
Constable, duties of township, 143, 144
Co-operative movement, beginning of, 194, 195
Corn mills in 13th and 14th century, 62
Cornholme, 207
—— Church, 208
Cotton industry, development of, 157–160
—— mill, first local, 158

INDEX

Court Baron, 69
—— Leet, 70
Cowell, Rev. Joseph, 175
Cross Stone Chapel, 85, 136, 137, 140, 175
—— School, 136, 137, 138, 196
Crossley, Alderman, 25
—— Anthony, 136, 155
—— David, 130
—— of Scaitcliffe, family of, 79, 103
Crowther, J., of Walsden, 45

Darney, William, 131
Day Schools, Establishment of, 200–202
Defoe's description of Halifax parish, 113
Deira, Anglian kingdom of, 35
Dewsbury, William, 126
Dialect, 41, 43, 44, 45
Domesday Book, 46–54
Domestic system of manufacture, 109
—— description of, 113
Druids, 28

Earth Circle, ancient, 25
Education Act of 1870, 201
Edwin, 37
Elmet, forest of, 35, 36, 37
Erringden township, 48, 56, 68, 75, 81, 108
Ethelburga, 37
Ethelfrith, 35

Factory Acts, 161, 165, 167
—— Schools, introduction of, 199
—— System, development of, 157–162
—— Cruelties of, 160–161
Farmhouses in 17th century, 123

Fault in Todmorden, 15
Fawcett, Dr., 134
Ferrar, Bishop of St. David's, 91
Feudalism, rise of, 40, 46
—— effect of Norman Conquest on, 46, 54
Fielden and Travis of Clough mill, 158
—— Art School, 214
—— Bros. Ltd., 207
—— family of, 232
—— Hospital, 212
—— John, M.P., 159, 163–168, 170, 173, 184, 190, 233
—— Joshua, 157, 159, 161, 233
—— Luke, 21
—— monument, 168
—— Mrs. Samuel, 201-2, 215
Flint implements, 21, 22, 25
—— nodules, 24
Foresters, position of, 56
Forests, importance in Norman times, 55
—— punishments for offences in, 57
Foster, John, 134
Friends, see Quakers
Fulling mills, early, 114

Gaddens reservoirs, 157
Gallows, right of, 75
Gamel, 53, 54
Gas, supply of, 212
Gastrell, Bishop, 130, 135
Gibbet law, 75
—— the Halifax, 76, 77
—— farm, 77
Gibson, Samuel, 204
Glacial Drift deposits, 18, 19, 20
Golden Lion Inn, 170, 177

INDEX

Gorpley reservoir, 214
Government, Celtic and Anglian methods compared, 38, 39
Great House in Stansfield, 128, 130
Grimshaw, William, 131, 132, 134
Guardians, Board of, 189, 190

Halifax, 48, 77, 81, 100, 109, 110, 113, 114, 121
—— Church, 66, 67
—— parish, value of Church lands in, 68
Hammerton, Mr., 172, 200
Hardman, Dr., 176, 184
Harley Wood Church, 208
Hebden Bridge, growth of, 208
Heptonstall, 67, 68, 75, 81, 120
—— during Civil War, 100–103
—— Methodism in, 131–133
—— Chapel, 68, 84, 85, 86, 87, 88, 89, 138, 141, 209
—— Chapelry, 68, 139
—— Grammar School, 115, 138, 196
Heywood, Oliver, of Coley Chapel, 128, 129
Heyworth, Dr. Heyworth, 151, 176
Hipping bequest, 140, 141
Holme, 67, 93
Horsfall, Lieut., 98, 99
Houses in the 14th century, 63
—— 16th and 17th century, 121–123
Hoyle, J.P., Caleb, 207
Hundreds, 39

Industrial revolution, 154 *et seq.*
Ingham, William, 191
Instaurator, 60
Iron smelting in 14th century, 63

Jackman, Mr., 21

Krabtree, Henry, Curate of Todmorden, 106, 116, 118–120, 127

Land, measurement of, 48
—— Bovate, 48
—— Carucate, 48, 52, 53, 67
—— Hide, 48, 53
Law, Robert, F.G.S., 21, 25, 204
Langfield township, 48, 68, 75, 81
Legend of Lady Sybil of Bernshaw Tower, 116–118
Lewes, Priory of, 61, 67, 68, 88
Lincoln, Henry de Lacy, Earl of, 57, 58
Lineholme Baptist Chapel, 175, 209
Local Board Districts, 211
Long Causeway, 32
Loyal Association in Elizabeth's reign, 93

Mackworth, Sir Francis, 100, 102, 103
Maiden Cross, 103
Mankinholes, 56, 60, 126, 209, 222
Manor Courts, Local, business of, 70–75, 78
Manors, 47
Maps, ordnance, 234
Markets in 14th century, 65
Mediæval times, buildings in, 63, 64
—— farming in, 60
—— markets, 65
—— prices in, 60, 63
—— rents in, 59, 63
—— wages in, 64
—— wool growing in, 61
Merlinus Rusticus, 118, 119
Methodists, first, 131

INDEX

Midgeley, Joseph, 91, 96, 116
—— Richard, 91, 92
—— township, 48, 81
Militia bounties, 181
—— clubs, 180
Millstone grit 9, 13, 14
—— Kinderscout, 9, 13, 14, 15
—— Middle, 9, 14, 15, 17
—— Rough Rock, 10, 15
Mineral wealth, 109
Mining industry in Middle Ages, 62, 63
—— in 16th century, 109
Mitchell, William, 130
Monasteries, 67
Mount Cross, 38, 66

Neolithic man, 21–24
Normans, influence of, in building churches, 66
Nowell, John, 204

Out of school exercises, 16, 17, 20
Overseer's accounts, 148–150
Overseers of the Poor in 18th century, duties of, 146–151

Packhorse roads, 123, 124
Pannage, 61
Parliamentary representation, 228–230
Patmos Chapel, 172, 175
Paulinus, 38
Paupers, treatment of, 147–151
Pennine Chain, 5, 12, 14, 15, 19
Pilgrimage of Grace 88
Pinder, 153
Pinfold, 153
Place names, 35, 42, 43, 58, 83

Plague, 120
'Plug drawers,' 163
Police, opposition to County, 193–4
Pollard's bequest, 140
Poll Tax, Richard II's reign, 80
Poorhouses in 18th century, 149, 150
Poor Law Amendment Act, 188–193
—— Union, 189–190, 220–221
—— Riots, 191–192
Post Office, the first, 177
Power looms, introduction of, 162, 164
Presbyterianism in Todmorden, 104, 107, 128, 130, 131
Press gang, 181
Prior's Court, 69
Pronunciation, local, 45
Protestantism, beginning of local, 90
Puritanism, growth of, 91, 92, 93, 94, 95

Quakers or Friends, 106, 107, 126, 127, 131
—— burial grounds, 127
—— meeting houses, 128, 170
—— sufferings of, 127, 128

Radcliffe, family of, 79, 91, 103, 169, 231–232
—— Joshua, 103, 232
—— Savile, 96, 122, 232
Railway, construction of, 177–179
Ramsbotham, Thomas, 173
Ramsbottom, Henry, 161
—— John, 205
Recedham (Rochdale), 53
Reform movement, 183–188
Ridgefoot mill, 207
Ripon, 109

INDEX

Roads, construction and repair of, 151, 155
Rochdale Grammar School, 115, 231
Rodhill End Chapel, 130, 131, 133, 175
Roger of Poitou, 52, 53, 54
Roman Catholic services illegal, 93
Roman coins, 32, 33
—— entrenchments, 32
—— roads, 30, 31, 32, 124
Russell, Dr., 25

St. Peter's Church, Walsden, 208
Salford, Hundred of, 52, 54, 55
Sandal Magna, Church at, 51
Scholefield, Jonathan, Curate of Cross Stone, 98, 99, 100
School Board, the first, 201
Serfs, 53
Sewage disposal works, 214, 216
Ship money, 96, 112
Shore Baptist Chapel, 134, 176
Smith, Richard, 134
Sokemen, 47, 49, 51
Sowerby township, 48, 81
Spring Gardens Inn, 156, 169
Standing, James, 205
Stansfield, Abraham, 204
—— family of, 79, 85, 103
—— hall, 79
—— mill, 79
—— township, 48, 67, 68, 75, 81, 108
"Steam factory," the first, 161, 170
Stoodley Pike, 182, 183
Sunday Schools, 196–199
Superstitions local, 116, 118, 176
Surnames, beginning of, 61, 62, 81, 82, 83

Surveyor of highways, duties of, 151
—— difficulties of, 154
Surveyor's accounts, 152, 153

Taylor, Dan, 133
Todmorden "Advertiser," 203
—— animals, 225–227
—— changes in local government, 209–214
—— Chapel (St. Mary's), 85, 90, 104, 105, 106, 135, 138, 174, 208
—— climate, 221
—— coaches, 176, 177
—— Co-operative Society, 195, 213–214
—— cricket field, first, 172
—— death rate, 221
—— elevations, principal, 221–222
—— Endowed School, 136, 196
—— fairs, 146, 174
—— flowers, 223–225
—— Free Library, 214, 235
—— Hall, 79, 91, 122
—— hills, 12–16
—— in 18th century, 135
—— in 19th century, 169–177
—— Literary Society, 205
—— markets, 174
—— mayors, 214
—— Mechanics' Institute, 203
—— municipal debt, 217
—— name, first mention of, 78
—— National School, 200
—— Old Library, 203
—— parishes, 220
—— parliamentary divisions, 220
—— pastimes, 177
—— Political Union, 184–187

I

242 INDEX

Todmorden, population, 52, 80, 173, 174, 208, 209
—— rainfall, 221
—— religious life in, 174–176
—— Scientific Society, 205
—— Secondary School, 202, 215
—— Town Hall, 213
—— township divisions, 219–220
—— Urban Sanitary District, 210–211
—— waterworks, 212, 216
Towneley, Charles, 103
—— Sir John, 92
Township records, 234, 235
Turnpike road, the first, 154, 155,
—— tolls on, 156

Ulnagers, 112
Unitarian Chapel, 170, 209

Villeins, 47, 49, 52, 53, 60, 74, 108
Volunteer movement, 181, 182

Wadsworth township, 48, 67, 68, 75, 81, 108
Wager of law, 72
Wages in the 14th century, 64
Wakefield Church, 51
—— manor of, 48, 55

Wapentakes, 40
Warley township, 48, 81
Warren, family of, Earls of Surrey,
—— first earl, 67
—— second earl, 55, 67, 79
—— fifth earl, 56, 58, 75
Waterside mill, 159, 162, 170
Wesley, John, 131–133, 138
Wesleyan Chapel, Doghouse, 133
—— York Street, 175
West Lodge, 172
Whitehart Fold, 174
Whitehead, James, 203
Wilkinson, Mr., of Burnley, 25
Wilson, Lawrence, 173
Witchcraft, belief in, 116
Wolves in the 14th century, 64
Woollen manufacture, 61, 82, 83 109, 111, 112
Workhouses, opposition to, 183, 193
Working classes in early 19th century, condition of, 162

Yoredale rocks, 7, 9, 13, 15
Yorkshire, invasion of, by Angles and Danes, 35, 36, 37, 40, 41

Publications
OF THE
University of Manchester

SHERRATT & HUGHES

MANCHESTER UNIVERSITY PUBLICATIONS.

ANATOMICAL SERIES.

No. I. STUDIES IN ANATOMY from the Anatomical Department of the University of Manchester. Vol. iii. Edited by ALFRED H. YOUNG, M.B. (Edin.), F.R.C.S., Professor of Anatomy. Demy 8vo, pp. ix, 289, 23 plates. 10s. net. (Publication No. 10, 1906.)

"This forms the third volume of the Studies in Anatomy issued by the Council, and contains contributions of considerable interest. The volume is well printed and bound. It speaks well for the activity of investigation at Manchester."—*Lancet.*

"The volume is well got up and is evidence of the continuation of the excellent work which has been carried on for so long a period, under Professor A. H. Young's supervision, and has been encouraged and stimulated by his own work."—*British Medical Journal.*

BIOLOGICAL SERIES.

No. I. THE HOUSE FLY. *Musca domestica* (Linnæus). A Study of its Structure, Development, Bionomics and Economy. By C. GORDON HEWITT, D.Sc., Dominion Entomologist, Ottawa, Canada, and late Lecturer in Economic Zoology in the University of Manchester. Demy 8vo, pp. xiv. 200, 10 plates. 20s. net.
(Publication No. 52, 1910.)

"The book is concisely written and beautifully illustrated by coloured plates."—*Lancet.*

"In the first the author deals with the anatomy of the fly, in the second with the habits, development, and anatomy of the larva, and in the third with the bionomics, allies, and parasites of the insect, and its relations with human disease. .... The book affords an excellent illustration of the amount of original and useful work that may be done on the commonest and best known of animals."—*Nature.*

"Of the book itself, it may be said that it is a model of its kind."
—*Athenæum.*

CELTIC SERIES.

No. 1. AN INTRODUCTION TO EARLY WELSH. By the late Prof. J. STRACHAN, LL.D. Demy 8vo, pp. xvi. 294. 7s. 6d. net.
(Publication No. 40, 1908.)

"The Grammar as a whole is of course a very great advance on the pioneer work of Zeuss; Dr. Strachan had fuller and more accurate texts to work with, and possessed a knowledge probably unsurpassed of the results of recent progress in Celtic philology, which he himself did so much to promote."—Professor Morris Jones in the *Manchester Guardian.*

"The work is an excellent introduction to the study of early Welsh. We can strongly recommend it to Welsh students; it is undoubtedly a work which no student of Celtic literature can afford to be without."
—*North Wales Guardian.*

"The work is destined, of course, to become the text-book in early Welsh wherever taught."—*Western Mail.*

34, Cross Street, Manchester

MANCHESTER UNIVERSITY PUBLICATIONS.

CELTIC SERIES.

No. II. THE LANGUAGE OF THE ANNALS OF ULSTER. By TOMÁS O'MÁILLE, M.A., Professor of Irish in University College, Galway. Demy 8vo, pp xiii. 220. 7s. 6d. net.

(Publication No. 53, 1910.)

The objects of this dissertation are firstly to investigate the date at which certain old-Irish phonological developments took place, and secondly to give an account of old-Irish declension as evidenced by the language of the Annals of Ulster. An Appendix on the analysis of Irish personal names is appended.

"As a valuable book, the work of an excellent scholar, as treating of a most interesting period of the Irish language, as containing apart from its very great academic use a surprising amount of matter that must fascinate all who have any feeling for the blend of old and new in Modern Irish, this elaborate treatise must be welcomed with joy. . . . . Learned the book is, patiently methodical, full of the invaluable statement of "document," widely enlightening for the scholars, and they already know that, and need no pushing towards the book, for which they and their special works have been impatiently waiting."

—*Freeman's Journal.*

"The book is a painstaking and accurate piece of work, and does honour to its author and the University which has printed it."

—*The Athenæum.*

"It is a work of fine scholarship, which will prove of great service to the student of early and middle Irish, and it is a valuable testimony of the interest which is being taken in our day in Irish letters."

—*Scotsman.*

"Obviously we have here an invaluable guide to the early history of the language. The book is carefully indexed, and will be found invaluable as a work of reference."—*Irish Times.*

"It is one of the most important contributions to old Irish studies issued in recent years The author had the enormous advantage of knowing modern Irish from childhood, and his investigations of the language of the annals are evidence of the advantage."

—*Irish Independent.*

"The book is notable as extending the lines of investigation, chiefly directed upon Old Irish, with which we have grown familiar in the last ten or twelve years."—*Manchester Guardian.*

CLASSICAL SERIES.

No. I. A STUDY OF THE BACCHAE OF EURIPIDES. By G. NORWOOD, M.A , Assistant Lecturer in Classics. Demy 8vo, pp. xx, 188. 5s. net. (Publication No. 31, 1908.)

"The interest of Mr. Norwood's book, which . . . is a very welcome addition to the bibliography of Euripides, and a scholarly and interesting

MANCHESTER UNIVERSITY PUBLICATIONS.

CLASSICAL SERIES.

A STUDY OF THE BACCHAE OF EURIPIDES (continued).

piece of work, displaying erudition and insight beyond the ordinary, lies in the way in which, by applying Dr. Verrall's methods . . . . he first shows up difficulties and inconsistencies, some of which have hardly been noticed before . . . and then produces his own startling theory, which he claims is the great solvent of all the perplexities."
—*Saturday Review.*

"Unless very strong evidence can be produced against Mr. Norwood's view, it must be accepted as the true solution of the problem. . . . Mr. Norwood is generally clear, and abounds in illuminating thoughts. He has added a full bibliography (running to twenty-three pages) of writings on Euripides, and for this every scholar will offer his sincere thanks. . . . He has done a very good piece of work."—*Athenæum.*

"This volume forms the first of a Classical Series projected by the Manchester University, who are to be congratulated on having begun with a book so original and full of interest. . . . It is admirably argued, and is instinct with a sympathetic imagination. It is, at the very least, an extremely able attempt to solve a very complex problem."
—*Manchester Guardian.*

"Mr. Norwood's book has even in the eyes of a sceptic the considerable merit of stating the hypothesis in a very thoroughgoing and able manner, and at least giving it its full chance of being believed."
—Professor Gilbert Murray in the *Nation.*

"L'interprétation de M. Norwood est certainement très ingénieuse; elle est même très séduisante."—*Revue Critique.*

ECONOMIC SERIES.

No. I. THE LANCASHIRE COTTON INDUSTRY. By S. J. CHAPMAN, M.A., M. Com., Stanley Jevons Professor of Political Economy and Dean of the Faculty of Commerce. Demy 8vo, pp. vii. 309. 7s. 6d. net.   (Publication No. 4, 1904.)

"Such a book as this ought to be, and will be, read far beyond the bounds of the trade."—*Manchester Guardian.*

"There have been books dealing with various phases of the subject, but no other has so ably treated it from the economic as well as from the historical point of view."—*Manchester Courier.*

"The story of the evolution of the industry from small and insignificant beginnings up to its present imposing proportions and highly developed and specialised forms, is told in a way to rivet the attention of the reader . . . . . the book is a valuable and instructive treatise on a fascinating yet important subject."—*Cotton Factory Times.*

SHERRATT & HUGHES

MANCHESTER UNIVERSITY PUBLICATIONS.
ECONOMIC SERIES.

(GARTSIDE REPORT, No. 1.)

No. II. COTTON SPINNING AND MANUFACTURING IN THE UNITED STATES OF AMERICA. By T. W. UTTLEY, B.A., Gartside Scholar. Demy 8vo, pp. xii. 70. 1s. net.

(Publication No. 8, 1905.)

"The writer gives ample details concerning wages and other features connected with typical mills . . . and the information thus gathered is of interest and value to the factory operative as well as the student and economist."—*Cotton Factory Times.*

"Mr. Uttley describes how he visited the mills in various States in very systematic and detailed manner. Altogether the report makes an admirable and welcome collection of information, and will be found on many occasions worthy of reference."—*Textile Mercury.*

(GARTSIDE REPORT, No. 2.)

No. III. SOME MODERN CONDITIONS AND RECENT DEVELOPMENTS IN IRON AND STEEL PRODUCTION IN AMERICA, being a Report to the Gartside Electors, on the results of a Tour in the U.S.A. By FRANK POPPLEWELL, B.Sc., Gartside Scholar. Demy 8vo, pp. xii. 126. 1s. net.

(Publication No 21, 1906.)

"Mr. Popplewell gives a clear exposition of the results of specialisation in production, of the development of ore-handling machinery, and of the general use of the charging machine, features that characterise American practice. He shows, too, that the colossal blast-furnace with huge yield due to high-blast pressure, regardless of consumption of steam and boiler coal, is giving place to a blast furnace of more modest dimensions. . . .

"The impression derived from reading Mr. Popplewell's report is that many of the most striking developments, admirable as they are, were designed to meet special wants, and are not necessarily applicable in Great Britain."—*Nature.*

(GARTSIDE REPORT, No. 3.)

No. IV. ENGINEERING AND INDUSTRIAL CONDITIONS IN THE UNITED STATES. By FRANK FOSTER, M.Sc., Gartside Scholar. Demy 8vo, pp. ix. 106. 1s. net.

(Publication No 22, 1906.)

"The report under review is of very great interest to those connected with the manufacturing branch of engineering in this country, many of whom will have to relinquish their preconceived notions regarding American methods, if Mr. Foster's conclusions are to be accepted."

—*Electrical Review.*

34, Cross Street, Manchester

SHERRATT & HUGHES

MANCHESTER UNIVERSITY PUBLICATIONS.
ECONOMIC SERIES.

No. V. THE RATING OF LAND VALUES. By J.D. CHORLTON, M.Sc.
Demy 8vo, pp. viii. 177. 3s. 6d. net. (Publication No. 23, 1907.)

"The first half of this book deserves to become a classic . . . . . . is one of the best books on a practical economic question that has appeared for many years. It is not only scientifically valuable, but so well written as to be interesting to a novice on the subject."—*The Nation.*

"A very businesslike and serviceable collection of essays and notes on this intricate question."—*Manchester Guardian.*

"Mr. Chorlton deals clearly and concisely with the whole subject of rating and land values."—*The Standard.*

"The impartiality and candour of Mr. Chorlton's method are beyond dispute, and his book will repay careful study by all who are interested in the question, from whatever motive."—*Westminster Gazette.*

GARTSIDE REPORT, No. 4.)
No. VI. DYEING IN GERMANY AND AMERICA. By SYDNEY H. HIGGINS, M.Sc., Gartside Scholar. Demy 8vo, pp. xiii. 112.
1s. net. (Publication No. 24, 1907.)

"The book will . . make a valuable addition to the technical literature of this country."—*Tribune.*

"The work is one which . . . . should receive the attention of those who desire a general view of the German and American dyeing industries."—*Textile Manufacturer.*

No. VII. THE HOUSING PROBLEM IN ENGLAND. By ERNEST RITSON DEWSNUP, M.A., Professor of Railway Economics in the University of Chicago. Demy 8vo, pp. vii. 327. 5s. net.
(Publication No. 25, 1907.)

"Professor Dewsnup's book on the housing problem consists of three distinct parts, each of which is a valuable contribution to economic science. In Part I, Professor Dewsnup tries to give a clear and definite account of the evil with which authorities in England are called upon to cope. Avoiding all special pleading and all evidence of the sensational kind which is apt to give a false idea of the extent and intensity of the evil of overcrowding, he does not on the other hand fall into the error of minimizing the evil.

"In Part II, Professor Dewsnup gives a most excellent and well-digested summary of the legislation which has been passed by Parliament since 1851 to cope with the evils of overcrowded houses, and of overcrowded areas.

"In Part III, the strictly informational and statistical work of the previous parts is utilized by the author to support his own conclusions as to the best methods of dealing with the problem of overcrowding.

"Whether or not the reader agrees with Professor Dewsnup in the conclusions he draws from his data, every student of economics must be grateful to him for the accuracy and care which have gone into the collection and arrangement of his material."—*The American Political Science Review*, vol. iii, No. 1, February, 1909.

SHERRATT & HUGHES

MANCHESTER UNIVERSITY PUBLICATIONS.
ECONOMIC SERIES.

(GARTSIDE REPORT, No. 5.)
No. VIII. AMERICAN BUSINESS ENTERPRISE. By DOUGLAS KNOOP, M.A., Gartside Scholar. Demy 8vo, pp. viii. 128. 1s. 6d. net.
(Publication No. 30, 1907.)

"The book is calculated to give a clear and accurate description, "essentially intended for the general reader," and the author has quite rightly eliminated everything of a technical character, giving his theme both the simplicity and the interest that are required. . . . The work might well have been doubled in length without any loss of interest. . . . Invaluable as a text-book."—*The Economic Journal.*

"Should on no account be missed, for it is a very good attempt at a survey of the enormous field of American business in the true and judicial spirit."—*Pall Mall Gazette.*

(GARTSIDE REPORT, No. 6.)
No. IX. THE ARGENTINE AS A MARKET. By N. L. WATSON, M.A., Gartside Scholar. Demy 8vo, pp. viii. 64. 1s. net.
(Publication No. 33, 1908.)

"A valuable and thorough examination of the conditions and future of Argentine commerce."—*Morning Leader.*

(GARTSIDE REPORT, No. 7.)
No. X. SOME ELECTRO-CHEMICAL CENTRES. By J. N. PRING, M.Sc., Gartside Scholar. Demy 8vo, pp. xiv. 137. 1s. 6d. net.
(Publication No. 41, 1908.)

"Concise, business-like, and furnished with some valuable papers of statistics, the report will prove well worthy of the study of anyone specially interested in this subject."—*Scotsman.*

". . . . . The reviewer says unhesitatingly that this Gartside Report . . . . . is the best all-round book on industrial electro-chemistry that has so far come to his notice."—*Electro-chemical and Metallurgical Industry*, May, 1909.

(GARTSIDE REPORT, No. 8.)
No. XI. CHEMICAL INDUSTRY ON THE CONTINENT. By HAROLD BARON, B.Sc., Gartside Scholar. Demy 8vo, pp. xi. 71. 1s. 6d. net. (Publication No. 44, 1909.)

"Well informed, well systematised, and written with businesslike precision, it deserves the attention of everyone interested in its subject."—*Scotsman.*

"For a good general account of the chemical industry on the Continent we think this report, so far as it goes, to be an excellent one and is, moreover, unlike many works on the subject, interesting to read."
—*Chemical Trades Journal.*

"Clearly and intelligently handled."—*The Times.*

SHERRATT & HUGHES

MANCHESTER UNIVERSITY PUBLICATIONS.
ECONOMIC SERIES.

No. XII. UNEMPLOYMENT. By Prof. S. J. CHAPMAN, M.A., M.Com., and H. M. HALLSWORTH, M.A., B.Sc. Demy 8vo, pp. xvi. 164. 2s. net, paper, 2s. 6d. net, cloth. (Publication No. 45, 1909.)

"On the whole, the authors offer a solid contribution, both as regards facts and reasoning, to the solution of a peculiarly difficult and pressing social problem."—*Cotton Factory Times.*

". . . reproduces in amplified form a valuable set of articles, giving the results of an investigation made in Lancashire, which lately appeared in the *Manchester Guardian*. By way of Introduction we have an examination, not previously published, of the Report of the Poor-law Commission on Unemployment. There is a large accompaniment of Charts and Tables, and indeed the whole work bears the mark of thoroughness."
—*Guardian.*

(GARTSIDE REPORT, No. 9.)

No. XIII. THE COTTON INDUSTRY IN SWITZERLAND, VORALBERG AND ITALY. A Technical and Economic Study. By S. L. BESSO, LL.B. Demy 8vo, pp. xv. 229. 3s. 6d. net.
(Publication No. 54, 1910.)

"The large amount of information gathered has been carefully arranged. . . . The work is a worthy one, interesting to the general reader, and valuable to the captain of commerce, and inevitably suggests the desirability of having the remaining countries of the Continent similarly surveyed . . . . this volume, which is well worth careful study by all who are interested in the social and economic conditions of textile workers abroad."—*The Cotton Factory Times.*

"This volume may be heartily commended to the attention of all persons interested in every phase of cotton mill economics, and we congratulate Mr. Besso on the admirable manner in which he has set forth the results of his painstaking investigations. In these days of international comparisons, a series of volumes dealing in this way with every industrial country would be of considerable value to students of industrial and commercial affairs."—*The Textile Mercury.*

". . . . the facts and statistics the author marshals so clearly . . . . a skilled investigator. For the rest, this volume does infinite credit alike to the author and to his University."—*Morning Leader.*

MANCHESTER UNIVERSITY PUBLICATIONS.
EDUCATIONAL SERIES.

No. I. CONTINUATION SCHOOLS IN ENGLAND & ELSEWHERE. Their place in the Educational System of an Industrial and Commercial State. By MICHAEL E. SADLER, M.A., LL.D., Professor of the History and Administration of Education. Demy 8vo, pp. xxvi. 779. 8s. 6d. net. (Publication No. 29, 1907.)

This work is largely based on an enquiry made by past and present Students of the Educational Department of the University of Manchester. Chapters on Continuation Schools in the German Empire, Switzerland, Denmark, and France, have been contributed by other writers.

". . . . . gives a record of what the principal nations are doing in the prolongation of school work. It is invaluable as a *corpus* of material from which to estimate the present position of the world—so far as its analogies touch Britain—in 'further education,' as the phrase is."
—*The Outlook.*

"The most comprehensive book on continuation schools that has yet been issued in this country"—*Scottish Review.*

"The whole question is discussed with an elaboration, an insistence on detail, and a wisdom that mark this volume as the most important contribution to educational effort that has yet been made."
—*Contemporary Review.*

"The subject of the work is one that goes to the very heart of national education, and the treatise itself lays bare with a scientific but humane hand the evils that beset our educational system, the waste of life and national energy which that system has been unable in any sufficient degree to check."—*The Spectator.*

"It is a treasure of facts and judicious opinions in the domain of the history and administration of education."—*The Athenæum.*

No. II. THE DEMONSTRATION SCHOOLS RECORD. No. I. Being Contributions to the Study of Education from the Department of Education in the University of Manchester. By J. J. FINDLAY, M.A., Ph.D. Sarah Fielden Professor of Education. Demy 8vo, pp. viii. 126. 1s. 6d. net. (Publication No 32, 1908.)

"Professor Findlay and his skilled and experienced collaborators give an interesting account of the uses of the demonstration classes, the nature and scope of the work done in them, and the methods adopted (as well as the underlying principles) in some of the courses of instruction."—*The Athenæum.*

"The book gives an instructive account of the attempts made to correlate the subjects of school instruction, not only with each other, but also with the children's pursuits out of school hours. . . . The problem Professor Findlay has set himself to work out in the Demonstration School is, How far is it possible by working with the children through successive culture epochs of the human race to form within their minds not only a truer conception of human history, but also eventually a deeper comprehension of the underlying purpose and oneness of all human activities?"—*Morning Post.*

SHERRATT & HUGHES

MANCHESTER UNIVERSITY PUBLICATIONS.
EDUCATIONAL SERIES.

No. III. THE TEACHING OF HISTORY IN GIRLS' SCHOOLS IN NORTH AND CENTRAL GERMANY. A Report by EVA DODGE, M.A., Gilchrist Student. Demy 8vo, pp. x. 149. 1s. 6d. net.
(Publication No. 34, 1908.)

"We cordially recommend this most workmanlike, and extremely valuable addition to pedagogic literature."—*Education.*

"Miss Dodge has much of interest to say on the limitations and defects of history-teaching in girls' schools, but the real contribution of this book is its revelation of how the history lesson can be made a living thing."—*Glasgow Herald.*

"Gives a clear and detailed account of two well-organised schemes of historical teaching in Germany."—*School World.*

No. IV. THE DEPARTMENT OF EDUCATION IN THE UNIVERSITY OF MANCHESTER, 1890-1911. Demy 8vo, 146 pp. 1s. 6d. net, paper; 2s. 6d. net, cloth.
(Publication No. 58, 1911.)

This book, published in commemoration of the twenty-first anniversary of the education department, includes an article nearly 50 pages long by Prof Sadler on University Training Colleges, their origin, growth and influence, a history by Mr. W. T. Goode of the department of education in the University, a register of past and present students and a record of the publications issued from the department. It is illustrated by photographs of the University and some of the leading persons connected with the education department.

No. V. OUTLINES OF EDUCATION COURSES IN MANCHESTER UNIVERSITY. Demy 8vo, pp. viii., 190. 3s. net.
[Publication No. 61, 1911.

No. VI. THE STORY OF THE MANCHESTER HIGH SCHOOL FOR GIRLS, 1871—1911. By SARA A. BURSTALL, M.A. Demy 8vo., pp. xx. 214, with 18 Plates. 5s. net. (Publication No. 63, 1911.)

ENGLISH SERIES.

No. I. THE LITERARY PROFESSION IN THE ELIZABETHAN AGE. By PH. SHEAVYN, M.A., D.Lit., Special Lecturer in English Literature and Tutor for Women Students; Warden of the Hall of Residence for Women Students.

A series of brief studies dealing with the conditions amidst which the profession of literature was pursued under Elizabeth and James I. It treats of their relations with patrons, publishers, and reading public, and with various authorities exercising legal control over the press; and discusses the possibility of earning a sufficient livelihood, in this period. by the proceeds of literary work. Demy 8vo, pp. xii. 221. 5s. net.
(Publication No. 49, 1909.)

". . . . scholarly and illuminating book. It opens a new series ir the Manchester University publications, and opens it with distinction. A more elaborately documented or more carefully indexed work need not be desired. The subject is an engrossing one; and, although the author has aimed rather at accuracy and completeness than at the arts of entertainment, the result remains eminently readable."
—*Manchester Guardian.*

SHERRATT & HUGHES

MANCHESTER UNIVERSITY PUBLICATIONS.
ENGLISH SERIES.

No. II. BEOWULF : Edited, with Introduction, Notes, and Glossary, by W. J. SEDGEFIELD, Litt.D., Lecturer in English Language. Demy 8vo, pp. xii. 300. 9s. net. (Publication No. 55, 1910.)

"It is his carefulness in this matter of the text that will win Mr. Sedgefield the chief thanks of students. This record of variants is full and accurate, and the fuller notes which follow the text itself should be very helpful both to the pupil and the expert. In the glossarial index Mr. Sedgefield has accomplished a task hitherto unattempted in England. . . . Mr. Sedgefield's edition of "Beowulf" maintains admirably the standard of scholarliness which Miss Sheavyn's recent volume set her followers in the new English series of Manchester University studies, and we need no longer reproach ourselves with the necessity of going to Germany for a fully edited text of the greatest monument of our early literature. All scholars must be grateful."—*Manchester Guardian.*

"Too often, the philologist and the man of letters find themselves at variance, and it is rare indeed to find the two combined in one personality, but, brief as Mr. Sedgefield's introductory essays necessarily are, they suffice to show that the poem appeals to him in its literary as well as in its linguistic aspect. His criticisms are admirably suggestive, and his notes on the metre, origin, authorship and date are models of clearness and condensation. The Bibliography and Glossary are admirably full."—*Guardian.*

". . . His hope that it will find acceptance with a larger public, if not already fulfilled, certainly will be, for the edition is incomparably better than any yet produced in England, and so complete in glossary, bibliography, and other explanatory matter as to stand in no fear of a rival."—*Journal of Education.*

"It is a scholarly piece of work, embodying the results of the latest researches and containing an excellent bibliography. The introduction provides an admirable analysis of the composition and structure of the poem. It is the best English edition available of the oldest extant epic of the English tongue."—*Scotsman.*

"Mr. W. J. Sedgefield's new edition of "Beowulf" is a great step forward in the study of Beowulf in particular and the general popularisation of the study of Anglo-Saxon in general. It may be said that in each of its various sections the introduction, the notes, the glossary, and the appendices, this work is much more complete than any other English edition which has hitherto been published, and it should prove the greatest help to students of this grand old epic poem . . . a work which essentially conforms to the spirit of modern science."
—*Commentator.*

"The notes handle all the chief difficulties frankly."
—*Educational Times.*

"The Bibliography deserves high praise."—*The Athenæum.*

No. III. PATIENCE: A West Midland Poem of the Fourteenth Century. With an Introduction, Notes, and Glossary, by HARTLEY BATESON, M.A. [*In the Press.*

SHERRATT & HUGHES

MANCHESTER UNIVERSITY PUBLICATIONS.
HISTORICAL SERIES.

No. I. MEDIÆVAL MANCHESTER AND THE BEGINNINGS OF LANCASHIRE. By JAMES TAIT, M.A., Professor of Ancient and Mediæval History. Demy 8vo, pp. x. 211. 7s. 6d. net.
(Publication No. 3, 1904.)

"Patient and enlightened scholarship and a sense of style and proportion have enabled the writer to produce a work at once solid and readable."—*English Historical Review.*

"A welcome addition to the literature of English local history, not merely because it adds much to our knowledge of Manchester and Lancashire, but also because it displays a scientific method of treatment which is rare in this field of study in England."—Dr. Gross in *American Historical Review.*

"La collection ne pouvait débuter plus significativement et plus heure. usement que par un ouvrage d'histoire du Moyen Age dû à M. Tait, car l'enseignement mediéviste est un de ceux qui font le plus d'honneur à la jeune Université de Manchester, et c'est à M. le Professeur Tait qu'il faut attribuer une bonne part de ce succès."—*Revue de Synthése historique.*

No. II. INITIA OPERUM LATINORUM QUAE SAECULIS XIII., XIV., XV. ATTRIBUUNTUR. By A. G. LITTLE, M.A., Lecturer in Palæography. Demy 8vo, pp. xiii. 273 (interleaved). (Out of print.)
(Publication No. 5, 1904.)

"Whoever has attempted to ascertain the contents of a Mediæval miscellany in manuscript must often have been annoyed by the occurrence of a blank space where the title of the treatise ought to be. Mr. Little has therefore earned the gratitude of all such persons by making public a collection of some 6,000 incipits, which he arranged in the first instance for his private use, in compiling a catalogue of Franciscan MSS."
—*English Historical Review.*

No. III. THE OLD COLONIAL SYSTEM. By GERALD BERKELEY HERTZ, M.A., B.C.L., Lecturer in Constitutional Law. Demy 8vo, pp. xi. 232. 5s net. (Publication No. 7, 1905.)

"Mr. Hertz gives us an elaborate historical study of the old colonial system, which disappeared with the American Revolution. . . . . He shows a remarkable knowledge of contemporary literature, and his book may claim to be a true history of popular opinion."—*Spectator.*

"Mr. Hertz's book is one which no student of imperial developments can neglect. It is lucid, fair, thorough, and convincing."
—*Glasgow Herald.*

"Mr. Hertz's 'Old Colonial System' is based on a careful study of contemporary documents, with the result that several points of no small importance are put in a new light . . . . it is careful, honest work . . . . The story which he tells has its lesson for us."—*The Times.*

"Both the ordinary reader and the academic mind will get benefit from this well-informed and well-written book."—*Scotsman.*

"Mr. Hertz has made excellent use of contemporary literature, and has given us a very valuable and thorough critique. The book is interesting and very well written."—*American Political Science Review.*

33, Soho Square, London, W.

MANCHESTER UNIVERSITY PUBLICATIONS.
HISTORICAL SERIES.

No. IV. STUDIES OF ROMAN IMPERIALISM. By W. T. ARNOLD, M.A. Edited by EDWARD FIDDES, M.A., Lecturer in Ancient History, with Memoir of the Author by Mrs. HUMPHRY WARD and C. E. MONTAGUE. With a Photogravure of W. T Arnold. Demy 8vo, pp. cxxiii. 281. 7s. 6d. net
(Publication No. 16, 1906.)

"Mrs. Humphry Ward has used all her delicate and subtle art to draw a picture of her beloved brother; and his friend Mr. Montague's account of his middle life is also remarkable for its literary excellence."
—*Athenæum.*

"The memoir .... tenderly and skilfully written by the 'sister and friend,' tells a story, which well deserved to be told, of a life rich in aspiration, interests, and friendships, and not without its measure of actual achievement."—*Tribune.*

"This geographical sense and his feeling for politics give colour to all he wrote."—*Times.*

"Anyone who desires a general account of the Empire under Augustus which is freshly and clearly written and based on wide reading will find it here."—*Manchester Guardian.*

"Nothing could be better than the sympathetic tribute which Mrs. Humphry Ward pays to her brother, or the analysis of his work and method by his colleague Mr. Montague. The two together have more stuff in them than many big books of recent biography."
—*Westminster Gazette.*

The Memoir may be had separately, price 2s. 6d net

No. V. CANON PIETRO CASOLA'S PILGRIMAGE TO JERUSALEM IN THE YEAR 1494. By M. M. NEWETT, B.A., formerly Jones Fellow. Demy 8vo, pp. viii. 427. 7s. 6d. net.
(Publication No. 26, 1907.)

"Tra mezzo ai tanti libri esteri di semplici divulgazione su fatti e figure della storia italiana, questo emerge piacevalmente e si legge volontieri. E diverso di carattere e di trattazione. Esume .... dalla polvere degli archivi e delle biblioteche qualche cosa che ha un valore fresco ed interessante, un valore storico e un valore umano."
—A.A.B. in the *Archivio Storico Italiano*

"L'introduction se termine par toute une dissertation du plus grand intérêt documentée à l'aide des archives vénitiennes, sur le caractère commercial des pelérinages, dont les armateurs de Venise assumèrent, jusqu 'au XVIIe siècle l'entreprise."
—J.B. in the *Revue de Synthèse historique.*

"Miss Newett has performed her task admirably, preserving much of the racy humour and shrewd phrasing which mark the original, and adding, in the introduction, a general treatise on the Venetian pilgrim industry, and in the notes copious illustrations of the text."
—Horatio Brown in the *English Historical Review.*

SHERRATT & HUGHES

MANCHESTER UNIVERSITY PUBLICATIONS.
HISTORICAL SERIES.

CANON PIETRO CASOLA'S PILGRIMAGE TO JERUSALEM IN THE YEAR 1494.—Continued.

"Miss Newett's introduction is an admirable bit of work. She has studied carefully what the archives of Venice have to say about pilgrim ships and shipping laws, and her pages are a mine of information on such subjects."—Dr. Thomas Lindsay in the *Scottish Historical Review*.

"This is a deeply interesting record, not merely of a Syrian pilgrimage, but of Mediterranean life and of the experiences of an intelligent Italian gentleman at the close of the Middle Ages—two years after the discovery of America. It would not be easy to find a more graphic picture, in old days, of a voyage from Venice to the Levant."
—*American Historical Review*.

No. VI HISTORICAL ESSAYS. Edited by T. F. TOUT, M.A., Professor of Mediæval and Modern History, and JAMES TAIT, M.A., Professor of Ancient and Mediæval History. Demy 8vo, pp. xv. 557. 6s. net. Reissue of the Edition of 1902 with index and New Preface (Publication No. 27, 1907.)

"Diese zwanzig chronologisch geordneten Aufsätze heissen in der Vorrede der Herausgeber *Festchrift*, behandeln zur Hälfte ausser-englische Themata, benutzen reichlich festländische Literatur und verraten überall neben weiten Ausblicken eine methodische Schulung die der dortigen Facultät hohe Ehre macht."—Professor Liebermann in *Deutsche Literaturzeitung*.

"Imperial history, local history, ecclesiastical history, economic history and the methods of historical teaching—all these are in one way or another touched upon by scholars who have collaborated in this volume. Men and women alike have devoted their time and pains to working out problems of importance and often of no slight difficulty. The result is one of which the university and city may be justly proud."—The late Professor York Powell in the *Manchester Guardian*.

"Esso contiene venti lavori storici dettati, quattro da professori e sedici da licenziati del Collegio, e sono tutto scritti appositamente e condotti secondo le più rigorose norme della critica e su documenti."—R. Predelli in *Nuovo Archivio Veneto*.

"Le variété des sujets et l'érudition avec laquelle ils sont traités font grand honneur à la manière dont l'histoire est enseigné à Owens College."
—*Revue Historique*.

"Par nature, c'est un recueil savant, qui témoigne du respect et de l'émulation que sait exercer pour les études historiques la jeune et déjà célèbre université."—*Revue d'histoire ecclésiastique* (Louvain).

"All these essays reach a high level; they avoid the besetting sin of most of our present historical writing, which consists of serving up a hash of what other historians have written flavoured with an original spice of error. . . . . They are all based on original research and written by specialists."—Professor A. F. Pollard in the *English Historical Review*.

"Sie bilden einen schönen Beweis fur die rationelle Art, mit der dort dieses Studium betrieben wird."—Professor O. Weber in *Historische Zeitschrift*.

The index can be purchased separately, price 6d. net.

33, Soho Square, London, W.

MANCHESTER UNIVERSITY PUBLICATIONS.
HISTORICAL SERIES.

No. VII. STUDIES SUPPLEMENTARY TO STUBBS' CONSTITUTIONAL HISTORY. Vol. i. By CH. PETIT-DUTAILLIS, Litt.D., rector of the University of Grenoble. Translated from the French by W. E. RHODES, M.A., and edited by Prof. JAMES TAIT, M.A. Demy 8vo, pp. xiv. 152. 4s. net.
(Publication No. 38, 1908. Second Edition, 1911).
" The volume will be virtually indispensable to teachers and students of history."—*Athenæum*.

" This task has been carefully and well performed, under the supervision of Professor Tait, who has written a short but adequate introduction. This little book, ought, without delay, to be added to every public or private library that contains a copy of the classic work to which it forms an indispensable supplement."
—Dr. W. S. McKechnie in the *Scottish Historical Review*.

" These supplementary studies impress one as a discreet and learned attempt to safeguard a public, which is likely to learn all that it will know of a great subject from a single book, against the shortcomings of that book."—Professor A. B. White in the *American Historical Review*.

" C'est un complément indispensable de l'ouvrage de Stubbs, et l'on saura gré à l'Université de Manchester d'avoir pris l'initiative de cette publication."—M. Charles Bémont in *Revue Historique*.

" Ce sont des modèles de critique ingénieuse et sobre, une mise au point remarquable des questions les plus importantes traitées jadis par Stubbs."—M. Louis Halphen in *Revue de Synthèse historique*.

" Zu der englischen Ubersetzung dieser Excurse, durch einen verdienten jüngeren Historiker, die durchaus leicht wie Originalstil fliesst, hat Tait die Vorrede geliefert und manche Note, die noch die Literatur von 1908 berücksichtigt. Die historische Schule der Universität, Manchester, an Rührigkeit und strenger Methode von keiner in England übertroffen, bietet mit der Veröffentlichung der werthvollen Arbeit des Franzosen ein treffliches Lehrmittel."—Professor F. Liebermann, in *Deutsche Literaturzeitung*.

No. VIII. MALARIA AND GREEK HISTORY. By W. H. S. JONES, M.A. To which is added the History of Greek Therapeutics and the Malaria Theory by E. T. WITHINGTON, M.A., M.B. Demy 8vo, pp. xii. 176. 5s. net. (Publication No 43, 1909.)

" Mr. W. H. S. Jones is to be congratulated on the success with which he has conducted what may be described as a pioneering expedition into a practically unexplored field of history . . . . the publishers are to be congratulated on the admirable way in which the book has been turned out—a joy to handle and to read."—*Manchester Guardian*.

" This interesting volume is an endeavour to show that the decline of the Greeks as a people for several centuries before and after the Christian era was largely due to the prevalence of malaria in its various forms."—*Glasgow Herald*.

" [The author] . . . . has amassed a considerable store of valuable information from the Greek classics and other sources which will prove extremely useful to all who are interested in his theory."
—*Birmingham Daily Post*.

MANCHESTER UNIVERSITY PUBLICATIONS
HISTORICAL SERIES.

No. IX. HANES GRUFFYDD AP CYNAN. The Welsh text with translation, introduction, and notes by ARTHUR JONES, M.A., Jones Fellow in History. Demy 8vo, pp. viii. 204. 6s. net.
(Publication No. 50, 1910.)

"No Welsh historian of the future can afford to neglect this scholarly attempt to give the work of Griffith ap Cynan a true historical setting. The introduction is an ideally well-balanced estimate of a singularly quaint and beautiful piece of history."—*Glasgow Herald*.

"The Editor has prefaced his text with a comprehensive and nearly always convincing introduction of more than 100 pages, besides copious notes. Nearly every page of both contains matter of Irish history, sometimes really new, since taken from the document never deeply studied before, and always valuable from the new light thrown by the collation of independent, 'international' testimonies. . . . It will at once be seen that we have here a document of the first interest to ourselves; the University and the Editor have put us in their debt for a valuable contribution to our history."—*Freeman's Journal*.

"Mr. Jones prints the Welsh text in a scholarly recension, and accompanies it page by page with a faithful version into English, explains its obscurities and personal and local allusions in notes always concise and to the point, and brings it in with an interesting introduction, which treats fully of the transmission of the text, of its value as an historical document, and of its relation to other remaining original authorities for the history of the Norman Conquest."—*Scotsman*.

"Mr. Jones's enterprise is the result of the happy union in the University of Celtic and of historical studies. . . The textual editing, the annotations, and the translation have all been admirably done, and the work is a credit alike to the author, the University, and to the Press."—*Manchester Guardian*.

"Hearty thanks are due for a most useful and satisfactory edition."
—*Archæologia Cambrensis*.

No. X. THE CIVIL WAR IN LANCASHIRE. By ERNEST BROXAP, M.A. Demy 8vo, pp. xv. 226. 7s. 6d. net.
(Publication No. 51, 1910.)

"By a judicious use of it he has produced an eminently readable and informing work. . . . The University of Manchester, which, but for the pressure of the political situation, would have been founded in 1642, is to be congratulated upon its choice of an historian of the war in Lancashire."—*Athenæum*

"Mr. Broxap's monograph must be welcomed as the most important of those hitherto given to history to illuminate the county aspect of the Civil War. . . . . . The whole book is very carefully revised and accurate in its details, full and satisfactory, and the order in which the story is told is excellent. The index is also sufficient, and the whole study is amply annotated. Altogether, both the author and the Manchester University Press are to be thoroughly congratulated upon the volume."—*Morning Post*.

MANCHESTER UNIVERSITY PUBLICATIONS.
HISTORICAL SERIES.

THE CIVIL WAR IN LANCASHIRE (continued).

"It is clear that Mr. Broxap has minutely studied all available original materials and that he uses them with care and discrimination. . . . the highest praise that can be given to the author of a historical monograph is that he set out to produce a book that was wanted, does that extremely well, and does nothing else, and to this praise Mr. Broxap is fully entitled."—*Westminster Gazette*.

No. XI. A BIOGRAPHY OF THOMAS DEACON, THE MANCHESTER NON-JUROR. By Henry Broxap, M.A. Demy 8vo, pp. xix. 215, 2 plates. 7s. 6d. net. (Publication No. 59, 1911.)

"It has the signal merit, as history, of dealing with real historical questions and bringing research and historical methods to bear upon them. The author's motive has never been to concoct a book for the circulating library, but to illustrate by a single instance the strong and noble characteristics of a sect which Johnson and Macaulay despised."—*Manchester Guardian*.

"The materials for a biography of Thomas Deacon are not too plentiful, but Mr. Broxap has made the best possible use of the available sources, and weaves into his story many interesting glimpses of the social and religious life of the period."—*Glasgow Herald*.

No. XII. THE EJECTED OF 1662: Their Predecessors and Successors in Cumberland and Westmorland. By B. NIGHTINGALE, M.A. In two volumes, demy 8vo, pp. xxiv. 1490. 28s. net.
(Publication No. 62, 1911.)

No. XIII. GERMANY IN THE NINETEENTH CENTURY. Lectures by J. HOLLAND ROSE, Litt.D., C. H. HERFORD, Litt.D., E. C. K. GONNER, M.A., and M. E. SADLER, M.A., LL.D. With an Introductory Note by Viscount HALDANE. Demy 8vo, pp. xxi. 142. 2s. 6d. net. (Publication No. 65, 1912.)

No. XIV. A HISTORY OF PRESTON IN AMOUNDERNESS. By H. W. CLEMESHA, M. A. Demy 8vo., 7s. 6d. net.
(Publication No. 67, 1912.)

THE LOSS OF NORMANDY, 1189—1204. By F. M. POWICKE, M.A., Professor of History in the University of Belfast. [*In the Press.*

DOCUMENTS RELATING TO IRELAND UNDER THE COMMONWEALTH. By ROBERT DUNLOP, M.A., Lecturer on Irish History. In 2 volumes, demy 8vo.
This work will consist of a series of unpublished documents relating to the History of Ireland from 1651 to 1659, arranged, modernized, and edited, with introduction, notes, etc., by Mr. DUNLOP.

[*In Preparation.*

SHERRATT & HUGHES

MANCHESTER UNIVERSITY PUBLICATIONS.
MEDICAL SERIES.

No. I. SKETCHES OF THE LIVES AND WORK OF THE HONORARY MEDICAL STAFF OF THE ROYAL INFIRMARY. From its foundation in 1752 to 1830, when it became the Royal Infirmary. By EDWARD MANSFIELD BROCKBANK, M.D., M.R.C.P. Crown 4to. (illustrated), pp. vii. 311. 15s. net.
(Publication No. 1, 1904.)
" Dr. Brockbank's is a book of varied interest. It also deserves a welcome as one of the earliest of the 'Publications of the University of Manchester.' "—*Manchester Guardian.*

No. II. PRACTICAL PRESCRIBING AND DISPENSING. For Medical Students. By WILLIAM KIRKBY, sometime Lecturer in Pharmacognosy in the Owens College, Manchester. Crown 8vo, pp. iv. 194. 5s. net.
(Publication No. 2, 1904, Second Edition, 1906.)
"The whole of the matter bears the impress of that technical skill and thoroughness with which Mr. Kirkby's name must invariably be associated, and the book must be welcomed as one of the most useful recent additions to the working library of prescribers and dispensers."
—*Pharmaceutical Journal.*
" Thoroughly practical text-books on the subject are so rare, that we welcome with pleasure Mr. William Kirkby's 'Practical Prescribing and Dispensing.' The book is written by a pharmacist expressly for medical students, and the author has been most happy in conceiving its scope and arrangement."—*British Medical Journal.*

No. III. HANDBOOK OF SURGICAL ANATOMY. By G. A. WRIGHT, B.A., M.B. (Oxon.), F.R.C.S., Professor of Systematic Surgery, and C. H. PRESTON, M.D., F.R.C.S., L.D.S., Lecturer on Dental Anatomy; Assistant Dental Surgeon to the Victoria Dental Hospital of Manchester. Crown 8vo, pp. ix. 205. 5s. Second edition. (Publication No. 6, 1905.)
"Dr. Wright and Dr. Preston have produced a concise and very readable little handbook of surgical applied anatomy. . . . The subject matter of the book is well arranged and the marginal notes in bold type facilitate reference to any desired point."—*Lancet.*

No. IV. A COURSE OF INSTRUCTION IN OPERATIVE SURGERY in the University of Manchester. By WILLIAM THORBURN, M.D., B.S. (Lond.), F.R.C.S., Lecturer in Operative Surgery. Crown 8vo, pp. 75 (interleaved), 26 Figures in the Text. 2s. 6d. net. (Publication No. 11, 1906.)
"This little book gives the junior student all that he wants, and nothing that he does not want. Its size is handy, and altogether for its purpose it is excellent."—*University Review.*

No. V. A HANDBOOK OF LEGAL MEDICINE. By W. SELLERS, M.D. (London), of the Middle Temple, and Northern Circuit, Barrister-at-law. With 7 Illustrations. Crown 8vo, pp. vii. 233. 7s. 6d. net. (Publication No. 14, 1906.)
"This is quite one of the best books of the kind we have come across."—*Law Times.*

MANCHESTER UNIVERSITY PUBLICATIONS.

MEDICAL SERIES.

No. VI. A CATALOGUE OF THE PATHOLOGICAL MUSEUM OF THE UNIVERSITY OF MANCHESTER. Edited by J. LORRAIN SMITH, M.A., M.D. (Edin.), Professor of Pathology. Crown 4to, 1260 pp. 7s. 6d. net. (Publication No. 15, 1906.)

"The catalogue compares very favourably with others of a similar character, and, apart from its value for teaching purposes in an important medical school such as that of the University of Manchester, it is capable of being of great assistance to others as a work of reference."
—*Edinburgh Medical Journal*

"In conclusion we need only say that Professor Lorrain Smith has performed the most essential part of his task—the description of the specimens—excellently and an honourable mention must be made of the book as a publication."—*British Medical Journal.*

No. VII. HANDBOOK OF DISEASES OF THE HEART. By GRAHAM STEELL, M.D., F.R.C.P., Professor of Medicine, and Physician to the Manchester Royal Infirmary. Crown 8vo, pp. xii. 389, 11 plates (5 in colours), and 100 illustrations in the text. 7s. 6d. net. (Publication No. 20, 1906.)

"It more truly reflects modern ideas of heart disease than any book we are acquainted with, and therefore may be heartily recommended to our readers."—*Treatment.*

"We regard this volume as an extremely useful guide to the study of diseases of the heart, and consider that no better introduction to the subject could possibly have been written."
—*Medical Times and Hospital Gazette.*

No. VIII. JULIUS DRESCHFELD. IN MEMORIAM. Medical Studies by his colleagues and pupils at the Manchester University and the Royal Infirmary. Imperial 8vo, pp. vi. 246. With a Photogravure and 42 Plates. 10s. 6d. net. (Publication No. 35, 1908.)

"A worthy memorial of one who left no small mark upon the study of clinical pathology in this country."—*British Medical Journal.*

"The papers which compose the bulk of the volume have been reprinted from the 'Manchester Chronicle,' vol. xiv, and they are of both interest and permanent value."—*Scottish Medical Journal.*

"The editor, Dr. Brockbank, can be congratulated upon editing a volume that will fitly perpetuate the memory of his eminent colleague."
—*Medical Review.*

SHERRATT & HUGHES

MANCHESTER UNIVERSITY PUBLICATIONS.
MEDICAL SERIES.

No. IX. HANDBOOK OF INFECTIOUS DISEASES. By R. W. MARSDEN, M.D. Crown 8vo, pp. vi. 296. 5s. net.
(Publication No. 39, 1908.)

"This book aims at giving a practical account of the various infectious diseases, suitable for ready reference in everyday work, and the author has, on the whole, succeeded admirably in his attempt."—*The Lancet.*

"Throughout the book the information given seems thoroughly adequate, and especial attention is paid to diagnosis."
—*Scottish Medical Journal.*

"The subject matter is well arranged and easy of reference."
—*The Medical Officer.*

No. X. LECTURES ON THE PATHOLOGY OF CANCER. By CHARLES POWELL WHITE, M.A., M.D., F.R.C.S. Imperial 8vo, pp. x. 83, 33 plates. 3s. 6d. net. (Publication No. 42, 1908)

"The volume is a model of scientific self-restraint. In four chapters the author covers in simple language much that is of main interest in the present phase of investigation of cancer . . .

"The volume . . . is well illustrated with statistical charts and photomicrographs, and its perusal must prove profitable to all who wish to be brought up-to-date in the biology of cancer."—*Nature.*

"Full of scholarly information and illustrated with a number of excellent black-and-white plates."—*Medical Press.*

"These lectures give a short résumé of recent work on the subject in an easily assimilable form."—*St. Bartholomew's Hospital Journal.*

No. XI. SEMMELWEIS: HIS LIFE AND HIS DOCTRINE. A chapter in the history of Medicine. By Sir WILLIAM J. SINCLAIR, M.A., M.D., Professor of Obstetrics and Gynæcology in the University of Manchester. Imperial 8vo, pp. x. 369, 2 plates. 7s. 6d. net.
(Publication No. 46, 1909.)

"Semmelweis has found a worthy biographer who has made a noteworthy contribution to medical literature, and whose understanding of the work and sympathy for the trial of his subject are obvious."
—*Dublin Journal of Medical Science.*

"Das wahrhaft vornehm geschriebene Buch des auch bei uns in Deutschland hochverehrten englischen Kollegen spricht für sich selbst. Es ist berufen, in dem Vaterlande Lister's auch dem grossen Märtyrer Semmelweis Gerechtigkeit zuteil werden zu lassen."
—*Zentralblatt für Gynäkologie.*

"There should be a wide public, lay as well as medical, for a book as full of historical, scientific and human interest as this 'Life of Semmelweis.' . . . Sir William Sinclair's book is of the greatest interest, and we are glad to welcome an adequate English appreciation of Semmelweis, who certainly ranks among the 'heroes of medicine.'"
—*Nature.*

"It is a book all obstetricians and research men should read."
—*Scottish Medical Journal.*

"A most instructive and interesting biography of the discoverer of the cause of puerperal fever. . . . The book is well printed and bound."
—*Medical Review.*

SHERRATT & HUGHES
MANCHESTER UNIVERSITY PUBLICATIONS.
MEDICAL SERIES.

No. XII. MODERN PROBLEMS IN PSYCHIATRY. By. E. LUGARO, Professor of Nervous and Mental Diseases in the University of Modena. Translated from the Italian by DAVID ORR, M.D., Assistant Medical Officer and Pathologist to the County Asylum, Prestwich; and R. G. ROWS, M.D., Assistant Medical Officer and Pathologist to the County Asylum, Lancaster. With an introduction by T. S. CLOUSTON, M.D., Physician Superintendent, Royal Asylum, Morningside, and Lecturer on Mental Diseases in Edinburgh University. Imperial 8vo, pp. viii. 305, 8 plates. 7s. 6d. net. (Publication No. 47, 1909.)

"Professor Lugaro is to be congratulated upon the masterly and judicious survey of his subject which he has given to the world in this work. Not only have we a succinct and clear exposition of the present state of our knowledge, but we are confronted with a tale of the inexhaustible work that lies before us."—*Lancet.*

"The work should be on the shelf of every pathologist and asylum physician; it is thoughtful, suggestive and well written. The translation also is excellent."—*Nature.*

"The book is a very distinct addition to the literature of psychiatry, and one which will well repay careful study."
—*Californian Medical Journal.*

"The whole book is suggestive in the highest degree, and well worthy of careful study. Dr. David Orr and Dr. R. G. Rows, the translators, are to be heartily congratulated on the manner in which they have rendered the original into terse and idiomatic English."—*Athenæum.*

No. XIII. FEEBLEMINDEDNESS IN CHILDREN OF SCHOOL AGE. By C. PAGET LAPAGE, M.D., M.R.C.P. With an Appendix on Treatment and Training by MARY DENDY, M.A. Crown 8vo. pp. xvi. 359, 12 Plates. 5s. net. (Publication No. 57, 1911.)

"There is indeed much of practical interest in the book, which is well printed at the Manchester University Press and is admirably illustrated and got up."—*British Medical Journal.*

"It will be thus seen that the author covers much ground and it is surprising how much interesting information is included. Taken as a whole the book is excellent and will, we feel sure, meet with a ready sale. . . . . . We cordially welcome this volume as an admirable contribution to the literature of the subject."—*Medical Times*

. . . . . "We consider these objects have been achieved. The book is a clear and accurate short account of the characteristics of feebleminded children, which cannot fail to be of service to those for whom it is intended. . . . The Appendix contributed by Miss Dendy is, as we should expect, clear and practical, and is a valuable addition to the book."
—*British Journal of Children's Diseases.*

No. XIV. DISEASES OF THE NERVOUS SYSTEM. By JUDSON S. BURY, M.D. (Lond.). F.R.C.P. Demy 8vo., pp. xx. 788. 15/- net.
(Publication No. 66, 1912.)

34, Cross Street, Manchester

SHERRATT & HUGHES

MANCHESTER UNIVERSITY PUBLICATIONS.
PHYSICAL SERIES.
No. I. THE PHYSICAL LABORATORIES OF THE UNIVERSITY OF MANCHESTER. A record of 25 years' work. Demy 8vo, pp. viii. 142, with a Photogravure, 10 Plates, and 4 Plans. 5s. net.
(Publication No. 13, 1906.)

This volume contains an illustrated description of the Physical, Electrical Engineering, and Electro-Chemistry Laboratories of the Manchester University, also a complete Biographical and Bibliographical Record of those who have worked in the Physics Department of the University during the past 25 years.

"The book is excellently got up, and contains a description of the department of physics and its equipment, a short biographical sketch of the Professor with a list of his scientific writings and a well-executed portrait and a record of the career of students and others who have passed through Dr. Schuster's hands. Alumni of Owens will welcome the volume as an interesting link with their alma mater."—*Glasgow Herald*.

"This interesting and valuable contribution to the history of the Manchester University also contains several illustrations, and forms the first of the 'physical series' of the publications of the University of Manchester."—*The Times*.

"It is a memorial of which any man would be justly proud, and the University of which he is both an alumnus and a professor may well share that pride."—*Manchester Guardian*.

No. II. LABORATORY EXERCISES IN PHYSICAL CHEMISTRY. By J. N. PRING, D.Sc. Crown 8vo. 4s. net.
(Publication No. 64, 1912.)

PUBLIC HEALTH SERIES.
No. I. ARCHIVES OF THE PUBLIC HEALTH LABORATORY OF THE UNIVERSITY OF MANCHESTER. Edited by A. SHERIDAN DELÉPINE, M.Sc., M.B., Ch.M., Director of the Laboratory and Proctor Professor of Comparative Pathology and Bacteriology. Crown 4to. pp. iv. 451. £1. 1s. net.
(Publication No. 12, 1906.)

"The University of Manchester has taken the important and highly commendable step of commencing the publication of the archives of its Public Health Laboratory, and has issued, under the able and judicious editorship of Professor Sheridan Delépine, the first volume of a series that promises to be of no small interest and value alike to members of the medical profession and to those of the laity. . . . Original communications bearing upon diseases which are prevalent in the districts surrounding Manchester, or dealing with food- and water-supplies, air, disposal of refuse, sterilisation and disinfection and kindred subjects, will be published in future volumes; and it is manifest that these, as they successively appear, will form a constantly increasing body of trustworthy information upon subjects which are not only of the highest interest to the profession but of supreme importance to the public."
—*The Lancet*.

33, Soho Square, London, W.

MANCHESTER UNIVERSITY PUBLICATIONS.
THEOLOGICAL SERIES.

No. I. INAUGURAL LECTURES delivered during the Session 1904-5, by the Professors and Lecturers of the Faculty of Theology, viz. :—
Prof. T. F. Tout, M.A.; Prof A. S. Peake, B.D.; Prof. H. W. Hogg, M.A; Prof T. W. Rhys Davids, LL.D.; Rev. W. F. Adeney, D.D.; Rev. A. Gordon, M.A.; Rev. L. Hassé, B.D.; Rev. Canon E. L. Hicks, M.A.; Rev. H. D. Lockett, M.A.; Rev. R. Mackintosh, D.D.; Rev. J. T. Marshall, D.D.; Rev. J. H. Moulton, D.Litt.
Edited by A. S. PEAKE, B.D., Dean of the Faculty.
Demy 8vo, pp. xi. 296. 7s. 6d. net. (Publication No. 9, 1905.)

"The lectures, while scholarly, are at the same time popular, and will be found interesting and instructive by those who are not theologians. . . . . The entire series is excellent, and the volume deserves a wide circulation."—*Scotsman.*

"The lectures themselves give a valuable conspectus of the present position of Theological Research. . . . They are, of course, not addressed to experts, but they are exceedingly valuable, even when allowance is made for their more or less popular form."—*Examiner.*

"This is a most interesting and valuable book, the appearance of which at the present moment is singularly significant. . . . But it is impossible in a brief review to indicate all the treasures of this rich volume, to read which carefully is to be introduced to the varied wealth of modern Biblical scholarship."—*Baptist.*

LECTURES.

No. I. GARDEN CITIES (Warburton Lecture). By RALPH NEVILLE, K.C. 6d. net. (Lecture No. 1, 1905.)
No. II. THE BANK OF ENGLAND AND THE STATE (A Lecture). By Sir FELIX SCHUSTER. 6d. net. (Lecture No. 2, 1905.)
No. III. BEARING AND IMPORTANCE OF COMMERCIAL TREATIES IN THE TWENTIETH CENTURY. By Sir THOMAS BARCLAY. 6d. net. (Lecture No. 3, 1906.)
No. IV. THE SCIENCE OF LANGUAGE AND THE STUDY OF THE GREEK TESTAMENT (A Lecture). By JAMES HOPE MOULTON, M.A., Litt.D. 6d. net. (Lecture No. 4, 1906.)
No. V. THE GENERAL MEDICAL COUNCIL: ITS POWERS AND ITS WORK (A Lecture). By DONALD MACALISTER, M.A., M.D., B.Sc., D.C.L., LL.D. 6d. net. (Lecture No. 5, 1906.)
No. VI. THE CONTRASTS IN DANTE (A Lecture). By the Hon. WILLIAM WARREN VERNON, M.A. 6d. net. (Lecture No. 6, 1906.)
No. VII. THE PRESERVATION OF PLACES OF INTEREST OR BEAUTY (A Lecture). By Sir ROBERT HUNTER. 6d. net.
(Lecture No. 7, 1907.)
No. VIII. ON THE LIGHT THROWN BY RECENT INVESTIGATIONS ON ELECTRICITY ON THE RELATION BETWEEN MATTER AND ETHER (Adamson Lecture). By J. J. THOMSON, D.Sc., F.R.S. 6d. net. (Lecture No. 8, 1908)

MANCHESTER UNIVERSITY PUBLICATIONS.
LECTURES.

No. IX. HOSPITALS, MEDICAL SCIENCE, AND PUBLIC HEALTH (A Lecture). By Sir CLIFFORD ALLBUTT, K.C.B., M.D. (Cantab.). 6d. net. (Lecture No. 9, 1908.)
No. X. ENGLISH POETRY AND GERMAN PHILOSOPHY IN THE AGE OF WORDSWORTH (Adamson Lecture). By A. C. BRADLEY, Litt.D. 6d. net. (Lecture No. 10, 1909.)
No. XI. THE EVOLUTION OF SURGERY. By WILLIAM THORBURN, F.R.C.S. 6d. net. (Lecture No. 11, 1910.)
No. XII. LEIBNIZ AS A POLITICIAN. By A. W. WARD, Litt.D., F.B.A. 6d. net. (Lecture No. 12, 1911.)
Lecture No. XIII. OLD TOWNS AND NEW NEEDS, by PAUL WATERHOUSE, M.A., F.R.I.B.A., and THE TOWN EXTENSION PLAN, by RAYMOND UNWIN, F.R.I.B.A. 1s. net.

CALENDAR OF THE VICTORIA UNIVERSITY OF MANCHESTER. Session 1904-5. Demy 8vo, 1100 pp. 3s. net.
(Publication No. 17.)
CALENDAR OF THE VICTORIA UNIVERSITY OF MANCHESTER. Session 1905-6. Demy 8vo, 1200 pp. 3s. net.
(Publication No. 18.)
CALENDAR OF THE VICTORIA UNIVERSITY OF MANCHESTER. Session 1906-7. Demy 8vo, 1300 pp. 3s. net.
(Publication No. 19.)
CALENDAR OF THE VICTORIA UNIVERSITY OF MANCHESTER. Session 1907-8. Demy 8vo, 1400 pp. 3s. net.
(Publication No. 28.)
CALENDAR OF THE VICTORIA UNIVERSITY OF MANCHESTER. Session 1908-9. Demy 8vo, 1460 pp. 3s. net.
(Publication No. 37.)
CALENDAR OF THE VICTORIA UNIVERSITY OF MANCHESTER. Session 1909-10. Demy 8vo. 1470 pp. 3s. net.
(Publication No. 48.)
CALENDAR OF THE VICTORIA UNIVERSITY OF MANCHESTER. Session 1910-11. Demy 8vo, 1550 pp. 3s. net.
(Publication No. 56.)
CALENDAR OF THE VICTORIA UNIVERSITY OF MANCHESTER. Session 1911-12. Demy 8vo, 1570 pp. 3s. net.
(Publication No. 60.)

SHORT HISTORY OF TODMORDEN. By J. HOLDEN, M.A.
[*In the Press.*

THE REGISTER OF GRADUATES OF THE UNIVERSITY OF MANCHESTER UP TO JULY 1908. 2s. 6d. net, cloth 3s. 6d. net.
(Publication No. 36.)

SHERRATT & HUGHES

Publications of the John Rylands Library issued at the University Press.

THE JOHN RYLANDS LIBRARY : Memorial of the Inauguration, 6th October, 1899. [Printed for private circulation.] 8vo, pp. 24.

CATALOGUE OF THE MANUSCRIPTS, BOOKS, AND BOOK-BINDINGS EXHIBITED AT THE OPENING OF THE JOHN RYLANDS LIBRARY, MANCHESTER, 6th October, 1899. 8vo, pp. 42. [Out of Print.

CATALOGUE OF THE PRINTED BOOKS AND MANUSCRIPTS IN THE JOHN RYLANDS LIBRARY, MANCHESTER. 1899. 3 vols. 4to. 31s. 6d. net

CATALOGUE OF BOOKS IN THE JOHN RYLANDS LIBRARY ... PRINTED IN ENGLAND, SCOTLAND, AND IRELAND, AND OF BOOKS IN ENGLISH PRINTED ABROAD, TO THE END OF THE YEAR 1640. 1895. 4to, pp. iii. 147. 10s. 6d. net.

THE ENGLISH BIBLE IN THE JOHN RYLANDS LIBRARY, 1525 to 1640. With 26 facsimiles and 39 engravings. [Printed for private circulation.] 1899. Folio, pp. xvi. 275. In levant Morocco, 5 guineas net.

THE JOHN RYLANDS LIBRARY : A Brief Description of the Building and its Contents, with a Descriptive List of the Works Exhibited in the Main Library. [Printed for private circulation.] July 1902. 8vo, pp. 48. [Out of Print.

JOHN RYLANDS LIBRARY. . . . JOHANN GUTENBERG AND THE DAWN OF TYPOGRAPHY IN GERMANY. Lecture by the Librarian, 14th October, 1903. (Synopsis of Lecture.—List of works exhibited . . . to illustrate the work of the first typographers in Germany. . .—A selection from the works in the John Rylands Library bearing upon the subject.) 1903. 8vo, pp. 15.
[Out of Print.

THE JOHN RYLANDS LIBRARY : THE MOVEMENT OF OLD TESTAMENT SCHOLARSHIP IN THE NINETEENTH CENTURY. [Synopsis of] a lecture by Prof. A. S. Peake, . . . 11th November, 1903—Some leading dates in Pentateuch criticism, 1903. 8vo, pp. 8. [Out of Print.

WORKS UPON THE STUDY OF GREEK AND LATIN PALÆO-GRAPHY AND DIPLOMATIC IN THE JOHN RYLANDS LIBRARY. . . . Reprinted from the "Quarterly Bulletin of the John Rylands Library." 1903. 4to, pp. 16. [Out of Print.

THE JOHN RYLANDS LIBRARY. . . . Catalogue of an Exhibition of Bibles illustrating the history of the English versions from Wiclif to the present time. Including the personal copies of Queen Elizabeth, General Gordon, and Elizabeth Fry. 1904. 8vo, pp. 32.
[Out of Print.

THE JOHN RYLANDS LIBRARY. . . . Catalogue of the Manuscripts and Printed Books exhibited on the occasion of the visit of the National Council of the Evangelical Free Churches. 1905. 8vo, pp. 38. [Out of Print.

34, Cross Street, Manchester

SHERRATT & HUGHES

THE JOHN RYLANDS LIBRARY. . . . A brief historical description of the Library and its contents, with Catalogue of the selection of early printed Greek and Latin Classics exhibited on the occasion of the visit of the Classical Association. . . 1906. 8vo, pp. 89. Illus. 1s. net.
  Full bibliographical descriptions of the first printed editions of the fifty principal Greek and Latin writers; of the first printed Greek classic ("Batrachomyomachia," 1474) the only known copy is described.

THE JOHN RYLANDS LIBRARY. . . . Catalogue of an Exhibition of Bibles illustrating the history of the English versions from Wiclif to the present time, including the personal copies of Queen Elizabeth, Elizabeth Fry, and others. 1907. 8vo, pp. vii. 55. [*Out of Print.*]

THE JOHN RYLANDS LIBRARY. . . . Catalogue of the selection of Books and Broadsides illustrating the early history of printing exhibited on the occasion of the visit of the Federation of Master Printers and Allied Trades. 1907. 8vo, pp. vi. 34. [*Out of Print.*]

THE JOHN RYLANDS LIBRARY. . . . A brief historical description of the Library and its contents. 1907. 8vo, pp. 53. Illus.
[*Out of Print.*]

THE JOHN RYLANDS LIBRARY. . . . Catalogue of an Exhibition of Illuminated Manuscripts, principally Biblical and Liturgical, on the occasion of the Church Congress. 1908. 8vo, pp. vi. 82. 6d. net.

THE JOHN RYLANDS LIBRARY. . . . Catalogue of an Exhibition of original editions of the principal works of John Milton arranged in celebration of the tercentenary of his birth. 1908. 8vo, pp. 24. 6d. net.

THE JOHN RYLANDS LIBRARY. . . . Catalogue of an Exhibition of the works of Dante Alighieri [with list of a selection of works on the study of Dante]. 1909. 8vo, pp. xii. 55. 6d. net.

THE JOHN RYLANDS LIBRARY. . . . Catalogue of an Exhibition of original editions of the principal English Classics [with list of works for the study of English Literature]. 1910. 8vo, pp. xvi. 86. 6d. net.

A CLASSIFIED CATALOGUE OF THE WORKS ON ARCHITECTURE AND THE ALLIED ARTS IN THE PRINCIPAL LIBRARIES OF MANCHESTER AND SALFORD, with Alphabetical author list and subject index. Edited for the Architectural Committee of Manchester by Henry Guppy and Guthrie Vine. 1909. 8vo, pp. xxv. 310. 3s. 6d. net, or interleaved 4s. 6d. net.

THE JOHN RYLANDS LIBRARY. . . . An analytical catalogue of the contents of the two editions of "An English Garner," compiled by Edward Arber (1877-97), and rearranged under the editorship of Thomas Seccombe (1903-04). 1909. 8vo, pp. viii. 221. 1s. net.

BULLETIN OF THE JOHN RYLANDS LIBRARY. Vol. i. (1903-08). 4to, pp. 468. 6s. net.

33, Soho Square, London, W.

SHERRATT & HUGHES

AN ACCOUNT OF A COPY FROM THE FIFTEENTH CENTURY [now in the John Rylands Library] of a map of the world engraved on metal, which is preserved in Cardinal Stephen Borgia's Museum at Velletri. By A. E. Nordenskiöld (copied from "Ymer," 1891). *Stockholm*, 1891. 4to, pp. 29, and facsimile of map. 7s. 6d. *net.*

CATALOGUE OF THE COPTIC MANUSCRIPTS IN THE JOHN RYLANDS LIBRARY. By W. E. Crum. 1909. 4to, pp. xii. 273. 12 plates of facsimiles, in collotype. 1 guinea *net.*

Many of the texts are reproduced *in extenso*. The collection includes a series of private letters considerably older than any in Coptic hitherto known, in addition to many MSS. of great theological and historical interest.

CATALOGUE OF THE DEMOTIC PAPYRI IN THE JOHN RYLANDS LIBRARY. With facsimiles and complete translations. By F. Ll. Griffith. 1909. 3 vols. 4to.
1. Atlas of facsimiles in collotype.
2. Lithographed hand copies of the earlier documents.
3. Key-list, translations, commentaries, and indexes. 3 guineas *net.*

This is something more than a catalogue. It includes collotype facsimiles of the whole of the documents, with transliterations, translations, besides introductions, very full notes, and a glossary of Demotic, representing the most important contribution to the study of Demotic hitherto published. The documents dealt with in these volumes cover a period from Psammetichus, one of the latest native kings, about 640 B.C., down to the Roman Emperor Claudius, A.D. 43.

CATALOGUE OF THE GREEK PAPYRI IN THE JOHN RYLANDS LIBRARY. By Arthur S. Hunt. Vol. i : Literary texts (Nos. 1-61) 1911. 4to, pp. xii. 204. 10 plates of facsimiles in collotype. 1 guinea *net.*

The texts are reproduced *in extenso*. The collection comprises many interesting Biblical, liturgical, and classical papyri, ranging from the third century B.C. to the sixth century A.D. Included are probably the earliest known text of the "Nicene Creed," and one of the earliest known vellum codices, containing a considerable fragment of the "Odyssey," possibly of the third century A.D.

CATALOGUE OF THE GREEK PAPYRI IN THE JOHN RYLANDS LIBRARY. By Arthur S. Hunt. Vols. 2 and 3 : Non-literary documents. [*In Preparation.*

THE JOHN RYLANDS FACSIMILES : A series of reproductions of unique and rare books in the possession of the John Rylands Library.

The volumes consist of minutely accurate facsimile productions of the works selected, preceded by short bibliographical introductions.

The issue of each work is limited to five hundred copies, of which three hundred are offered for sale, at a price calculated to cover the cost of reproduction.

SHERRATT & HUGHES

1. PROPOSITIO JOHANNIS RUSSELL, printed by William Caxton, circa A.D. 1476. Reproduced from the copy preserved in the John Rylands Library. . . . With an introduction by Henry Guppy. 1909. 8vo, pp. 36, 8. 3s. 6d. net.

    This "proposition" is an oration, pronounced by John Russell, Garter King of Arms, on the investiture of Charles, Duke of Burgundy, with the Order of the Garter, in February, 1469, at Ghent. The tract consists of four printed leaves, without title-page, printer's name, date, or place of printing. It is printed in the type which is known as Caxton's type "No. 2," but whether printed at Bruges or at Westminster has yet to be determined.

    For many years the copy now in the John Rylands Library was considered to be unique. Indeed, until the year 1807 it lay buried and unnoticed in the heart of a volume of manuscripts, with which it had evidently been bound up by mistake. Since then, another copy has been discovered in the library at Holkham Hall, the seat of the Earl of Leicester.

2. A BOOKE IN ENGLYSH METRE, of the Great Marchaunt man called "Dives Pragmaticus". . . . 1563. Reproduced in facsimile from the copy in the John Rylands Library. With an introduction by Percy E. Newbery; and remarks on the vocabulary and dialect, with a glossary by Henry C. Wyld. 1910. 4to, pp. xxxviii. 16. 5s. net.

    The tract here reproduced is believed to be the sole surviving copy of a quaint little primer which had the laudable object of instructing the young in the names of trades, professions, ranks, and common objects of daily life in their own tongue. The lists are rhymed, and therefore easy to commit to memory, and they are pervaded by a certain vein of humour.

3. A LITIL BOKE the whiche traytied and reherced many gode thinges necessaries for the . . . Pestilence . . . made by the . . . Bisshop of Arusiens. . . [London], [1485 ?]. Reproduced in facsimile from the copy in the John Rylands Library. With an introduction by Guthrie Vine. 1910. 4to, pp. xxxvi. 18. 5s. net.

    Of this little tract, consisting of nine leaves, written by Benedict Kanuti, Bishop of Västerås, three separate editions are known, but only one copy of each, and an odd leaf are known to have survived.

    There is no indication in any edition of the place of printing, date, or name of printer, but they are all printed in one of the four type employed by William de Machlinia, who printed first in partnership with John Lettou, and afterwards alone, in the city of London, at the time when William Caxton was at the most active period of his career at Westminster.

THE ELLESMERE CHAUCER: Reproduced in Facsimile. Price £50 net.

LE PELERIN DE VIE HUMAINE. (Privately printed for the Roxburghe Club).

33, Soho Square, London, W.

SHERRATT & HUGHES

TRANSACTIONS OF THE INTERNATIONAL UNION FOR CO-OPERATION IN SOLAR RESEARCH (Vol. i., First and Second Conferences). Demy 8vo, 260 pp. and plate. 7s. 6d. net.

TRANSACTIONS OF THE INTERNATIONAL UNION FOR CO-OPERATION IN SOLAR RESEARCH (Vol. ii., Third Conference.) Demy 8vo. 7s. 6d. net.

TRANSACTIONS OF THE INTERNATIONAL UNION FOR CO-OPERATION IN SOLAR RESEARCH (Vol. iii., Fourth Conference.) Demy 8vo. 7s. 6d. net.

EXCAVATION OF THE ROMAN FORTS AT CASTLESHAW (near Delph, West Riding), by SAMUEL ANDREW, Esq., and Major WILLIAM LEES, J.P. First Interim Report, prepared by F. A. BRUTON, M.A. Demy 8vo, pp. 38, 20 plates and plans. 1s. net.

EXCAVATION OF THE ROMAN FORTS AT CASTLESHAW (near Delph, West Riding), by SAMUEL ANDREW, Esq., and Major WILLIAM LEES, J.P. Second Interim Report, prepared by F. A. BRUTON, M.A. Demy 8vo, pp. 93, 45 plates and plans. 3s. 6d. net.

THE ROMAN FORT AT MANCHESTER. Edited by F. A. Bruton. Demy 8vo. 6s. net.

THE ROMAN FORT AT RIBCHESTER. Edited by J. H. HOPKINSON, M.A. Demy 8vo. 6d. net.

THE MOSTELLARIA OF PLAUTUS. Acting edition with a translation into English verse. Edited by G. NORWOOD, M.A. 1s. net.

THE VICTORIA UNIVERSITY OF MANCHESTER MEDICAL SCHOOL. 6d. net.

THE BOOK OF RUTH (Unpointed Text). 6d. net.

THE BOOK OF AMOS (Unpointed Text). 6d. net.

SCENES FROM THE RUDENS OF PLAUTUS, with a Translation into English Verse. Edited by R. S. CONWAY, Litt.D., Professor of Latin in the University. 6d. net.

THE POEMS OF LEOPARDI. By FRANCIS BROOKS, M.A. Price 3s. 6d. net.

MANCHESTER UNIVERSITY DIARY, 1911-12. 1s. net.

A TARDINESS IN NATURE AND OTHER PAPERS. By MARY CHRISTIE. Edited, with Introductory Note and Memoir, by MAUD WITHERS. Crown 8vo, 331 pp. 3s. net.

MUSICAL CRITICISMS. By ARTHUR JOHNSTONE. With a Memoir of the Author by HENRY REECE and OLIVER ELTON. Crown 8vo, 225 pp. 5s. net.

MANCHESTER BOYS. By C. E. B. RUSSELL. With an Introduction by E. T. CAMPAGNAC. Crown 8vo, pp. xvi. 176, 19 plates 2s. 6d. net.

MANCHESTER BANKS · ANALYSIS OF THE PUBLISHED BALANCE SHEETS FOR 1908, 1909, 1910, and 1911. By D. DRUMMOND FRASER, M.Com. 1s. net each.

JOURNAL OF THE MANCHESTER ORIENTAL SOCIETY, No. 1, 1911. 5s. paper, 6s. cloth.

Lightning Source UK Ltd.
Milton Keynes UK
UKHW010639280422
402201UK00002B/333